Great Britain and Mexico in the Era of Porfirio Díaz

Great Britain and Mexico in the Era of Porfirio Díaz

Alfred Tischendorf

Duke University Press   *Durham, North Carolina*   *1961*

©1961, Duke University Press

HF
3508
.M6
T5
1961

Cambridge University Press, London N. W. 1, England

Library of Congress Catalog Card Number 61-6224

Printed in the United States of America
by the Seeman Printery, Inc., Durham, N. C.

To the memory of my brother,
David Lee Tischendorf

The publication of this book was assisted by funds from the grant to the Duke University Press by the Ford Foundation.

Preface

This volume does not represent an attempt to survey every aspect of the relations between Great Britain and Mexico in the years from 1876 to 1911. It is concerned mainly with economic affairs and with the diplomatic difficulties which attended British interest in the Republic during the Díaz epoch. Anglo-Mexican relations were severed in 1867 and until 1884 no official intercourse existed between the two countries. The opening chapter is concerned with efforts to produce a rapprochement without which much of Britain's penetration of Mexico before 1911 would not have occurred. Later chapters examine the investments and enterprises of British citizens during the Díaz period, the promotional aspects of this enterprise, the problems which capitalists and technologists faced in pressing their objectives, something of their profits and losses, and the story of the aid which they expected and sometimes received from the Foreign Office. Companies organized by Englishmen have been emphasized, as have significant ventures formed in Canada with the aid of English capital. Consideration of the twenty-three Scottish companies registered in Edinburgh to operate in Mexico has been omitted except to record their presence in tabular form. None of them was important. The story of the loss of British pre-eminence in the Mexican market after 1876 has been summarized in one chapter. In the concluding chapter I have presented a summary and appraisal of the British activities in Mexico.

The topic presented has at least two larger ramifications. The obstacles which plagued British investors and the impact of British capital on Mexican progress are not without interest for those concerned with contemporary problems of the underdeveloped areas. The reader also should be reminded of the long rivalry of the United States and Great Britain in Mexico. Despite the work of diplomats, merchants, and investors, Britain seldom competed successfully with the dollar in Mexico after 1876, and a contest dating back to the 1820's was settled before Porfirio Díaz fled into exile. British investments had not yet reached their peak in 1911, but only a few Britons remained to dispute seriously the undoubted supremacy of the United States.

In preparing this volume I have become indebted to many people. The Research Council of Duke University and Rotary International provided the funds for study in Mexico and England. I am indebted to the staffs of the Public Record Office, Stock Exchange Library, British Museum, Company Registration Office, and the Institute of Mining and Metallurgy in London for their valued assistance. I wish to thank Dr. Henry Stanley Ferns, author of the recently published *Great Britain and Argentina in the Nineteenth Century*, for his counsel and hospitality while I was in Birmingham, England. My stay in that city was also made more enjoyable by the kindness of Denis Mitchell, Eric Skinner, and J. Kenneth Walker and their families. The staffs of the Biblioteca Nacional, The Archivo Nacional, the library of the Ministry of Foreign Relations, and the Hemeroteca Nacional in Mexico City deserve special mention. They labor under difficulties. It was not their fault that the materials available in their repositories failed to shed more light on the topic being examined. The obligations incurred in the United States are too numerous to catalogue. Special acknowledgments must, however, be given to the persons who assisted me in the Library of Congress and the National Archives in Washington, and to J. Fred Rippy, Professor Emeritus of the University of Chicago, Professor Robert Crane, University of Michigan, and Dr. George Wythe, Washington D. C., all of whom read and criticized the manuscript. Mr. Paul Fairchild of Ohio State University drew the maps and Dr. Ransom Patrick of Duke University prepared the original layout for the jacket. My principal debt is to my wife, Joyce Fuller Tischendorf, who was always there to offer her encouragement when the pace tended to slacken.

Alfred Tischendorf

Durham, North Carolina

Concerning footnotes

Short titles, abbreviations, and initials are used after the first citation for sources that frequently appear in the text. For full bibliographical information on the terms cited, see the bibliography.

AAMMG	*Anglo-American and Mexican Mining Guide*
CRO	Company Registration Office, Bush House, London
FO 50	Public Record Office, London, Foreign Office Archives, Mexico
FO 203-205	Public Record Office, London, Foreign Office Archives, Consular Despatches, Mexico
GBDCR AS	Great Britain, Diplomatic and Consular Reports, Annual Series
GBDCR MS	Great Britain, Diplomatic and Consular Reports, Miscellaneous Series
HAHR	*Hispanic American Historical Review*
IAEA	*Inter-American Economic Affairs*
JEH	*Journal of Economic History*
MF	*Mexican Financier*
MJ	*Mining Journal*
MM	*Mining Magazine*
MRC	Mexican Railway Company
MW	*Mining World and Engineering Record*
RJ	*Herapath's Railway and Commercial Journal*
SAJ	*South American Journal*
SEL	Stock Exchange Library, London
SEYB	*Stock Exchange Year-Book*
TR	*Two Republics*

Table of Contents

1. *The Renewal of Diplomatic Relations* —3
2. *British Enterprise during the Diplomatic Imbroglio* —21
3. *Rails, Rivalries, and Pools, 1885-1910* —42
4. *The Mining Story, 1885-1910* —71
5. *A Disastrous Adventure in Real Estate and Rubber* —96
6. *Some British Investments in the later Díaz Period: Utilities, Factories, and Petroleum* —111
7. *The Loss of British Commercial Pre-eminence* —128
8. *The Balance Sheet* —139
   Appendix —147
   Selected Bibliography —175
   Index —185

List of Tables

1. *British limited companies organized to work in Mexico prior to January 1, 1876, and on the Company Registrar's list on that date* —22
2. *British limited companies organized between January 1, 1876, and December 31, 1884, to work in Mexico* —23

3. *British limited companies registered to work in Mexico, end of 1884* —*23*

4. *Dividend record of the Mexican Railway Company, 1876-1884* —*35*

5. *Dividend record of the Mexican Railway Company, 1885-1910* —*48*

6. *Dividends paid on selected shares and debentures of the Interoceanic Railroad, 1892-1910* —*59*

7. *British dividend mining companies, 1885-1910* —*72*

8. *British investments in Mexico, 1876-1910: Amount of paid-up capital* —*140-141*

9. *Total registered British limited companies and non-British companies in which British capital was invested, 1876-1910* —*141*

List of Maps

1. *Approximate location of British-controlled limited mining companies, end of 1884* —*26*

2. *The Mexican Railway* —*33*

3. *Railroad map of Mexico: 1876-1911* —*37*

4. *Profitable British mining companies: 1885-1910* —*79*

5. *El Oro mining district* —*87*

6. *Location of active British ranching and colonization companies: 1885-1910* —*98*

Great Britain and Mexico in the Era of Porfirio Díaz

1. The Renewal of Diplomatic Relations

When Porfirio Díaz entered Mexico City on November 23, 1876, the relations of Great Britain and Mexico were in a most unsatisfactory state. For nearly nine years diplomatic intercourse had been suspended and neither government indicated it would make the first move to repair the break. In August, 1867 a British consul, Frederick Glennie, appearing before a judge in Mexico City to discuss the intestate property of a British subject, was informed that he could not be recognized in his official capacity. When Glennie requested an explanation from the Minister of Foreign Affairs he was told that Benito Juárez' government would have no communication with agents of those powers that had recognized the ill-fated regime of the Archduke Ferdinand Maximilian.[1] On October 25, 1867, the British Foreign Secretary, Lord Stanley, informed Britain's legation in Mexico City that: ". . . the decision of the Mexican Government . . . renders it no longer compatible with the dignity of Her Majesty's Government to keep up in Mexico even the semblance of a Diplomatic Mission."[2] On December 8 President Juárez told the Mexican Congress of the decision that had been conveyed to Glennie in August. Juárez, motivated by financial considerations and widespread resentment toward those nations which had participated in the first stages of the intervention in 1861, also declared that treaties and conven-

---

[1] Great Britain, House of Commons Sessional Papers, 1867-68, LXXIII, *Paper relating to the withdrawal of the British mission from Mexico*, 1867-68 [cmd. 3989].
[2] *Ibid.*

tions between Mexico and these countries were cancelled.[3] The action brought little response from the press in Mexico City; one newspaper mentioned only that Britain probably would soon take the initiative in calling for a renewal of relations.[4]

Among the agreements disavowed by Juárez was the English Convention of 1851. His repudiation of assignments of customs duties made to Mexico's foreign creditors prior to 1861 fell squarely on the Convention bondholders. Also affected were the London bondholders, like the Convention group heirs to decades of Mexican revolution and financial chaos. The par value of Mexican government securities held by London bondholders at the time of the diplomatic rupture was £22,341,322, and those held by the Convention bondholders was £996,983.[5] A brief history of these bonds is essential to an understanding of Anglo-Mexican relations following Lord Stanley's note of October 25.

The Convention bondholders were originally those Britons who suffered economic or physical injuries in Mexico before 1842 and whose claims were protected officially by the British government.[6] A settlement of these claims was arranged in 1842 but the agreement was never carried out. In 1851, however, claims totaling £996,983 were consolidated into the "Doyle" or "English" Convention. Twelve per cent of the annual maritime customs revenue was assigned to the Convention bondholders. In 1852, after Mexico defaulted, she agreed to assign an additional 3 per cent of the customs revenue to pay

[3] Edgar Turlington, *Mexico and Her Foreign Creditors* (New York, 1930), pp. 173-74.

[4] *El Siglo XIX*, n.d., in R. Middleton (British Minister to Mexico) to Stanley, No. 3 in No. 4, Dec. 9, 1867, Great Britain, House of Commons Sessional Papers, 1867-68, LXXIII [cmd. 3989].

[5] Edward Kohzevar, *Report on the Republic of Mexico to the Council of Foreign Bondholders* (London, 1886), p. 9; John Walsham (Foreign Office librarian), Observations on the question of a renewal of relations with Mexico and its connection with the obligation of the Republic to recognize the claims of British creditors, Confidential, Nov. 15, 1881, Public Record Office, London, Foreign Office Archives, Mexico (cited hereinafter as FO 50), Volume 437. During the preparation of this monograph these archives could be examined to December 31, 1902.

[6] A Mexican viewpoint regarding the bondholders may be found in Joaquín D. Cassasús, *Historia de la deuda contraída en Londres* (México, 1885), pp. 353-84; also see Francisco Bulnes, *La deuda inglesa—colección de artículos publicados en El Siglo XIX* (México, 1885). A survey of the activities of the bondholders after 1824 is found in Turlington, pp. 1-170, and Edward Hertslet (Foreign Office librarian), Memorandum as to how far Her Majesty's Government are bound to support the claims of British subjects against Mexico, Confidential, Nov. 9, 1881, FO 50, Vol. 437.

off the arrears. Default again occurred in the wake of political strife and no important arrangements were made with the Convention bondholders until 1859. On January 22 of that year the "conservative" faction placed General Felix Zuloaga in the presidential chair in Mexico City. Despite Juárez' claim to the same office it was from the Zuloaga government that British Minister L. C. Otway secured an agreement to give the bondholders 6 per cent interest a year. The annual customs house allotment was increased to 16 per cent a year and the Otway Convention was approved by the British government.

The London bondholders represented the loans made to Mexico in 1824 and 1825. They then amounted to approximately £10,000,000.[7] The London bondholders' security for the repayment of the loans was not based on an international agreement as was that of the Convention bondholders, but only on a private agreement with the Mexican government.[8] On October 14, 1850, following frequent conversions and recurrent default, a law providing the basis of a settlement of Mexico's foreign debt was passed by Congress. The payment of interest on the London securities again ceased in 1854, and four years later the assignments mortgaged to the bonds were appropriated by the so-called Juárez government.

Until 1859 the paths of the Convention and London bondholders were clearly separate, with only the former having the protection of the British government. In 1859 a contingent of the British navy anchored off Veracruz and its captain demanded that the Juárez "government" pay interest on both the London and Convention debt.[9] After two weeks of discussion 25 per cent of the customs revenue was set aside for the London bondholders and 16 per cent for those who held Convention bonds.[10] In 1860 the Mexicans also assented to an additional assignment of 10 per cent of the import duties collected at Veracruz and Tampico. The two arrangements later were referred to as the Dunlop-Aldham Convention.

The fortunes of the Convention and London bondholders

---

[7] For a list of the loans made to Mexico, see Corporation of Foreign Bondholders, *Annual Report* (London, 1877).

[8] Hertslet memorandum, Nov. 9, 1881, FO 50, Vol. 437.

[9] *Ibid.*

[10] Casasús, pp. 334-35.

again diverged after 1860. The next significant phase in the history of the Convention debt came in 1867 when Juárez canceled the English Convention and withdrew the assignment of all customs duties. His decree, Juárez insisted, did not mean that Mexico repudiated its obligation to pay the Convention bondholders. It meant that *Mexico denied the international character of the agreement and thus no longer considered the Convention bondholders under the protection of the British government.*[11] The position of the London bondholders was more complicated and proved an increasing source of concern and annoyance to the Foreign Office. The London bondholders insisted that as a result of the Dunlop-Aldham agreements they, like the Convention bondholders, also fell under the international agreements recognized by Great Britain.[12] The London group offered further evidence which they believed bolstered their claim to official protection. The United States, in an effort to halt the European tripartite intervention of 1861, had volunteered to undertake for a short period the payment of interest due to Mexico's creditors. Britain's Prime Minister, Lord Russell, refused the offer. The London bondholders declared that while they agreed to Russell's right as their trustee to reject the proposal, the British government had assumed all responsibility of the trust as a result of his action.[13]

Benito Juárez took another view of the problem. In 1864 the London bondholders were the chief supporters of a loan floated by the Maximilian regime. On the day the Archduke approved a contract with a London banking house for the loan, a decree converted the London debt into new 3 per cent bonds totaling £4,864,000. Three years later when Juárez repudiated the assignment of customs duties made under the Dunlop-Aldham agreement, he did so on grounds that the bondholders had released the Republic from this arrangement by their dealings with Maximilian. The London bondholders maintained that the settlement of 1864 related only to arrears on the

---

[11] Foreign Office, unsigned memorandum on the proposed renewal of diplomatic relations with Mexico, March 14, 1883, FO 50, Vol. 443.

[12] The British government traditionally did not often interfere on behalf of those who freely lent their money to foreign nations, although it might do so under certian conditions. See Sir John Williams, *International Law and International Financial Obligations Arising from Contract*, II (Leyden, 1923), 10-11.

[13] Hertslet memorandum, Nov. 9, 1881, FO 50, Vol. 437.

1850 debt and not to the debt itself. Juárez countered this statement by replying that his administration would be willing to consider new arrangements for paying its debts.[14] In this situation it was inevitable that the London bondholders, anxious to receive interest on their securities, would push vigorously for a restoration of diplomatic relations and a settlement of their grievances.[15]

The London bondholders began to agitate for a renewal of relations as soon as British diplomats withdrew from Mexico in 1867. Their cause was championed mainly by the Mexican Bondholders' Committee, a group that included naval officers and a few members of Parliament. The committee's agent, E. J. Perry, was sent to Mexico City and through him the bondholders made at least four unsuccessful attempts before 1876 to induce Mexico to resume payment of interest on the bonds. The committee also exerted pressure on the Foreign Office and was in frequent contact with persons outside England who might assist their cause. William H. Seward and Hamilton Fish, for example, were approached in an attempt to obtain their interposition in the diplomatic stalemate.[16]

The London bondholders received little encouragement from their discussions with the Foreign Office before 1876. Lord Stanley stated in 1868 that Britain was not responsible for the diplomatic break; Mexico had chosen, unwisely he thought, to view the British recognition of Maximilian as an act of hostility against the Republic. A simple matter of Britain's self-respect would not allow the Foreign Office to ask Mexico to reconsider the decision: "All I can say is that whenever they may think it right to take what I will . . . call a more rational view, and show a wish to make up this difference, they will not find any difficulty in the way of a reconciliation on our part."[17]

[14] Turlington, p. 174.

[15] The Foreign Office felt that a group other than the Convention and London bondholders also had some right to official consideration. On June 26, 1866, an Anglo-Mexican treaty providing for the settlement of various claims by British citizens against the Republic after 1842 was signed. One British source estimated that the claims totaled about £270,000. No decision as to the exact sum involved had been made when Juárez disavowed the agreement in 1867. See Hertslet memorandum, Nov. 9, 1881, FO 50, Vol. 437; Foreign Office memorandum, March 19, 1883, FO 50, Vol. 443.

[16] The attempt failed. Perry's correspondence with Seward's aide may be found in FO 50, Vol. 439. Also see Simon Stevens (Tehuantepec Railway Company) to Foreign Secretary, Jan. 8, 1877, FO 50, Vol. 439.

[17] Foreign Office memorandum, April 14, 1869, FO 50, Vol. 439.

On October 9, 1869, Lord Clarendon, then Foreign Secretary, told representatives of the London bondholders that Mexico had put an end to diplomatic relations in an offensive manner. If she wished to resume normal intercourse, Mexico should make known her willingness in proper form, perhaps through the German or Italian Ministers in Mexico City. Mexico would have to recognize all conventions and treaties made with Great Britain or at least substitute others mutually agreed on.[18] This seemed unlikely since Juárez had taken the opposite view regarding the first demand, and Mexican public opinion in the 1870's was in no mood to consider new proposals for paying old debts.[19]   *El Época* in Mexico City felt, however, that because Mexico was held in "high esteem" in England—a rather unfortunate choice of words under the circumstances—a renewal of relations might occur momentarily.[20] The Mexican Minister of Foreign Relations offered no public statements concerning the imbroglio during the early 1870's, but the British Foreign Office continued to express its willingness in Parliament to renew relations, always with the stipulation that the formal initiation come from Mexico.[21] Yet when Porfirio Díaz became President of Mexico in April, 1877, British-Mexican relations stood exactly where they had at the beginning of the decade.

The Foreign Office had little reason to modify its position prior to the Díaz Revolution. Few British investors were concerned with Mexican enterprise between 1867 and 1876, and Mexico was seldom mentioned in London financial magazines as a field for profitable investment. The number of Britons in

[18] Foreign Secretary to Law Officers of the Crown, Sept. 15, 1871, FO 50, Vol. 489; Law Officers to Foreign Secretary, Oct. 5, 1871, FO 50, Vol. 439.
[19] Graham Dunlop (British resident in Mexico City) to Foreign Secretary, May 12, 1874, FO 50, Vol. 439.
[20] May 10, 1877.
[21] Statements made in the British Parliament may be found in *Hansard's Parliamentary Debates*, 1868-69, CXCV, 845; CXCVII, 110; CXCVIII, 897; 1871, CCVII, 1883; 1883, CCXVII, 1563; 1874, CCXVIII, 1878. Mexican records relative to relations with Britain before the renewal of relations are scanty. The complete records are in the Archivo general, Mexico City, but the most accessible source is México, Secretaría de Relaciones Exteriores, *Memoria que en cumplimiento del precepto constitucional presentada al duodécimo congreso de la unión El C. Ignacio Mariscal* (México, 1885), Anexos 27-48. Most of the Mexican correspondence during the 1870's concerned alleged Indian encroachments on the British territory of Honduras. This problem did not deter the renewal of relations. See México, Secretaría de Relaciones Exteriores, *Correspondencia diplomática cambiada entre el gobierno de la república y el de su majestad británica con relación del territorio llamado de Belice, 1872-78* (México, n.d.).

Mexico was small and the Foreign Office received little correspondence of any sort from those living in the country. Most of the protests sent to the Foreign Office by Britons were directed against state governments, and the Office reasoned that the central Mexican authorities were powerless to obtain damages even if claims were made.[22]

The pattern of Anglo-Mexican relations changed in various ways between 1876 and 1880. This resulted in the first unofficial attempt by British diplomats to restore diplomatic intercourse in the latter year. In 1876 the Foreign Office had reason to believe that a victory by Díaz in his revolutionary adventure might create an atmosphere favorable to a renewal of relations.[23] This optimism pervaded certain business circles in England. On December 12, 1876, a memorial from the Association of Chambers of Commerce of the United Kingdom called attention to the volume of trade between Britain and Mexico. Fifty-two branches of the Association pointed out that approximately two hundred ships from Britain annually were registered at Mexican ports—far more than by any other European country.[24] If diplomatic relations were restored the presence of British diplomats would obviate the need for merchants to make deputations through foreign consulates. Their main complaints were directed toward Mexico's strict regulations regarding ships' manifests. The slightest infraction brought heavy fines and it was difficult for even the most zealous company to avoid considerable loss each year. Until diplomatic protection was available the merchants could expect no answer other than the one given to Jenkins and Son Company by the Foreign Office: "We have no representative in Mexico and Mexico none in England. I do not see therefore that we can help the shippers being robbed. They must comply with the Mexican regulations as best they may."[25]

Between 1876 and 1880 London financial publications inten-

[22] Foreign Office memorandum, List of claims made by British citizens on the Government of Mexico subsequent to the rupture of relations, Oct. 10, 1883, FO 50, Vol. 443.

[23] C. E. Bourdillon (attorney in Mexico City) to Derby, Feb. 16, 1876, FO 50, Vol. 429.

[24] Memorial from the Association of Chambers of Commerce to Derby, Dec. 12, 1876, FO 50, Vol. 429. Britain dominated the Mexican market in 1876.

[25] Derby to Board of Trade, Oct. 10, 1877, FO 50, Vol. 429. The complaint was sent by Jenkins and Son Company to Board of Trade, Oct. 4, 1877, FO 50, Vol. 429.

sified their verbal thrashing of the Mexican government for its failure to honor its obligations to the bondholders.[26] Letters from the bondholders themselves to the Foreign Office pointed to the possibility of Britons investing in Mexico, but demanded the settlement of financial problems and a restoration of diplomatic relations as necessary prerequisites. Alexander Grant of Norwood, one of the letter writers, feared that capitalists from the United States and merchants from Germany would gain the upper hand in Mexico if relations were not soon restored. Britain could not afford to ignore a country which because of its "geographical and other advantages . . . will someday become of great importance."[27]

The London bondholders continued to press the Foreign Office for assistance from 1876 to 1880, but during these years the bondholders focused their main efforts on direct negotiations with the Díaz administration. Mexico was aware of the necessity of attracting foreign capital for internal improvements. In December, 1878, E. J. Perry concluded a strange agreement with the Mexican government which made the adjustment of the debt dependent on the bondholders' lending money for the construction of a railroad from Mexico City to the Pacific coast.[28] The bondholders rejected this financial blackmail and a modified proposal was turned down by the Mexican Congress. Then in the summer of 1880 a commission was appointed by the Mexican government to study the nation's foreign debts. The significance of this was not lost on the British Foreign Office, for if a settlement between the London bondholders and Mexico were made privately, the British government would not need to consider the matter during parleys for a diplomatic renewal.

The years between 1876 and 1880 brought an increase in the number of complaints of mistreatment from Britons living in the Republic. Squabbles on the northern frontier occasionally affected British interests. The Foreign Office did not attempt to appeal to Mexican justice in these cases, but instead sent a form letter calculated to stifle British complaints: "I am to

[26] *Mining Journal*, L (Feb. 21, 1880), 220, suggested that perhaps the bondholders might have been wiser to have invested their capital in developing the Empire.
[27] Grant to Derby, Jan. 24, 1876, FO 50, Vol. 429; Grant to Derby, Nov. 8, 1877, FO 50, Vol. 430.
[28] Corporation of Foreign Bondholders, *Annual Report, 1878*, pp. 36-37.

state that, as diplomatic relations are suspended between Her Majesty's Government and that of Mexico, His Lordship regrets that he is unable to tender you any assistance in this matter."[29] Aside from the border troubles, a case involving a deserter from the Royal Navy, and a few protests from companies trading in Mexico, the other call for protection came in 1879 from La Paz, Lower California, where Mexican bandits were preventing the shipment of ore from the port.[30] As British interests expanded in Mexico such requests for diplomatic assistance also would increase.

British investors who between 1876 and 1880 organized eight companies to work in the Republic combined with other Britons to urge that the Foreign Office take the first step toward a renewal of relations. On April 30, 1877, Lord Huntley, a shareholder in the Trojes Mining and Smelting Company, sent a petition signed by twenty-one Englishmen to the Foreign Office. This petition called for the establishment of a diplomatic staff in Mexico to provide protection for investors.[31] On June 8, 1877, Simon Stevens of the Tehuantepec Railway Company, a Mexican concern in which many Britons held shares, emphasized the need for action in a letter to the Foreign Secretary:

> The future prosperity of Mexico, rich as that country is in natural resources, and the success of public works . . . are so evidently dependent on the restoration of friendly relations with Great Britain that I must ask . . . pardon for my earnestness in proposing the consideration of this matter.[32]

Two weeks later Foreign Secretary Derby received a delegation of British investors, bankers, and members of Parliament to discuss Anglo-Mexican affairs. Derby sympathized with their desire for diplomatic relations as likely to be conducive to British activities in Mexico, but he insisted that Mexico would have to give some indication of a desire to renew relations.[33]

---

[29] Foreign Secretary to William Ross (Scottish-born cattle rancher in Mexico), Aug. 31, 1877, FO 50, Vol. 430.

[30] The diplomatic records note that the Admiralty, at the request of the Foreign Office, dispatched a warship to La Paz "with the desired result." Foreign Secretary to the Admiralty, Dec. 29, 1879, FO 50, Vol. 435; Woolrich Company to Foreign Secretary, March 14, 1880, FO 50, Vol. 436.

[31] Huntley to Derby, April 30, 1877, FO 50, Vol. 436.

[32] Stevens to Derby, June 8, 1877, FO 50, Vol. 439.

[33] Foreign Office memorandum, deputations to Derby, June 25, 1877, FO 50, Vol. 439.

Old agreements such as the English Convention would have to be recognized. Derby put his views in writing in August when Robert Geddes, Manager of the London Bank of Mexico and South America, returned to Mexico City. He authorized Geddes to use the letter in any way he thought proper. When Geddes showed the letter to Mexico's Secretary of Foreign Affairs, he was told that, although the Mexican government wished to break the diplomatic deadlock, this could be accomplished only on the basis of new treaties.[34]

In summary, petitions and letters from British merchants to the Foreign Office between 1876 and 1880 mentioned the possibility of increasing British-Mexican trade, but diplomatic relations were needed to instil the confidence necessary to push trading operations. Holders of Mexican bonds insisted that any future investment by Britons in the Republic had to be preceded by a settlement of their grievances and a restoration of diplomatic relations. By 1880 adjustment of the London debt by bondholders and the Mexican government seemed possible, and the Foreign Office was therefore relieved of the necessity of involving the bondholders' claims in discussions leading to a resumption of relations. The need for a diplomatic corps was indicated by the increasing number of complaints from Britons in Mexico from 1876 to 1880. Opportunities for capital investment in the Republic were growing and seemed partly to depend on Britain's renewing relations as quickly as possible. Added to these factors was the belief in the Foreign Office by 1880 that Mexico desired to offset American influence by expanding her intercourse with European nations.[35]

In late 1880, following the renewal of diplomatic accord between Mexico and France, the most important of the intervening powers in 1861, Emilio Velasco was appointed Mexican Minister to Paris. The British Foreign Office saw his

[34] Derby to Geddes, Private, Aug. 27, 1877, FO 50, Vol. 439; Geddes to Derby, Oct. 30, 1877, FO 50, Vol. 439. The Mexicans were consistent; see José Fernández (acting Secretary of Foreign Affairs) to Ignacio Mariscal (Mexican special envoy to Great Britain), June 12, 1883, in México, Secretaría de Relaciones Exteriores, *Memoria . . . presentada al duodécimo congreso de la unión El C. Ignacio Mariscal*, Anexo Numero 30.

[35] Evidence of this was offered in *El Época*, May 10, 1877; Bourdillon to Derby, April 14, 1876, FO 50, Vol. 429; Bourdillon to Derby, July 16, 1877, FO 50, Vol. 430; Bourdillon to Derby, July 30, 1878, FO 50, Vol. 439; Bourdillon to Lord Salisbury (Foreign Secretary), July 30, 1878, FO 50, Vol. 439.

appointment as an opportunity to make more direct contact with the Mexican government than it had since 1867. Lord Lyons, the British Ambassador in France, was instructed to learn the views of the Mexican government regarding a renewal of relations from Señor Velasco. The talks were to be private and unofficial.[36]

The first meeting of the diplomats, on December 13, 1880, was arranged by the German Ambassador in Paris. For nearly two years Velasco and Lyons sporadically discussed Anglo-Mexican difficulties.[37] Velasco admitted that Mexico wished to attract foreign capital. He told Lyons that his country feared territorial encroachments by the United States, saying that to prevent this Mexico was favoring American dollars and commerce. Velasco felt it was not safe to allow Mexican trade to fall almost entirely into American hands or to allow the foreign capital employed in Mexico to come exclusively from the United States. When talk turned to the problem of a renewal of Anglo-Mexican relations, Velasco explained that Great Britain and other nations had committed an unjustifiable act of war against Mexico when they recognized Maximilian's government. Each of these countries had to take the initiative in calling for a diplomatic agreement; Britain could not be given special treatment.

The Foreign Office in London considered its next move. Sir Charles Dilke wanted Mexico opened to British investors and merchants. He believed that Mexico preferred English capital, but if the diplomatic break continued American dollars would, of course, be used. It was obvious, according to Dilke, that the demands of bondholders and other claimants covered by conventions made prior to 1867 would prove embarrassing to the British government since Mexico denied their existence. Dilke was willing to deny that any of these claims were supported by the British government.[38] Lord Tenterden felt that

---

[36] Foreign Secretary to Lyons, No. 1408, Oct. 23, 1880, FO 50, Vol. 440.

[37] The Mexican summary of the early Velasco-Lyons talks may be found in México, Secretaría de Relaciones Exteriores, *Memoria . . . presentada al duodécimo congreso de la unión El C. Ignacio Mariscal,* Anexo Numero 31. Also see Lyons to Earl Granville (Foreign Secretary), Confidential No. 1151, Dec. 14, 1880, FO 50, Vol. 440; Granville to Lyons, Dec. 7, 1881, FO 50, Vol. 444; Foreign Office memorandum, Confidential, Feb. 14, 1881, FO 50, Vol. 437.

[38] Dilke memorandum, Jan. 21, 1881, FO 50, Vol. 440; also see Dilke's note on Lyons to Granville, No. 543, June 1, 1881, FO 50, Vol. 440.

it would be a mistake to submit to the Mexican demands, despite the pressure on the Foreign Office for a renewal of relations.[39] Edward Hertslet, the author of numerous memoranda on Mexican affairs, agreed with Tenterden. He argued that the recognition by various British and Mexican administrations of treaties and conventions signed between 1842 and 1867 made it impossible for the British government to shake off its responsibility so easily.

On December 7, 1881, after carefully studying these various opinions, the Foreign Office informed Lord Lyons that Britain hoped Mexico would state her intention of making an arrangement with the London and Convention bondholders. Diplomatic relations could then quickly be renewed since the declaration would be a substitute for the old agreements that Mexico considered void. Velasco immediately declared that his government could not agree to any declaration that might directly or indirectly open the way for diplomatic intervention on behalf of the bondholders by the British government. In any case, he argued, such a declaration was of little practical importance. Most of the Convention bonds were now in Mexican hands, having been purchased at various intervals, while the London bondholders were negotiating privately with Mexico for a settlement. When Lyons reminded Velasco that it was difficult for the Foreign Office to waive the right of subjects under conventions without some assurance that their claims would be adjusted, the Mexican Minister asked that the meetings temporarily be adjourned.[40] This announcement coincided with letters to the London Foreign Office from Chambers of Commerce in England mentioning opportunities to supply railway materials to Mexico, the closing of British trading houses in the Republic, and the need for an Anglo-Mexican commercial treaty.[41] It also came when the London bondholders had reached an impasse with the Mexican government

---

[39] Tenterden memorandum, Jan. 29, 1881, FO 50, Vol. 440.

[40] Details of the later Lyons-Velasco talks may be found in Granville to Lyons, Dec. 7, 1881, FO 50, Vol. 444; Lyons to Granville, Confidential No. 1112, Dec. 13, 1881, FO 50, Vol. 444; Lyons to Granville, No. 107, Feb. 6, 1882, FO 50, Vol. 444; Lyons to Granville, No. 1270, Dec. 12, 1882, FO 50, Vol. 440.

[41] Wolverhampton Chamber of Commerce to Granville, Feb. 14, 1882, FO 50, Vol. 438; Birmingham Chamber of Commerce to Granville, Dec. 21, 1882, FO 50, Vol. 438.

on the vexatious matter of their securities.[42]

Anglo-Mexican relations did not enter a new phase until January, 1883, when Lionel Carden, later British consul in Mexico City, was in the Republic preparing a report on the commerce of the country. After a meeting with Ignacio Mariscal, the Minister of Foreign Affairs, Carden told the Foreign Office of his belief that the Mexican government was ready to renew relations.[43] Carden was correct. The Mexican government, with Porfirio Díaz hovering in the backgound while a puppet held the presidency, was eager to have British pounds invested in the country. Mariscal believed Díaz wished to establish "a counterpoise to northern imperialism."[44] Mexico was even willing to pass over the question of the boundary between British Honduras and Mexico, a problem about which Mexican Ministers often had written in acid terms to London during the 1870's. Mexican pride demanded, however, that the first move come from London.

Lionel Carden's appraisal was given to Sir Julian Pauncefote and Lord Edmund Fitzmaurice at the Foreign Office. Pauncefote and Fitzmaurice realized that the question of who would formally take the initiative in calling for a resumption of relations had been a stumbling block since 1867. Lord Lyons once had suggested that it might be necessary "to put our pride in our pockets" and say that Great Britain wanted a renewal of relations.[45] Pauncefote and Fitzmaurice concurred and proposed to the Foreign Secretary that Lionel Carden might determine whether a friendly response would be given to such a statement before he delivered a formal invitation to discuss a restoration of diplomatic relations.[46] Carden followed these instructions and in late April, 1883, delivered a letter from the British Foreign Secretary to Ignacio Mariscal. It was obvious, stated Lord Granville, that prolonging the diplomatic break

[42] The Mexican committee appointed to study the Republic's foreign debt accomplished nothing, but the London bondholders did not intend to allow Mexico to forget her creditors. See the letter from W. W. Holmes, Secretary of the London bondholders in the *Times* (London), July 4, 1882.

[43] Carden to Granville, Confidential, Feb. 26, 1883, FO 50, Vol. 442.

[44] A speech in the Mexican Congress by Mariscal quoted in Isidro Fabela, *Belice: defensa de los derechos de México* (México, 1944), pp. 296-300.

[45] Lyons to Tenterden, March 8, 1881, FO 50, Vol. 440.

[46] These instructions are found in Granville to Carden, April 19, 1883, FO 50, Vol. 442.

would have no practical effect. He wrote that "Her Majesty's government desires to take the first step to renew diplomatic relations."[47] Granville suggested that envoys be appointed simultaneously to London and Mexico City to conduct the negotiations. On May 18, 1883, Mariscal accepted the invitation, pointedly noting that Britain had taken the initiative.[48]

Britain and Mexico quickly selected their envoys for the special mission. Sir Spenser St. John, a career diplomat who had served in France and Peru, began the trip to Mexico City, while Ignacio Mariscal, armed with instructions from the President, left for London.[49] Mariscal's instructions set forth the Mexican government's program for a renewal of relations. The envoy was to inform the Foreign Office that the position of the Republic regarding treaties and conventions made with Britain prior to the diplomatic break remained the same; these agreements were cancelled. Secondly, Mariscal was to press for a new commercial treaty on the most-favored-nation basis. It also was hoped that Mariscal could persuade the Foreign Office not to uphold the private claims made by Britons against the Mexican government after 1842. These claims, over two hundred in number, included losses and damages arising from unjust arrest, plunder of trains carrying British funds, robberies of British homes by government troops, and forced loans and requisitions. The Foreign Office tentatively had agreed to put the power of the British government behind these claims shortly before the break in 1867.[50] Finally, the Mexican envoy was to refrain from a discussion of the Honduras question.

Sir Spenser St. John arrived in Mexico in early June and announced what everyone already knew—that the London and Convention bondholder issue would make negotiations for a diplomatic renewal extremely difficult.[51] St. John conferred

---

[47] Granville to Mariscal, April 19, 1883, in México, Secretaría de Relaciones Exteriores, *Memoria . . . presentada al duodécimo congreso de la unión El C. Ignacio Mariscal*, Anexo Numero 27.

[48] Mariscal to Granville, May 18, 1883, *ibid.*, Anexo Numero 28.

[49] Instructions to Mariscal, June 12, 1883, *ibid.*, Anexo Numero 30.

[50] Hertslet memorandum, Nov. 9, 1881, FO 50, Vol. 437; Foreign Office memorandum, March 19, 1883, FO 50, Vol. 443.

[51] St. John to Mr. Jervoise (Foreign Office), June 16, 1883, FO 50, Vol. 441. St. John was pessimistic in June because the London bondholders again had failed to reach an agreement with the Mexican government. Details may be found in *South American Journal*, XXI (May 24, 1883), 12; *Investors' Monthly Manual*, XIII (May 31, 1883), 39.

with Acting Minister of Foreign Affairs, José Fernández, in July and August, 1883. Fernández recited the familiar Mexican arguments. Mexico did not intend to "repudiate its obligations," but no claims that existed before the renewal of relations were to be made the subject of diplomatic representation.[52] If Britain would agree to the terms outlined in Mariscal's instructions, Mexico for her part:

... would cover with a veil the share which Great Britain took in the European intervention, and would consider the moment of the renewal of relations as ... the birth of two states to political life, forgetting all the previous more or less well grounded motives of complaint of one against the other.[53]

The British viewpoint was that the rights of her citizens stated in the various conventions, notably that of 1851, could not be abandoned by Her Majesty's government.[54] No new Anglo-Mexican commercial treaty could be signed until some assurance was given that the bondholders' claims would be settled.

Officials at the Foreign Office believed that the seeming necessity of upholding old agreements was proving an insuperable barrier to a renewal of diplomatic relations. Lord Fitzmaurice noted that under existing conditions British claimants were receiving no money and had little chance of getting what was owed to them while the diplomatic breach remained open. He reminded his colleagues that Britain's main concern was to renew relations for the sake of trade and investment.[55] The validity of his statement was emphasized by the letters that arrived at the Foreign Office in 1883. A memorandum from fifty-four Chambers of Commerce protested that British trade with Mexico was being ruined while the diplomats argued. A delegate from the British-owned Mexican Railway Company wrote that unless "some stimulus is given to British commerce" it would be driven out by the United States. Another correspondent reminded the Office that British ma-

[52] A summary of the St. John-Fernández discussions may be found in Law Officers of the Crown to Granville, Jan. 22, 1884, FO 50, Vol. 447.

[53] Enclosure in St. John to Foreign Secretary, July 31, 1883, FO 50, Vol. 441.

[54] Mariscal to Fernández, Nov. 4, 1883, in México, Secretaría de Relaciones Exteriores, *Memoria . . . presentada al duodécimo congreso de la unión El C. Ignacio Mariscal*, Anexo Numero 39.

[55] Mr. Jervoise, memorandum respecting the renewal of relations with Mexico with minutes by Sir Julian Pauncefote and Lord Edmund Fitzmaurice, Nov. 7, 1883, FO 50, Vol. 443.

chinery might play an important role in Mexico if a mining boom developed. When diplomatic intercourse was resumed Britain might induce Mexico to revise her high duties on foreign machinery. Other letters pointed to the plans for railroads, aqueducts, harbors, and canals that were being presented in Mexico City. The opportunities for British investment were growing.[56]

In January, 1884, Fitzmaurice and Sir Julian Pauncefote presented a plan for renewing diplomatic relations to the Law Officers of the Crown. The Law Officers were asked to answer one question: Could Britain abandon the Convention bondholders and other claimants if Mexico promised in the document restoring relations that she would impartially examine the claims of Britons against Mexico after 1842? The Law Officers believed that the conventions could be abrogated legally.[57] They reasoned that Mexico had no intention of carrying out the terms of the old agreements. The only alternative was to set the stage for making new arrangements that promised some hope for the creditors. The Foreign Office was heartened by this legal opinion. Lord Fitzmaurice knew that British citizens had no chance of being paid until there was a renewal of diplomatic relations.

On April 20, 1884, Sir Spenser St. John began to prepare the document that was to renew Anglo-Mexican relations. A new treaty of peace, commerce, and navigation was to be made and until such a treaty was concluded, or for at least seven years, the two countries were to extend to the other the most-favored-nation treatment in all matters.[58] The British government agreed to give up its rights under previous conventions and agreements with the understanding that:

> The Mexican Government will order an impartial investigation to be made with respect to all the pecuniary claims of British subjects based on acts of the Federal Government anterior to the exchange of the ratifications of these Preliminaries, and will provide for the liqui-

[56] Memorandum from the Association of Chambers of Commerce to the Foreign Office, March 12, 1883, FO 50, Vol. 443; A. Renshaw (Mexican Railway Company) to Foreign Secretary, April 4, 1883, FO 50, Vol. 443; Robert Griffin (Privy Council for Trade) to Granville, June 13, 1883, FO 50, Vol. 443; *Pall Mall Gazette*, March 22, 1883.

[57] Law Officers of the Crown to Granville, Jan. 22, 1884, FO 50, Vol. 446.

[58] The full text of the agreement is found in Great Britain, *State Papers*, LXXVI (1884-85), 908-10.

dation of the amounts which may be found to be due them, as well as for the payment of those already recognized by the same Federal Government.[59]

The term "claims" referred to the Convention debt and to complaints of mistreatment made by Britons after 1842; it did not refer to the London debt. This problem was to be settled by private negotiations between Mexico and the London bondholders.

The Mexican government accepted these proposals and on August 6, 1884, St. John and José Fernández signed the Preliminary Agreement renewing diplomatic relations. Pressure from British traders, investors, certain diplomats in the Foreign Office, disgruntled bondholders, and the Mexican government's fear of domination by the United States were major factors in the restoration of relations. On August 6 St. John wrote of his hope for Anglo-Mexican accord to a colleague at the Foreign Office:

> There is no doubt of the present political importance of the post, which will daily increase as the Mexicans lean on the moral support of England. But what is perhaps of greater importance to us, is the opening of this country to British commerce. The social influence which a minister can exercise aids him considerably in obtaining acceptance of his views on important political and commercial questions. And we have been taking advantage of the influence which social intercourse produces to endeavor to bring to our views personages so important as General Díaz . . . and Romero Rubio.[60]

The *South American Journal* added its opinion on August 14:

> Truly this is a land that ought not be neglected. It offers smiling welcome to British enterprise which has been too long estranged from a field affording so many splendid opportunities for the remunerative investment of British funds. With the resumption of diplomatic relations between Mexico and England . . . the gates of Mexico will be opened wide to the influx of British enterprise and capital, which have done so much for the progress and development of other Spanish-American states.[61]

St. John was appointed Minister to Mexico shortly after the

[59] *Ibid.* A similar article, II, which had no practical importance, referred to Mexican claims against Great Britain. It was expected that a mixed commission would be established to study the private British claims.

[60] St. John to Pauncefote, Private, Aug. 6, 1884, FO 50, Vol. 445.

[61] *SAJ*, XXIII (Aug. 14, 1884), 13.

renewal of relations while Ignacio Mariscal took up residence in London as his country's representative. British consuls were appointed and the most important post, in Mexico City, was given to Lionel Carden. Many problems still remained unsolved. The London bondholder's debt, the English Convention, the settlement of private British claims, and the possibility of a treaty of trade and navigation were reserved for future negotiations. The Foreign Office expected that these issues could be settled rapidly.[62] In March, 1885, St. John informed his superiors in London that a masked ball in honor of Mrs. Porfirio Díaz soon would be held at the British legation. There seemed no better way to publicize Anglo-Mexican friendship than by giving a party for the First Lady of the Republic.

[62] They were settled but not with the speed hoped for by the Foreign Office. On June 23, 1886, the London bondholders agreed to exchange the bonds issued to them in 1864 by Maximilian in satisfaction of arrears of interest, for new 3 per cent Mexican government bonds at 50 per cent of their face value. Interest due after July 1, 1866, by 1885 amounting to £6,144,990, was converted into new bonds at 15 per cent. St. John then suggested that Convention bondholders be permitted to turn in their securities for bonds of the new issue. This was done. See enclosure in St. John to Foreign Office, Sept. 17, 1894, FO 50, Vol. 448; México, Secretaría de Hacienda, *Memoria correspondiente al ejército fiscal de 1885 a 1886 presentado al congreso de la unión por Lic. Manuel Dublán* (México, 1887). The settlement helped to restore Mexican credit in Europe and Britons invested in various bonds issued by city, state, and the national governments from 1885 to 1911. J. Fred Rippy, "English Investments in Mexico: A Story of Bonanzas and Heartbreaks," *Journal of Business*, XXVI (Oct., 1952), 228-42, says that the total invested in Mexican bonds by Englishmen before 1911 was about £25,000,000. A higher figure was given in *SAJ*, LXVI (Feb. 27, 1909), 242-43. Whatever the amount, English bondholders did not profit much from their holdings; see Rippy, *Journal of Business*, XXVI, 228-29. The bondholders' settlement was followed by the signing of a treaty of friendship, navigation, and commerce in 1887. The most time-consuming problem proved to be the settlement of the private British claims originating after 1842 against the Mexican government. The Claims Commission headed by Lionel Carden and General Félix Berriozábal worked nearly thirty months examining 281 claims. Payment to the thirty-one claimants whose claims were allowed was made in Mexican government bonds. See the author's "The Anglo-Mexican Claims Commission, 1884-1895," *Hispanic American Historical Review*, XXXVII (Nov., 1957), 471-79.

2. British Enterprise during the Diplomatic Imbroglio

The masked ball in Mexico City was Sir Spenser St. John's way of saying that he understood the Latin American mind. St. John knew that during the diplomatic rupture the United States had replaced Britain as Mexico's chief supplier of goods. He realized that British capital investments in the Republic were meager and that this reflected the strained relations between the two countries. St. John's party, and his subsequent plea for the British government to make Her Majesty's legation in Mexico City a showplace for influential Britons and Mexicans, was part of a plan to increase Anglo-Mexican economic ties.

When Díaz entered the capital in 1876 eight British mining companies, three railway concerns, a land-colonization company, a brewery, and a branch of the London Bank of Mexico and South America were listed at the Company Registration Office in London to work in the Republic.[1] These enterprises had a total paid-in capital of £7,752,078, most of which was invested in two concerns, the United Mexican Mining Company of Guanajuato, and the Mexican Railway Company linking Veracruz and Mexico City.[2] While the diplomatic imbroglio

[1] See Table 1, p. 22. Records of limited companies that concluded business before 1917 are being transferred from the Company Registration Office in Bush House, London, to the Public Record Office. The location of any company may first be checked by going to Bush House, and the Bush House citation will be used in this volume. The first citation of a company in this volume will include its name and file number. Thereafter, only the file number will be used.

[2] The paid-up or paid-in capital includes shares issued fully paid as well as for cash. The location of the Mexican Railway's route is traced on Map 2, p. 33. A list of

continued from 1876 to 1884, sixteen new Mexican companies were organized in London, but few of the twenty ventures on the Registrar's list in 1884 were important.[3] Only seven of the mining companies, the Mexican Railway enterprise, and the branch of the London bank regularly sent in their annual reports. Yet the years 1876-84 in many ways established a paradigm for British capital investment during the remainder of the Díaz period. The techniques of promotion used before 1885 enticed Britons into Mexican enterprise after that date. The areas that attracted British sterling before the Preliminary Agreement was signed continued to do so until 1911, and the problems encountered by the British companies from 1876 to 1884 persisted and often became more serious.

Table 1. _British limited companies organized to work in Mexico prior to January 1, 1876, and on the Company Registrar's list on that date_

Type of enterprise	Mining	Railways	Land companies	Breweries	Banking
Number organized	8	3[a]	1	1	1
Authorized capital	£2,835,220	6,916,060	50,000	50,000	900,000
Paid-up capital	£1,435,348	5,816,730	—	—	500,000

[a] Two of these concerns, the Yucatan State Railway Company and the Yucatan Railway and Warehouse Company, were not active enterprises.

the British limited mining companies organized to work in Mexico prior to December, 1885, and on the Registrar's list on that date is found in the Appendix, Table A.

[3] See Table 2, p. 23; Table 3, p. 23.

Table 2. *British limited companies organized between January 1, 1876 and December 31, 1884, to work in Mexico*

Type of enterprise	Mining	Banking	Public utilities
Number organized	14	1	1
Authorized capital	£2,967,325	900,000	100,000
Paid-up capital	£246,176	500,000	100,000

Table 3. *British limited companies registered to work in Mexico, end of 1884*

Type of Enterprise	Mining	Railways	Banking	Land companies	Public utilities	Totals
Number registered	16	1	1	1	1	20
Paid-up capital	£1,642,902[a]	7,820,780	500,000	—	100,000	10.06[b]

[a] Most of this amount, £1,230,398, was in the United Mexican Mining Company.
[b] Millions of pounds.

The mining story before 1885

British direct investments before 1885 may conveniently be divided into mining and railway activity.[4] Mining fever had

---

[4] Banking investments might be included, but banking concerns frequently issued only a yearly balance sheet. Most of their profitable years came after 1884. Sixteen important banks operated in the Federal District during the Díaz period. The London Bank of Mexico and South America paid dividends of about 13 per cent a year from 1899 to 1909 on a capital of £350,000. Britons held less than two-fifths of the shares of the National Bank of Mexico, capitalized at £1,600,000 in the 1880's and 1890's and at £3,100,000 from 1905 to 1910. This bank's annual returns averaged about 15 per cent from 1883 to 1911. A few Britons held shares in the International and Mortgage Bank of Mexico, formed in 1888. This concern paid average dividends of 4.5 per cent a year from 1890 to 1911. See Great Britain, Diplomatic and Consular Reports, Miscel-

been endemic in Mexico for centuries when Britons first brought their energies and money into the country in the 1820's.[5] Most of them quickly drew back with burned fingers, but the reports of silver and gold bonanzas continued to work their magic: "During the waves of English enthusiasm . . . no discrimination was shown. Anything in the semblance of a mine that could be bought, optioned, or located, and some that did not exist, were floated. Many people were fooled and, as in a lottery, a few drew prizes."[6]

The fragmentary official records of the active companies from 1876 to 1884, and the lack of coverage in journals and newspapers, make it difficult to reconstruct their activities. The first task of any enterprise was to acquire property and promote its venture in England. The oldest working company in 1876, the United Mexican enterprise, purchased a silver mining area in Guanajuato from a defunct English company in 1827.[7] The mines had been worked for at least sixty years when the mining engineers, bankers, and London businessmen who formed the nucleus of the United Mexican Mining Company assumed owership. Another silver lode near Guaymas, Sonora, also had been exploited for sixty years when two Englishmen affiliated with the London Bank of Mexico and South America were convinced by prospectors in the Sierra Madre region that the mines could be revived by using new reduction methods. George Hockin and William Marshall raised enough capital in London and New York to purchase the property in 1869 for £43,000, and shortly thereafter to organize the Almada and Tirito Silver Mining Company.[8] The third British company operating in 1876 was launched eight years earlier by John

---

laneous Series No. 517, *Report on the Federal District, 1899* (London, 1900); Walter Flavius McCaleb, *Present and Past Banking in Mexico* (New York, 1920), contains an adequate summary of the subject. Dividend records may be found in F. C. Mathieson and Sons, eds., *Stock Exchange Ten Year Record of Prices and Dividends* (London, 1907, 1915), I, IX.

[5] J. Fred Rippy, "Latin America and the British Investment 'Boom' of the 1820's," *Journal of Modern History*, XIX (March, 1947), 122-29; W. A. Prichard, "Looking for Mines in Mexico," *Mining Magazine*, I (Nov., 1909), 205.

[6] Prichard, *MM*, I, 205.

[7] Company Record Office, File No. 2744, United Mexican Mining Company.

[8] The company's name was changed slightly after its registration. See CRO, File No. 4732, The Almada and Tirito Consolidated Silver Mining Company. Also see Stock Exchange Library, London, Prospectus for the Almada and Tirito Consolidated Silver Mining Company.

Potts, a merchant who lived in Mexico during the Maximilian era. Potts diligently sent out mining experts into the Guerrero district until they discovered a promising gold quartz and placer area near Cozuca, about 230 miles from Mexico City. The owners were content to take £15,000 in shares of the company organized by Potts and six other Britons.[9] The directors of the companies organized after 1876 usually excluded details of their purchase from the concern's files. Two of the ventures, and probably many more, purchased their property from American owners living in Texas and New York City.[10] The organizers of La Trinidad, Limited, attracted by an advertisement in the *Mining Journal* paid for by James T. Browne, a London promoter, bought the mines he owned near Guaymas, Sonora, and hoped that the £2,000,000 in silver allegedly taken from the lode before 1880 was a portent of future success.[11]

The promoting zeal of men such as James T. Browne was matched by mining company directors and publicists whose task was to encourage investment in their particular companies. The job of promoting a Mexican company between 1876 and 1884 by issuing a prospectus and buying space in the *Mining Journal* or other publications was an arduous one. Angry bondholders were publicizing Mexico's poor record as a credit risk; British subjects had no official protection in the country; and reports of forced loans, frequent robberies, excessive taxation, and general backwardness countinued to filter into the Foreign Office from British travelers and residents.[12] The two economic slumps that hit Britain in 1876 and 1883, bringing a dip in the nation's investments around the globe, also contributed to the chore of promoting Mexican enterprise.[13] The

[9] CRO, File No. 4478, Guerrero [*sic*] Gold Mining Company; SEL, Prospectus for the Guerrero [*sic*] Gold Mining Company.

[10] CRO, File No. 18783, The Anglo-Mexican Mining Company; CRO, File No. 19108, Santa Rita Company; CRO, File No. 19452, The North Mexican Silver Mining Company.

[11] The history of the mine is summarized in *Mining World and Engineering Record*, XXVIII (Feb. 28, 1885), 215-16; *MJ*, LIV (Nov. 29, 1884), 275; *ibid.* (Dec. 6, 1884), 1424; SEL, Prospectus for La Trinidad; CRO, File No. 20507, La Trinidad.

[12] See the letters of Bourdillon to Derby, 1876, FO 50, Vol. 429; J. J. Aubertin, *A Flight to Mexico* (London, 1882), pp. 23-24, 97, 124.

[13] Evidence of the drop in investments may be found in the author's "British Investments in Colorado Mines," *The Colorado Magazine*, XXX (Oct., 1953), 241-46; and "North Carolina and the British Investor, 1880-1910," *North Carolina Historical Review*, XXXII (Oct., 1955), 512-18.

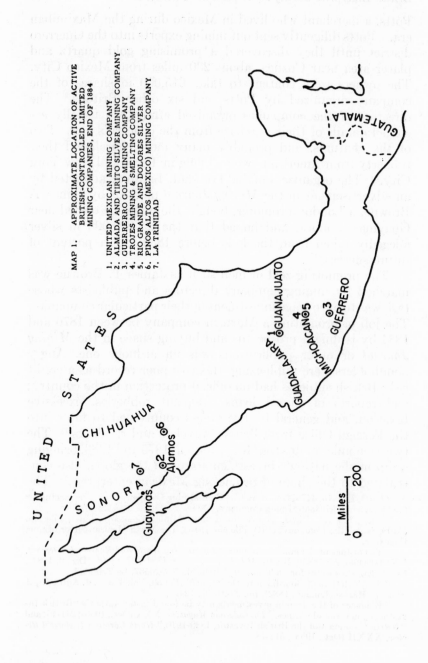

MAP 1. APPROXIMATE LOCATION OF ACTIVE
BRITISH-CONTROLLED LIMITED
MINING COMPANIES, END OF 1884

1. UNITED MEXICAN MINING COMPANY
2. ALMADA AND TIRITO SILVER MINING COMPANY
3. GUERRERO GOLD MINING COMPANY
4. TROJES MINING & SMELTING COMPANY
5. RIO GRANDE AND DOLORES SILVER
6. PINOS ALTOS (MEXICO) MINING COMPANY
7. LA TRINIDAD

Mexican prospectuses had a standard format. A prominent place was given to the list of company directors, particularly when they included members of Parliament, high-ranking military personnel, and men with business experience in Mexico. The availability of labor, water, and timber in the district was stressed, as was the degree of protection offered to Britons and their bullion and supply trains by state officials. Finally, investors were bombarded by testimonials from engineers, prospectors, and financiers who saw an El Dorado in every mine.[14]

The promotional effort of the North Mexican Silver Mining Company of Chihuahua, organized in 1884, was a model of sanguinary excellence. An advertisement in the *Mining Journal* on March 2, 1884, recalled "the thrilling adventures of Cortes in Mexico" and the tales of Spanish galleons laden with untold wealth, and implied that all this and more awaited Britons who invested in the North Mexican enterprise. Chihuahua was destined to become a marvel in the world of mining when the railroads then being constructed covered the state. Since labor was plentiful and cheap in Chihuahua, few skilled workers would have to be transported from other parts of Mexico or from Britain. After modern technology and efficiency corrected the mistakes made by the original owners who touched only the surface veins, investors could expect yearly dividends of at least 13 per cent on their capital. A "prominent engineer" admitted in the *Mining Journal* that he had never seen a better unwrought silver mining property in all his work in England, Brazil, and Colorado.[15]

Almost every major income and occupational group responded to calls for capital from the mining companies, but there was a preponderance of barristers, bankers, brokers, civil engineers, army officers, members of Commons, and London merchants in each of the pre-1885 active concerns. There was one significant change in the structure of the enterprises organized before 1876 and mining ore in that year, as compared to those formed between 1876 and 1884. Control of the shares

---

[14] Prospectuses are arranged without any order under particular years in the SEL. Lists of directors and the positions they held are found in *Directory of Directors, 1885* (London, 1886).

[15] *MJ*, LIV (March 2, 1884), 1280.

in the United Mexican and Almada companies was spread
evenly among 600 and 320 shareholders respectively in 1876,
and the situation altered but slightly during the next eight
years.[16] The newer concerns had fewer shareholders and control
in all the companies was centralized in the hands of a dozen or
less investors. This may have been planned, but it also is
conceivable that a general public apathy toward Mexican
enterprise dictated that a small block of shareholders take a
great many shares if the company was to survive.[17]

A glimpse of the problems encountered by the companies
working in Mexico provides a composite, although regrettably
hazy, picture of their operations.[18] The small British staff often
found that mining in an underdeveloped country produced a
variety of unexpected difficulties. A British manager was killed
by his own workers following the refusal of merchants in a
near-by town to take the scrip he had issued until money
arrived from England. Miners at another site persisted in
leaving the mines at harvest time to work on local haciendas;
and Indian raids in Sonora temporarily sapped the labor force
of three companies in 1883 when the governor conscripted
workers to quell the disturbances.[19] A perennial problem for
most companies was the lack of all-weather transportation
facilities. The La Trinidad Company began to build a 165-mile
wagon road from its property to the Sonora Railway in 1884
after a fruitless appeal to the Mexican government for aid.
Even the two oldest British companies did not solve their
transportation problems before 1885. A narrow-gauge railway
operated in a mile square area around the United Mexican camp

[16] File No. 2744; File No. 4732. There were exceptions. Anthony de Rothschild,
Sir Henry James, M. P., and Charles Custom of the London Stock Exchange held large
blocks of shares in the United Mexican Mining Company.
[17] See for example, CRO, File No. 11895, Rio Grande and Dolores Silver Company;
CRO, File No. 15178, La Gran Compana Gold and Silver Company; File No. 10768;
File No. 19452.
[18] The technological aspects of British mining in Mexico were mentioned infrequently
in company records or British journals. There was, in fact, only one reported example
of power machinery being used by a British venture. See *MJ*, LIV (Feb. 2, 1884),
Supplement. Three methods of treating silver ore were used at this time in Mexico:
lixiviation or the leaching process in which the silver was separated by washing with a
solvent; by smelting; and by amalgamating the ore with mercury. The last named, the
patio process, was used by most enterprises.
[19] *Two Republics,* July 12, 1884; *MW*, XXII (Jan. 7, 1882), 14-15; *MJ*, LIII (June 2,
1883), 55; David M. Pletcher, "The Development of Railroads in Sonora," *Inter-
American Economic Affairs*, I (March, 1948), 7-8.

in Guanajuato in 1884, but rails, other equipment, and provisions for the company were shipped by pack train from the capital as they had been since the 1820's.[20] The Almada concern in Sonora still was a hundred miles from a railroad after the completion of the Sonora line in the early 1880's. The company hoped that a railway might be constructed from their Alamos property westward to the coast. Then equipment could be brought by boat from San Francisco and transportation inland would be assured. The idea was considered in Mexico City before 1885 but nothing was done.[21]

Aside from reports of cave-ins, floods, and fires in the British mines, the other problem that concerned at least one company before 1885 was what the Chairman of the United Mexican enterprise termed "the loss on silver exchange."[22] His statement introduced a phenomenon that was an integral part of Mexico's economy throughout the Díaz period, and one that played an important part in the story of American and British enterprise from 1876 to 1910.[23] The fall in the value of silver, and particularly the Mexican peso, was caused, first of all, by the rising world production of silver after 1850, coupled with the relative decline in gold production. In the decade 1851-61 over 9.3 million kilograms of silver were produced; in the ten year period from 1881 to 1890 the figure rose to 31.2 million kilograms. In Mexico the most dramatic surge upward in silver production occurred in this latter decade following the passage of more liberal mining laws and the introduction of foreign capital. Secondly, at the same time more silver was flooding the market many countries began to substitute gold-standard currencies for bimetallism. To complete the triangle, the monopoly of the Mexican peso in the Far East was lost as countries such as Japan, the United States, and France, for various reasons, began to produce their own silver coin to replace the peso. These events did not occur simultaneously but their cumulative effect, according to David M. Pletcher,

[20] *MJ*, LIII (Nov. 3, 1883), Supplement; *ibid.* (Nov. 10, 1883), 1287.

[21] Manuel Dublán and José María Lozano, eds., *Colección legislativa completa de las disposiciones legislativas expedidas desde la independencia de la República* (México, 1876-1912), *XVI*, 17-26.

[22] *MJ*, XLVI (May 6, 1876), 511; *MW*, XXX (Oct. 30, 1886), 499, contains a brief summary of this problem.

[23] David M. Pletcher, "The Fall of Silver in Mexico, 1870-1910, and Its Effects on American Investments," *The Journal of Economic History*, XVIII (March, 1958), 33-55.

"was a continuous decline of the value of silver in terms of gold and of the value of the peso in terms of the American dollar, the British pound, and other standards of measure."[24] When a British company earning pesos in Mexico had to buy supplies, pay off its indebtedness, or issue dividends in pounds, it was adversely affected by an exchange rate that called for an increasingly larger amount of pesos to pay for a given amount of British pounds. Conversely, certain companies might counterbalance the silver handicap if they were in a position to draw most of their food, labor, and general supplies from Mexico. The cheap peso could be used to cover these expenses, as well as for buying whatever land was needed. The decline was not steady but the average price of an ounce of silver slipped from 52*d*. in 1876 to 50*d*. in 1884, 33*d*. in 1892, 22*d*. in 1898, 20*d*. in 1900, and 19½*d*. in 1902-3.[25]

The ramifications of the silver decline for each facet of British enterprise must be considered in their proper place. In the case of the British mining companies the effect of the silver inflation depended partly on whether enough ore other than silver could be mined and sold abroad at profits in gold to cover the expense of importing explosives, power equipment if any, and fuel. Ideally the silver from the mine could be used to pay expenses in Mexico; the other ores could be sold abroad for gold. The pre-1885 British ventures were not yet cushioned by the Mexican government's policy of buying up silver at a fixed rate nor were they in 1884 helped much by the lowering of taxes and the liberalizing of mining laws. Since the United Mexican Mining Company was mining silver almost exclusively in the year in which the chairman noted the loss on exchange, it is obvious that he felt the declining value of silver was *one factor* in the failure of the concern to return dividends in 1876. How then, given the decreasing value of silver from 1876 to 1884, can one explain the rise in the quotation of the company's shares in 1884 and the dividend of 5 per cent in that year? No single

---

[24] *Ibid.*, p. 38.

[25] These figures are taken from México, Secretaría de Hacienda, *Memoria correspondiente al sexagésimo noveno año económico de 1° de julio de 1893 a 30 de junio de 1894 presentada por el secretaría de hacienda al congreso de la unión* (México, 1894), 400-50, report by Joaquín Casasús; *SAJ*, XXVI (May 18, 1895), 197; *ibid.*, LIV (Dec. 12, 1903), 571; Great Britain, Diplomatic and Consular Reports, Annual Series No. 3039, *Report for the Year 1902 on the Trade and Commerce of Vera Cruz* (London, 1904).

cause explains this development, but it is significant that the company discovered a large silver lode in the summer of 1883 and that more than enough ore was mined to compensate for the depreciation in the value of silver that was taking place. The United Mexican's future depended on, among other things, how much ore could be drawn from the lode, and on what direction the price of silver would move. Only the United Mexican Company mentioned the silver issue prior to 1885, and it was not an important factor in the wretched dividend record of the other six British mining enterprises. The Almada company returned 5 per cent dividends to investors in 1876, but fires, floods, mismanagement involving high salaries for directors, exorbitant expenditures for equipment, and especially the lack of any highly productive veins, brought the concern close to bankruptcy in 1884.[26] The other companies simply found only a few traces of silver.

The Mexican Railway to 1885

The exiguous nature of British mining enterprise and the general economic backwardness of the country in the 1870's and early 1880's was in part an effect, and undoubtedly also a cause, of Mexico's inadequate transportation system. On August 20, 1864, Antonio Escandón, a wealthy Mexican *hacendado* who held a concession from the government to construct a line from Veracruz to Mexico City, transferred this right to English financiers. The Imperial Mexican Railway, Limited, was then organized in London with an authorized capital of £2,700,000.[27] Escandón was on the list of original subscribers that included a governor and director of the Bank of England and an associate of the famous firm of Baring Brothers. In 1868 the company accepted legal domicile in the Republic with the rights and obligations of a Mexican enterprise. The Mexican government

---

[26] *Ibid.* (May 19, 1883), 593; *MJ*, LIII (Jan. 13, 1883), 54.

[27] The word "Imperial" was dropped after Maximilian's execution. CRO, File No. 1543, The Mexican Railway Company. A summary of Mexico's early railroad history is found in J. Fred Rippy, *Latin America and the Industrial Age* (New York, 1947), pp. 142-51; also see *Herapath's Railway and Commercial Journal*, XXXVIII (May 13, 1876), 541.

contracted to pay a subsidy of 560,000 pesos a year for twenty-five years after the line was completed. Arrangements were made to carry federal troops and government freight at reduced rates, and maximum charges were established for all other types of goods and passenger classes. These rates could be reduced by government order whenever the company was able to pay more than 8 per cent annual dividends on its ordinary shares. A final clause in the contract contained the company's promise to construct a new dock at Veracruz in anticipation of the increased trade.[28]

The railroad was opened from coast to capital in 1873 after five years of hectic and sporadic building punctuated by high expenses, cries of foreign domination from Mexican politicians, and probably outright fraud on the part of the contractors.[29] Branch lines from Apizaco to Puebla and from Tejería to Jalapa, the latter a mule service, increased the length of the railroad to a total of 293 miles. The Mexican Railway was the only important line in a country that had less than 400 miles of track. The main line from Veracruz to Mexico City passed through some of the finest fruit, coffee, sugar cane, tobacco, wheat, and corn areas in the Republic. If a derailment did not delay the train, or if the soldiers who usually traveled as a protective escort were not called into action, passengers arrived in the capital after a journey of nineteen to twenty hours. They passed over 10 viaducts, 55 iron bridges, 43 wooden bridges, and through 15 tunnels.[30]

Reports of the railway's influence were made soon after it opened. Wagon trains were diverted from their old routes and brought goods from isolated areas to stations on the main line. Rumors were circulated that new industries would spring up

[28] David M. Pletcher, "The Building of the Mexican Railway," *HAHR*, XXX (Feb., 1950), 44; México, Ministerio de Fomento, Colonización y Comercio, *Decretos de concesión, 1876* (México, 1877), pp. 26-35.
[29] Pletcher, *HAHR*, XXX, 53-54. I am indebted to Professor Pletcher for permission to reproduce the map depicting the route of the Mexican Railway, see Map 2, p. 33. Readers who wish to examine the early history of the railroad in detail should see Francisco Calderón, *La vida económica*, in Daniel Cosío Villegas, *Historia moderna de México: La República restaurada* (México, 1955), pp. 608-70. This excellent volume also contains photographs of some of the early contractors and promoters of the railway concerns, see pp. 416-17. When complete, Villegas' six volume work will cover the history of Mexico from 1867 to 1911. Volume VI was not available in time for use in the writing of this monograph.
[30] File No. 1543, I; Aubertin, pp. 37-38; *El Monitor Republicano*, May, 6, 1881.

along the right of way. In 1873, 1874, and 1875 the company carried an average of 119,000 freight tons a year, 20 per cent of which was pulque, the "food, drink, and medicine" of thousands of Mexicans. Over 200,000 passengers used the railroad in one year, and in Orizaba and other key cities simple streetcar systems operating from the station to the town square were built by enterprising residents anxious to take advantage of the traffic.[31]

The company was governed in London by a board of ten directors, two of whom were appointed by the Mexican government under laws passed in 1867 and 1868. The authorized capital of the company stood at £6,266,060 in 1876, divided into 135,000 ordinary shares at £20; 127,705 first preference 8 per cent shares at £20; and 50,598 6 per cent second preference shares at the same price.[32] All of the first and second preference shares and 112,698 of the ordinary shares were taken up by 1876. The paid-up capital thus totaled £5,816,730, but despite the large number of shareholders in the company, the Mexican

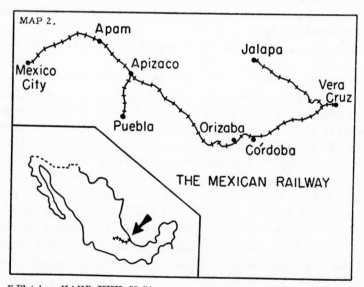

MAP 2.

Apam
Jalapa
Mexico City
Apizaco
Vera Cruz
Puebla
Orizaba
Córdoba

THE MEXICAN RAILWAY

---

[31] Pletcher, *HAHR*, XXX, 53-54.

[32] There also were mortgage bonds for which £2,000,000 Perpetual 6 per cent debenture stock was issued in 1880 at par. See File No. 1543, I.

Railway, like the British mining concerns organized between 1876 and 1884, was controlled by a few investors. Although there were 741 ordinary shareholders in 1876, the Mexican government, Antonio Escandón, William Barrón, a prominent Mexico City financier, Augustus Sillem, a company director, and the firm of Antony Gibbs in London, controlled more than 50 per cent of the ordinary shares.[33] The 127,705 first preference shares were distributed fully paid in 1874 to creditors of the company. There were 165 shareholders in 1876 but Escandón, George Gibbs, and George B. Crawley, whose company built part of the railroad, controlled 75 per cent of the shares. William Barrón, Antony Gibbs, and Escandón held a majority of the second preference shares that also were issued to cover company debts.[34]

The company's staff in Mexico consisted of a chief engineer, three superintendents of maintenance, a local superintendent in Jalapa, two locomotive superintendents, a chief accountant, and the head of company stores. It was this staff that watched helplessly as revolutionaries dynamited trains, destroyed freight, and robbed passengers in the melee preceding the overthrow of President Lerdo de Tejada.[35]

The comparative quiet that settled over the Republic following Díaz' victory was noted by the chairman of the company with unfeigned relief. Fifty per cent more passengers traveled on the Mexico City-Veracruz route in 1877 than in the preceding year, and the number of passengers and the total receipts continued to increase in 1878. The line carried 39,000 more tons of freight in 1877 than in 1876; in 1878 the figure was 50,000 more freight tons.[36] This was encouraging news for shareholders who had not yet received any returns on their investment, but it was offset by the Mexican government's inability to fully pay its promised subsidy in 1877 and 1878, the attempt of the workers in Veracruz harbor to prevent the opening of the company's dock facilities because it might threaten their

---

[33] *Ibid.* The Mexican government sold its shares in 1881 amidst complaints from the press; see *El Monitor Republicano*, May 3, 1881; *La Patria*, May 3, 1881.
[34] File No. 1543, I.
[35] *TR*, April 12, 1876; *ibid.*, May 17, 1876; *RJ*, XXXIX (Jan. 6, 1877), 7-8.
[36] See the chart in Matías Romero, *Railways in Mexico* (Washington, 1882), p. 201.

employment, and the slight but continued decline in the price of silver. [37]

The years 1879 and 1880 were the most profitable for investors since the railroad opened in 1873.[38] Careful management, a dip in foreign fuel prices, a substantial payment on the subvention by the Mexican government, and the long-delayed opening of the Veracruz dock contributed to this upswing.

Table 4. *Dividend record of the Mexican Railway Company, 1876-1884*

Year	First preference £2,254,100 (per cent)	Second preference £1,011,960 (per cent)	Ordinary £2,254,720 (per cent)
1876	Nil	Nil	Nil
1877	Nil	Nil	Nil
1878	Nil	Nil	Nil
1879	5-5	Nil	Nil
1880	8-8	5-5	½-½
1881	8-8	6 6	8-6½
1882	8-8	6-6	9½-14
1883	8-8	6-6	8-4
1884	8-8	6-Nil	1-Nil

More important than these and other factors was the railroad's position as a carrier of building materials used in the construction of the southern end of a railroad that was to link Mexico City to Ciudad Juárez near El Paso, Texas. In 1879 only 5,732 tons under this heading were transported; in 1880 the figure was 14,739 tons.[39] The improvement in the company's finances and the promise of greater revenues for a number of years as the

[37] The company believed that vested interests in Veracruz had successfully petitioned the government to protect them from competition. See *RJ*, XL (May 17, 1879), 544.

[38] Mexican Railway Company, *A Review of the Mexican Railway, 1879-1884* (London, 1885). This document is in the British Museum. It is a one-page summary of the half-year reports issued by the company. The semi-annual reports were published by the company, and some may still be examined in the files of the enterprise. The dividend record of the Mexican Railway, 1876-1884, is found in Table 4, p. 35.

[39] *Ibid.*

nation's railroad network expanded accounted for the rapid subscription to the £265,000 in 8 per cent bonds issued by the company in late 1879. Despite the loss on silver exchange that cost the company over £63,000 in 1879 and 1880, the net earnings were high enough to give holders of first preference shares 5 per cent dividends in June and December, 1879.[40] In 1880 the returns were increased to a total of 16 per cent. When second preference and ordinary shareholders received dividends in 1880 it was obvious, as one investor commented, that "a great change has come over the face of affairs in Mexico."[41]

The company continued to enjoy good times in 1881 and 1882. London's leading railway magazine documented its belief that the most important reason for the large dividends was the traffic in rail supplies sent to the Mexican Central's El Paso-Mexico City line, and to the Mexican National, another American line that was being constructed between Mexico City and Laredo, Texas.[42]. The Mexican Railway hauled 84,943 tons of railroad equipment in 1881 and 1882, four times as much as it carried in 1879 and 1880. The Chairman of the Mexican Railway, aware of the implications of these statistics, insisted that investors would have received dividends in 1882 even if no rails and supplies had been carried for the new concerns. He admitted, however, that the dividends for ordinary shareholders would have been 6 to 8 per cent rather than the 23 ½ per cent they received in 1882. The *Railway Journal* was skeptical, but it could hardly deny the existence of the quotation of 147 for ordinary shares on the Stock Exchange in January, 1883.[43]

The quotation began a downward spiral in February and by March, 1883, the figure barely reached 100. The *Mining Journal* attributed this to the public's realization that as the railways moved northward equipment would be shipped from Texas rather than Veracruz, and the Mexican Railway inevitably would lose its most important source of revenue. When the two railways ultimately were completed they would present the Mexican Railway with competition it could not stand.[44]

[40] *Ibid.*
[41] *RJ*, XLII (Dec. 18, 1880), 1456.
[42] *Ibid.*, XLIV (July 1, 1882), 783.
[43] *Ibid.*, XLV (Jan. 27, 1883), 115; *ibid.* (June 2, 1883), 642.
[44] *MJ*, LIII (March 10, 1883), 287.

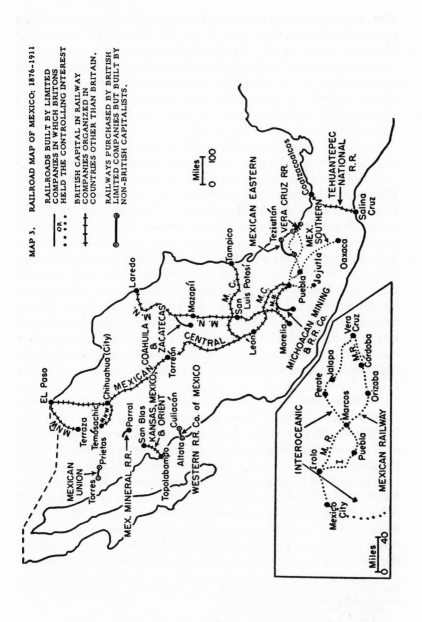

MAP 3. RAILROAD MAP OF MEXICO: 1876-1911

RAILROADS BUILT BY LIMITED COMPANIES IN WHICH BRITONS HELD THE CONTROLLING INTEREST

BRITISH CAPITAL IN RAILWAY COMPANIES ORGANIZED IN COUNTRIES OTHER THAN BRITAIN.

RAILWAYS PURCHASED BY BRITISH LIMITED COMPANIES BUT BUILT BY NON-BRITISH CAPITALISTS.

Miles
0   100

El Paso
Terraza
Temósachic
Prietos
Torres
Chihuahua (City)
MEXICAN UNION
M.N.W.
MEX. MINERAL R.R.
Parral
San Blas
KANSAS, MEXICO & ORIENT
Topolobampo
Altata
Culiacán
WESTERN R.R. Co. of MEXICO

MEXICAN COAHUILA & ZACATECAS
N.M.
W.
Torreón
Mazapíl
M. C.
San Luis Potosí
León
CENTRAL
M.C.
Morelia
MICHOACAN MINING & R.R. Co.
Puebla
Laredo
Tampico
MEXICAN EASTERN
Teziutlán
VERA CRUZ RR.
Coatzacoalcos
MEX. SOUTHERN
Jojutla
Oaxaca
Salina Cruz
TEHUANTEPEC NATIONAL R.R.

Miles
0   40

Mexico City
Irolo
INTEROCEANIC
M. R.
Puebla
Perote
Jalapa
Marcos
Orizaba
Córdoba
M.R.
Vera Cruz
MEXICAN RAILWAY

The company was, in fact, faced by more direct and immediate competition than that offered by the Mexican Central and Mexican National. By 1883 a Mexican enterprise was making slow progress on a railroad from Mexico City to Veracruz that was to follow a somewhat different route than the one taken by the Mexican.[45] A short line from Mexico City to Irolo was open in June and already a portion of the Mexican Railway's pulque traffic was being diverted.

These problems were discussed at the Mexican Railway's annual meeting in June, 1883. The chairman attempted to sound an optimistic chord. He doubted that goods from Europe would be sent to a seaport in the United States and then shipped by rail to Mexico City; they would continue to enter Mexico at Veracruz. Shareholders also were asked to consider the advantages of a larger railroad system in Mexico. The American lines eventually would raise the standard of living in areas through which they passed; this would increase the demand for foreign goods and the Mexican Railway would be on hand to haul the extra load. The consequences of having a competitor on the Mexico City-Veracruz route was not examined in open debate, but the chairman's announcement that the company was lowering freight rates from Mexico City to Irolo made it clear that the directors intended to fight for control of the traffic between the two points.[46]

Shareholders continued to receive a stream of bad news from Mexico between June and December, 1883. A yellow fever epidemic that struck Veracruz kept shippers from the port at the same time the needs of the new northern railway lines steadily declined. From January to June, 1883, about 28,000 tons of railroad supplies and equipment were carried inland from Veracruz; from July to December the figure fell to 16,391 tons.[47] Added to this was the continued drop in the price of silver, a drought that reduced the average yield of sugar, grain, and other produce outside Veracruz, and the continuing default of the Mexican government on the subsidy it owed the company

---

[45] A summary of the concessions granted by the government is found in Fred W. Powell, *The Railroads of Mexico* (Boston, 1921), pp. 139-43. See Map 3, p. 37, for a glimpse of the Irolo-Mexico City section.

[46] *RJ*, XLVI (June 2, 1883), 642, 645.

[47] MRC, *A Review of the Mexican Railway, 1879-1884* (London, 1885).

and on the sum due for carrying government freight.[48] The effect of the above factors was a diminution in company receipts of almost £130,000 during the last six months of 1883, a decline that took its heaviest toll on the ordinary shareholders. The company's net receipts in 1884 totaled £16,000 less than in the previous year. The most revealing statistics in the balance sheet were those that showed the company carried only 2,331 tons of railroad equipment for other lines within the Republic.[49] This was 47,000 tons less than in 1882, when the company returned its highest dividends. Only the first preference shareholders received a full return on their capital in 1884, and for the first time in five years no dividends were paid to the second preference or ordinary shareholders during the period July to December.

The progress of the Mexican Railway before 1885, or the lack of it, was a topic for bitter debate among Mexicans and Britons. The vagaries of available statistical data and the tendency of apologists and detractors of the line to overstate their case make it difficult to appraise the railroad's early role in Mexico. The company undoubtedly was a valuable addition to the Mexican economic and social scene. It contributed to the building of new railways, carried freight at speeds and with a degree of safety that previously had been impossible, and, although the impact is impossible to measure, the company increased the mobility of a portion of the Mexican population through its passenger service. In 1874, for example, there was one stagecoach capable of carrying twelve thin passengers operating between Mexico City and the village of Tlalnepantla, ten miles distant. Between 1876 and 1882 the Mexican Railway carried an average of almost five hundred persons each week between the village and the capital.[50]

The shareholders in the Mexican Railway Company received higher dividends for their efforts than investors in any important British or American line before 1911. These returns would have been greater had it not been for the silver exchange problem and the failure of the Díaz-González administrations to pay the

[48] *RJ*, XLV (Sept. 8, 1883), 1074; *ibid*. (Nov. 24, 1883), 1347; *The Mexican Financier*, VI (June 20, 1885), 189-90.
[49] MRC, *A Review of the Mexican Railway, 1879-1884* (London, 1885).
[50] Romero, p. 62.

company what it was owed. This does not negate the fact that
the dividends stemmed mainly from causes that no longer
existed by 1884.

Critics of the company complained that its rates were too
high and that it did not do enough for Mexico before 1885. In
1884 the lowest freight charges from Chicago to Mexico City via
the American-built Central line were only slightly higher than
the rates set by the Mexican Railway for the comparatively
short run from Veracruz to the capital.[51] Matías Romero
contended that selfishness and poor management were responsible for the high charges. He felt that the cost of the line
could have been cut 75 per cent if certain concessionaires had
not insisted that the railway pass through their estates. The
total costs also were boosted by beginning construction from
the capital and not the coast. Rates were kept high to pay off
the initial outlay and to take advantage of the company's
monopoly position, but the results for Mexican trade were
unfortunate. The diplomat and author insisted that the value
of Mexico's exports in the early 1880's expanded in spite of,
rather than because of, the Mexican Railway.[52]

The company directors countered by equating the rates
with the railway's high working costs. Engines were able to
carry only small loads over the rugged terrain on the main
route, but because of the constant climbing and braking the
fuel costs were high whatever weight was being hauled. The
railroad's maintenance bill was high, partly because of the
effects of tropical rains and falling rocks, two factors that the
company could scarcely control.[53] The directors did not mention that a more favorable exchange rate and the payment of
the government's debts might have eased their financial burden.
They did, however, reject the implication that a severe slash
in rates would stimulate agricultural production in eastern
Mexico, expand the consuming capacity of the Mexican population, and increase the company's revenues. They probably
were correct since Mexican agricultural progress in the late
nineteenth century was retarded by flaws in the economy that
lay outside the adjustment of company policy. Better and

[51] *Railroad Gazette* (Sept. 18, 1885), p. 6.
[52] Romero, pp. 5-10.
[53] *RJ*, XXXVIII (Jan. 1, 1876), 3; *ibid.*, XLI (Jan. 5, 1878), 8.

cheaper transportation was, of course, needed, but so too were more trained farmers, modern equipment, better irrigation, and capital for expansion. Equally plausible was the company's belief that the increased consumption of foreign imports did not depend on a diminution of the railroad's rates. Mexican tariff walls were enormous, and the adverse silver exchange rate made foreign luxuries the exclusive province of the wealthy. The millionaires would continue to purchase imports if the freight charges were lowered; the position of the peon and the urban white collar worker would not be affected. *The Times* (London) seemed to sum up the company's approach in 1884 when it wrote: "Years must elapse before there is much agricultural . . . produce to be carried by Mexican railroads or before the wants of the masses will fill many freight cars."[54]

The company's acceptance of this point of view may account for the campaign in 1884 to attract more passengers. Colored advertisements touting Puebla and Cholula as "the ancient site of the pyramids of the Aztecs" were placed in tourist agencies in Mexico and Europe, as were folders containing maps and timetables. Special excursion trains were arranged for local festivals, and passengers were told that they would pass through areas that compared in beauty to the wonders of Switzerland.[55] This campaign was in full swing when Anglo-Mexican diplomatic relations were restored.

[54] Feb. 1, 1883.
[55] *MF*, IV (Jan. 26, 1884), 270-72; *TR*, Dec. 21, 1884.

3. Rails, Rivalries, and Pools, 1885-1910

"Scenic route to the Gulf—The Most Picturesque Railway in this Republic and Probably in the World—Every Turn Associated with the Thrilling History of the Conquest—Magnificent Scenery." These advertisements beckoned travelers to a line whose future seemed extremely bleak in 1885. The trading community in Veracruz, the press in England and Mexico, and many diplomats in the Republic assembled a conglomeration of rumors, half-truths, and facts shortly after the renewal of diplomatic relations, and concluded that Mexico's leading eastern port city and the Mexican Railway Company that served it were about to be ruined. The Mexican Central had just dropped its charges for hauling freight to Mexico City below those quoted by the Mexican Railway for its shorter run and, according to *The Mexican Financier*, the Central was winning its battle to divert foreign trade bound for the capital to the northern route.[1] *La República* of Mexico City said on May 22, 1885, that freight trains which once carried full loads from Veracruz "now make the trip only to keep the locomotive wheels from rusting and parasite plants from becoming rooted in the tunnels." But what else could be expected of a line whose charges drove landowners and farmers to allow their surplus crops to rot rather than pay the company's fee for transporting it to other areas? A British consul conceded that a railway "that could be beaten in point of cheapness by pack

[1] *MF*, VI (April 11, 1885), 32; also see GBDCR, AS No. 146, *Report on the Trade of Vera Cruz for the Year 1886* (London, 1887).

animals is naturally not the railway to develop a country."[2]
La República also lampooned the railway's passenger service:

Everyone who wants to go to Europe goes via the Central, which
is neither easy nor cheap, but very natural, as that way they can
avoid . . . the bad service on the Mexican Railway. . . . Five years
ago [1880] the Mexican Railway decided to run night trains, and the
Pullman Company proposed to furnish them with sleepers. But for
some unknown reason the railway refused. Travelers complained . . .
of being unable to sleep, whereupon the management solved the
problem in a unique manner by abolishing the night trains.[3]

The Veracruz merchants were not particularly concerned
with the railway's lack of attention to its sleepy passengers,
much less with the jokes concerning the stale bread and atten-
uated coffee served by the company at most of its stations.
They argued vehemently that the Díaz government was ob-
ligated to protect the trading interests of their port.[4] The
Chamber of Commerce, careful to put self-interest in the back-
ground, reasoned that American commercial supremacy gained
through the northern railroads was certain to breed a desire for
political supremacy and Mexico would lose more of her territory
to the Yankee imperialists.[5] They insisted that the government give the Mexican Railway an ultimatum. Either the
company was to lower its rates or the government would rush
the completion of a rival line from Mexico City through Puebla
and Jalapa to Veracruz with the aid of European capital.[6] The
Veracruz lobbyists also asked President Díaz to authorize the
construction of a breakwater at the port and to take the steps
necessary to erase Veracruz' reputation as the most unhealthy
city in the world. Finally, they suggested that a slight reduction in the Mexican tariff might help to increase trade at the
port.[7]

Not all the crepe-hanging was justified. Veracruz was not
being pushed to the wall in 1885 and 1886, and the Mexican
Central and Mexican National companies were not doing as

[2] GBDCR, AS No. 146.
[3] *La República*, May 22, 1885.
[4] *Mexican Herald*, Sept. 26, 1885.
[5] Consul Baker to Salisbury, No. 15 Commercial Confidential, Aug. 29, 1887, FO
50, Vol. 461.
[6] GBDCR, MS No. 65, *Report on the Commerce of Vera Cruz and the Future of that
Port* (London, 1887).
[7] *MF*, VI (July 25, 1885), 259-60.

well as some of the Veracruz traders implied. Both ventures were, in fact, being reorganized to acquire more capital.[8] The Díaz administration and the Mexican Railway directors nevertheless realized the potential danger of the situation. The tariff on a few foreign goods was reduced, an extensive program of harbor improvements was outlined, and a vigorous assault on yellow fever at the port was promised by the President.[9] Late in 1887 he also announced that a London syndicate had agreed to finish a railroad from Veracruz to Mexico City under a bonus contract that placed a premium on speed. The Mexican Railway responded by cutting its rates for hauling freight approximately 18 per cent. Cuts were especially drastic on the first- and second-class freight hauled along the entire route from Veracruz to Mexico City.[10]

No amount of work on the harbor at Veracruz, adjustments in the Mexican tariff, or slices in the Mexican Railway's rates could have maintained the position the port once held as the only major center of Mexican commerce. Little was accomplished on the breakwater in the 1880's, and the reduction in Mexican Railway charges was countered by more severe rate slices by the Mexican Central.[11] Yet the complaints from commercial groups in Veracruz dwindled rapidly after 1886 and 1887. The value of the trade passing through Veracruz increased during these two years for the first time since the Mexican Central was opened; and, rightly or not, many observers felt that the lower tariff, the announcement of the construction of a new railroad, and the reduction of Mexican Railway rates were mainly responsible for the change.[12]

The record of the Mexican Railway from 1885 to 1892, the year when the last of the major lines in eastern Mexico built during the Díaz period was completed, shows that the lowering of its freight charges did not bring back the high returns of the early 1880's when the annual gross revenue reached 5.02 million pesos.[13] Following the diminution of traffic in rail supplies and

[8] *Ibid; RJ*, XLVII (May 23, 1885), 548-49; *Mexican Herald*, Aug. 13, 1887.
[9] Baker to Salisbury, No. 8 Commercial, April 19, 1887, FO 50, Vol. 461; also see *MF*, XI (Jan. 14, 1888), 253; *TR*, Feb. 12, 1889.
[10] *TR*, Feb. 7, 1888; GBDCR, AS No. 146.
[11] See the figures in the *Economist*, L (Aug. 13, 1892), 1033.
[12] GBDCR, AS No. 604, *Report for the Year 1888 on the Trade of Vera Cruz* (London, 1889). Also see *MF*, XI (Jan. 14, 1888), 253.
[13] Romero, p. 201.

equipment for the new American lines after 1882, the gross revenues rapidly declined to 3.79 million pesos in 1883.[14] The amount of goods, by weight, hauled on the Mexican Railway increased after 1884, but the total amount carried annually from 1885 to 1892 did not reach the level attained in 1881 or 1882. This, coupled with the lowering of the Mexican Railway's freight charges, and the slow increase of passenger travel, produced a gross revenue that did not climb above 4.1 million pesos in any year from 1885 to 1892.[15] This was discouraging and it was made more so by a fall in the price of silver from 50*d*. in 1884 to 33*d*. in 1892 that affected the all-important net receipts of the company. Editors of financial journals, company officials, and British consuls periodically played the perplexing game of estimating the amount in ordinary dividends lost by shareholders because of the silver problem.[16]

The source of the Mexican Railway's ordinary dividends, 1888-1891: the building of the Interoceanic and Mexican Southern Railroads

Holders of first and second preference shares earned rather steady returns from 1885 to 1892, and the ordinary shareholders received small dividends from 1888 to 1891.[17] The building of the Interoceanic and Mexican Southern railways enabled the company to pay these ordinary dividends despite its lower freight rates and the declining value of silver. The Chairman of the Mexican Railway admitted this in 1888 when he phlegmatically announced that the increased revenues for the year, enough to account for the ordinary dividend, came from "non-permanent" sources.[18] Specifically, the Mexican Railway was hauling machinery, fuel, and other supplies for two new British

[14] MRC, *Report of the Directors for the Half-Year Ended June 30, 1883* (London, 1883); *ibid., Report . . . for the Half-Year Ended December 31, 1883* (London, 1883); *TR*, Dec. 12, 1891. Published sources have been cited whenever possible.
[15] See the chart in *TR*, Dec. 12, 1891; also see *Economist*, LIX (Aug. 24, 1901), 1279.
[16] Examples of these statistical gyrations are found in GBDCR, AS No. 3039; *TR*, Dec. 12, 1891; *Economist*, LIX (Aug. 24, 1901), 1279; *SAJ*, XLIV (May 14, 1898), 374.
[17] Above, Table 5, p. 48, for the dividend record of the company.
[18] *SAJ*, XXIV (Nov. 10, 1888), 851; *MF*, XV (Oct. 26, 1889), 103.

railroad companies, one of them engaged in finishing a line from Veracruz to Mexico City, and the other constructing a line from Puebla to Oaxaca. This type of traffic had dipped to 2,331 tons in 1884; in 1889 it reached 54,723 tons, and a year later zoomed to 68,813 tons.[19]

The dream of a railroad from Acapulco to Veracruz furnished the impetus for several concessions from state governments and the federal administration to Mexican contractors between 1878 and 1880. Delfín Sánchez, an engineer, promoter, and financier who was married to one of Benito Juárez' daughters, managed to complete a line from the capital to Irolo in 1882. This was the road that gave the Mexican Railway its first taste of competition. Francisco Arteaga, another promoter, took on the job of extending the line southward from Irolo to Puebla, and other surveys and plans were made for laying track to Veracruz via Marcos, Perote, and Jalapa.[20]

On November 4, 1887, the Mexican government assigned all concessions to La Compañía del Ferrocarril Interoceánico de Acapulco a Veracruz, an enterprise headed by Delfín Sánchez. The other contractors were paid off, and Sánchez began a search for foreign capital to finance the remainder of the Mexico City-Veracruz construction. Two of his partners in the enterprise, President Díaz and Manuel Dublán, the Minister of Finance, were anxious to turn the task over to British investors and engineers.[21] Sánchez was sent to London in 1888 and there presented persuasive arguments to representatives of various London syndicates. The Interoceanic route, he noted, had fewer steep grades than did the Mexican Railway; her locomotives could haul two hundred tons of freight while the Mexican Railway could handle no more than sixty tons on each trip; and the new line would cost far less to finish since it did not cut through the rugged terrain followed by the older railroad. This meant that the Interoceanic could charge lower rates and yet earn larger profits than the Mexican Railway.[22]   On April 20,

    [19] *MF*, XVI (Oct. 25, 1890), 104-5; Great Britain, Public Record Office, Customs and Excise Documents, *Annual Statement of the Trade of the United Kingdom with Foreign Countries and British Possessions for the Year 1890* (London, 1890), 313.
    [20] Powell, pp. 139-43; CRO, File No. 26575, Interoceanic Railroad, I; United States, *Consular Reports*, XXXI (1889), 90. Also see above, Map 3, p. 37.
    [21] This was the opinion of Sir Spenser St. John; see St. John to Salisbury, No. 16 Diplomatic, May 4, 1888, FO 50, Vol. 465.
    [22] SEL, Prospectus for the Interoceanic Railroad.

1888, the concession held by Sánchez was transferred to the In-teroceanic Railroad, Limited, organized by Christian Murietta and Company of London. The price was £300,000 in cash and £500,000 in ordinary and preferred shares of the British concern. Most of the shares were taken by President Díaz, his father-in-law Romero Rubio, ex-President Manuel González, and Sánchez himself.[23] Over three hundred Britishers quickly took up the £800,000 in £10 preferred shares offered by the Interoceanic venture in June and July.[24]

On June 29, 1888, while Sánchez was hiring engineers and laborers, Frederick Issacson, a member of Commons and a shareholder in the Mexican Railway Company, appeared at the Foreign Office to assail the Interoceanic project. Issacson insisted that the concession granted to the Mexican Railway was violated by the one given to the Interoceanic Railroad. In 1868 the Mexican government promised "not to subsidize during 65 years the construction or working of any other railway between Veracruz and the city of Mexico or the intermediate points."[25] The Díaz regime had assigned such a subsidy to the Interoceanic company. The Office refused to interfere on behalf of the Mexican Railway, explaining that Article II of their concession left the way open for another capital-to-coast line *if it went through Puebla and Jalapa*. Sir Spenser St. John reminded Issacson that the Mexican Railway was accorded the opportunity of constructing such a road but had given up the right by agreement with Mexico on April 15, 1882. He brusquely dismissed Issacson with a lecture that placed respon-bility for the existence of the British Interoceanic company on the "monopoly manners" of the Mexican Railway.[26]

The Interoceanic enterprise confidently proceeded with its plans throughout the St. John-Issacson discussion. The section from Mexico City to Puebla was modernized in late 1888 under the direction of a British engineer from Brazil. Ten locomotives and 125 cars were ordered from Philadelphia and a "Business-man's Special" was put into service. A dining car was attached

---

[23] File No. 26575.

[24] *Ibid.* A bonus of £50,000 was promised to the contractor hired by the Inter-oceanic line if he could complete the entire job by December, 1892; see *MF*, XVI (Dec. 20, 1890), 303.

[25] Foreign Secretary to St. John, No. 23 Diplomatic, June 29, 1888, FO 50, Vol. 465.

[26] St. John to Salisbury, No. 30 Diplomatic, July 30, 1888, FO 50, Vol. 465.

Table 5.   *Dividend record of the Mexican Railway*
Company, 1885-1910[a]

Year	First preference £2,554,100 (per cent)	Second preference £1,011,960 (per cent)	Ordinary £2,254,720 (Average nominal capital) (per cent)
1885	8-6	3-Nil	Nil-Nil
1886	5.5-8	Nil-Nil	Nil-Nil
1887	8-8	3.5-5.5	Nil-Nil
1888	8-8	6-6	.5-Nil
1889	8-8	6-6	1.75-Nil
1890	8-8	6-6	Nil-3
1891	8-7.5	6-Nil	1.5-Nil
1892	4.5-1.5	Nil-Nil	Nil-Nil
1893	2-1.25	Nil-Nil	Nil-Nil
1894	.75-.50	Nil-Nil	Nil-Nil
1895	1.75-.50	Nil-Nil	Nil-Nil
1896	.75-.50	Nil-Nil	Nil-Nil
1897	2-2.5	4-Nil	Nil-Nil
1898	1.8-2.7	Nil-Nil	Nil-Nil
1899	2.4-3.8	Nil-Nil	Nil-Nil
1900	3-3.75	Nil-Nil	Nil-Nil
1901	2.3-2.5	Nil-Nil	Nil-Nil
1902	.5-2.2	Nil-Nil	Nil-Nil
1903	2.1-1.8	Nil-Nil	Nil-Nil
1904	4.1-6	Nil-Nil	Nil-Nil
1905	5-6.2	Nil-Nil	Nil-Nil
1906	6.1-8	Nil-3.7	Nil-Nil
1907	8-8	3.8-5.7	Nil-Nil
1908	8-8	5.7-1.7	Nil-Nil
1909	6.3-8	Nil-2.5	Nil-Nil
1910	8-8	2.8-6	Nil-1.5

[a] F. C. Mathieson and Sons, I, IX; File No. 1543; *Stock Exchange Year-Book, 1886-1911* (London, 1887-1912).

for the convenience of Puebla residents who could ride to
Mexico City in the morning, spend five hours in the capital, and
return home for a late dinner.[27] The Puebla-Perote route was
assigned to Scott, Read, Campbell & Company of London on

[27] *MF*, XII (Aug. 18, 1888), n. p.

September 19, 1888, and completed a year later, while the remainder of the line to Veracruz was finished by the Sullivan and Hampson Contractors Company at the end of 1892.[28] Nearly 500 miles of track, including a 123-mile spur south from the capital to Jojutla, was ready for business in December, 1892, when a private car complete with kitchen—the reputation of the cuisine on the route was no secret—carried Mexican and British dignitaries along the line while a band entertained them with popular tunes of the day.

The building of the Mexican Southern, Limited, from Puebla to Oaxaca provided the other "non-permanent" source of revenue that produced the Mexican Railway Company's ordinary dividends in the late 1880's and early 1890's.[29] For more than three years after June, 1889, the Mexican Railway carried equipment for the Southern from Veracruz to Puebla. In the long run, although it had no choice, the Mexican Railway was cutting its own financial throat by linking the Southern with Puebla, a station on both the Interoceanic and Mexican Railway routes. This became apparent when the Southern, still in the early phases of its construction, made special arrangements with the Interoceanic to carry the Southern's freight from Puebla to Veracruz when the line was finished.[30]

The Mexican Southern grew out of a government plan to connect a point south of Veracruz with a western port, an idea that attracted Jay Gould and Ulysses S. Grant.[31] When their venture collapsed in 1884 Mexico offered a subsidy for the construction of a shorter 228-mile line from Puebla to Oaxaca. Albert J. Campbell and H. Rudston Read, who helped with the building of the Interoceanic, acquired the concession in May, 1888. They placed a deposit of £150,000 in Mexican government bonds in the National Bank of Mexico to guarantee that the line would be completed in ten years and that no British diplomats in that period would be asked to intervene officially in disputes between the Mexican government and the com-

[28] *Ibid.*, XVI (Sept. 13, 1890), 659; *TR*, June 10, 1890.

[29] The Southern's route may be traced on Map 3, p. 37. CRO, File No. 28880, Mexican Southern Railway.

[30] *MF*, XIX (Dec. 19, 1891), 303-4.

[31] Osgood Hardy, "Uylsses S. Grant, President of the Mexican Southern Railroad," *Pacific Historical Review*, XXIV (May, 1955), 111-21.

pany.[32] The £600,000 in 6 per cent debenture stock and £500,000 in 7 per cent preference shares issued by the Southern in June, 1888, was grabbed up in twenty-four hours by London investment and trust companies, members of the peerage, and a smattering of army and navy officers.[33]

Read and Campbell were confident that the Puebla-Oaxaca area could support a narrow-gauge railroad that had the advantage of a monopoly position. Small soap and chocolate factories were located in the city of Oaxaca, and more sugar cane, henequen, coffee, wheat, corn, and beans reportedly were grown along the railroad's right of way than could be consumed by the local population. Coal and iron deposits were awaiting exploitation and over a hundred silver mines were believed closed because of the prohibitive cost of transporting ore to the north on wagon trains.[34]

Four teams of American and English engineers were commissioned to build the railroad and they in turn hired twelve hundred Mexican laborers. The iron for bridges, the air compressors used to cut several long tunnels, and the rolling stock were shipped from England, but the company took advantage of the silver depreciation to buy its other supplies in Mexico.[35] Sections of the line were opened whenever they were completed and tested by the engineers, and coffee, ore, and marble from adjacent villages were being hauled to Puebla a year before the entire line was finished. In June, 1892, Oaxaca businessmen raised 40,000 pesos for a fiesta to celebrate the driving of the last spike. On November 12 President Díaz, Romero Rubio, the British contractors, and a carload of newsmen arrived in Oaxaca on board a Mexican Southern train for the inauguration ceremonies. During his three-day visit the President briefly outlined the advantages of the railroad in a vigorous speech, reviewed the local military unit, and made a well-publicized call on the city's orphan asylum.[36]

Railways in the Republic never achieved what their backers expected of them. The Mexican Southern was no exception,

[32] File No. 28880.
[33] *SAJ*, XXVI (Aug. 10, 1889), 173.
[34] Francis Denys, Foreign Office memorandum, Dec. 5, 1889, FO 50, Vol. 469; *MF*, XVIII (Oct. 20, 1890), 35-36.
[35] *TR*, Dec. 13, 1889; *MF*, XVIII (Feb. 14, 1891), 491-92.
[36] *MF*, XX (June 4, 1892), 246; *ibid.*, XXI (Nov. 19, 1892), 198-99.

despite good relations with the Díaz dictatorship and the occasional payment of ordinary dividends that averaged 2 per cent annually between 1891, the year the Southern's capital was set at £1,000,000, and 1910, shortly after the line was leased to the Interoceanic Railroad.[37] A small percentage of the Southern's revenue came from carrying passengers on trips that were highlighted, according to the reporter for *El Ferrocarrilero*, by the behavior of conductors who alternated between selling whiskey to travelers and protecting the women from those who drank the brew.[38] The Mexican Southern's main revenue came from its freight traffic, but the narrow-gauge railroad's receipts, judged by contemporary standards, were never large. The British consuls who praised the impact of the line on the economy of Oaxaca may have been correct, but in its most lucrative year the railway earned less than 1.2 million pesos, or about one-seventh the total grossed by the Mexican Railway in its best year over a route only sixty-five miles longer than that followed by the Southern.[39]

The Southern directorate claimed that the company's chief handicap, aside from its overcapitalization, recurrent depressions in Puebla and Oaxaca, and the failure of the Mexican government to abide by the subvention arrangements, was the depreciation of silver. One of their first reports called the downward trend in the price of silver "a source of exceeding anxiety" to shareholders.[40] The directors explained that the railway's receipts were entirely in silver and calculated that a drop of 1*d.* in the value of the metal meant a loss of £1,000 in the net receipts for a half year. In 1903, as the price of silver hovered around 19*d.* and 20*d.*, the *South American Journal* used the Southern as an example of the damage wreaked by the collapse of silver. The gross receipts for two recent nine month periods in which working costs remained static showed receipts for the second span were 88,000 pesos greater than during the first period. But because of the drop in the price of silver the sterling net receipts were £1,500 less in the second, as compared

---

[37] The dividend record can be checked in the *Stock Exchange Year-Book*, published yearly in London.
[38] *El Ferrocarrilero*, Dec. 8, 1905.
[39] *SAJ*, LXII (Feb. 2, 1907), 132; *ibid.*, LXIX (Oct. 15, 1910), 33-34; *MJ*, LXXXVI (July 17, 1909), 79.
[40] *MF*, XX (July 15, 1893), 399-400.

to the first, period.[41] The editor's grumbling ceased only when
the Mexican government's adoption of the gold standard in
1905 promised to stabilize the price of silver. No one, unfortunately, could legislate into being the traffic needed by
the Southern.

All this lay in the future when Díaz gave the Mexican
Southern his official blessing in late 1892. To the north the
Interoceanic Railroad was open from Veracruz to Mexico City.
The Mexican Central's branch line to Tampico had just been
joined to the company's main track while the Mexican National
Railway, buoyed after 1887 by English as well as American
capital, carried passengers and freight from Laredo to Mexico
City. Ordinary and second preference shareholders in the
Mexican Railway Company received no dividends in 1892, and
what they long had feared—a full-scale rate war involving the
Central, National, Interoceanic, and themselves—had become a
reality. It was in this atmosphere that the two largest British-
organized lines, the Mexican Railway and the Interoceanic
Railroad, entered a decade of pools.

Pooling and rate fixing, 1892-1902

The policy of reducing charges to gain traffic instigated by
the Mexican Central in the 1880's culminated in the rate battle
that enveloped Mexico's four major railroads in 1892. The
Central's directors were convinced in that year that freight
from the United States would always move mainly through the
northern customs houses, but they also were convinced that the
Central's future depended on capturing a large segment of the
European traffic as well. In June the Central dropped its rates
for hauling freight to Mexico City from Tampico or El Paso to
an average of one-fourth the charges set by the Mexican Railway Company for carrying freight to the same destination.[42]
It was a short-term bargain that the Central planned to withdraw once shippers and manufacturers were accustomed to the

[41] *SAJ*, LIV (Jan. 17, 1903), 66.
[42] *Economist*, L (Aug. 13, 1892), 1033.

service offered by the line. The inevitable reaction occurred; within two months the Mexican, Interoceanic, and National roads were adjusting rates each day in an attempt to keep up with their competitors.[43]

The British Mexican and Interoceanic lines called for a conference of Mexico's Big Four in London in mid-August to fashion a compromise agreement. The request coincided with a poor harvest in eastern Mexico and a drop in the price of silver to its lowest point since Díaz first became President.[44] The Central was willing to attend such a meeting since its losses during the rate conflict proved greater than the directors were willing to accept.[45]

Uniform charges were established in London for hauling traffic of European origin destined for competitive points in Mexico. The rate, for example, for carrying second class European freight to Mexico City was set at 34.30 pesos, about 26 pesos less than the charge levied by the Mexican Railway in 1876 and 6 pesos less than its rate in 1885.[46] The gross receipts were to be pooled and a fixed percentage allotted to each company. Eight pesos on each ton carried was to go to the railroad doing the actual hauling; 45 per cent of the remaining receipts were to go to the Mexican, 20 per cent to the Interoceanic, 22 per cent to the Central, and 12 per cent to the National.[47] No arrangements were made to pool the receipts from traffic entering Mexico from the United States, but it was agreed that shipments to the capital or its environs from Veracruz, Tampico, or from the two northern termini of the American lines would all be hauled at the same rate, depending on the class of goods involved. The Mexican Railway and the Interoceanic Railroad also agreed to set fixed rates on all Mexican or "national" goods carried to competitive points.[48] President Díaz privately expressed his disapproval of the pactomania that had gripped the

---

[43] Enclosure in Consul Bland to Lord Rosebery (Foreign Secretary), Oct. 10, 1892, FO 50, Vol. 484; *Economist*, LIV (Oct. 31, 1896), 1421.

[44] Bland to Rosebery, Oct. 10, 1892, FO 50, Vol. 484.

[45] *Ibid.* These events were summarized in the *Economist*, LIII (May 4, 1895), 583.

[46] *Economist*, L (Aug. 13, 1892), 1033; *ibid.*, LIV (Oct. 31, 1896), 1421; *SAJ*, XXXIX (Nov. 23, 1895), 553.

[47] *SAJ*, XX (Aug. 13, 1892), 489; *Economist*, LIII (June 1, 1895), 712-13; *ibid.*, LIV (Oct. 31, 1896), 1421-22.

[48] *MF*, XX (May 27, 1893), 233.

floundering enterprises, but he allowed the agreements to go into immediate effect.[49]

The arrangements made in the British capital that involved all four companies lasted until June, 1895. It was evident after three years that the American Central and National lines carried only about 10 per cent of the European traffic that landed in Mexico; yet they received over 30 per cent of the gross receipts from the traffic.[50] The Mexican Railway and the Interoceanic Railroad also complained that their rivals constantly broke the agreement for hauling American traffic to Mexico City. When the two British companies suggested an adjustment of the European pool and the institution of a pool for American traffic, the Central promptly announced its withdrawal from all contracts with the other railways.[51] Three months later, in September, 1895, the Mexican and Interoceanic ventures set up their own temporary pool of receipts derived from hauling goods of American and European origin from Veracruz to Mexico City.[52]

The Mexican Central renewed the rate war just after its action in June, 1895. Agreements were made with several European shippers to haul their goods from Tampico to Mexico City for six months at an average rate of 5 pesos to 8 pesos per ton, 25 pesos per ton less than the rate levied under terms of the pooling agreement in 1892. The Mexican and Interoceanic railroads retaliated with average charges of 9 pesos from Veracruz to the capital.[53] The experiment was one year old when the Central's board of directors in New York suggested a return to the pool system and a stabilization of rates at a reasonable level. The Central did not seem to realize, wrote one British diplomat, that its scheme to divert European traffic from Veracruz generated more trouble than was warranted by the economic facts of life in Mexico. The country's trade was expanding and even the most ineptly prepared statistics indicated sizable yearly increases in the value of trade entering

---

[49] Bland to Rosebery, Oct. 10, 1892, FO 50, Vol. 484; also see Frank Tannenbaum, *Mexico: The Struggle for Bread and Peace* (New York, 1950), p. 211.

[50] *Economist*, LIII (June 1, 1895), 713.

[51] The Central did not deny the charge; see *MF*, XXIX (June 13, 1896), 160.

[52] *SAJ*, XXXIX (Nov. 23, 1895), 553.

[53] *Economist*, LV (April 24, 1897), 602-3.

both Tampico and Veracruz.[54] Veracruz was the natural point
of entry for European goods moving into southern Mexico; it
would continue to play this role no matter what policies were
pursued by the Central.[55]

A revised arrangement for pooling receipts from European
traffic and maintaining similar rates on merchandise reaching
Mexico from the United States was signed in October, 1896.
The contract relating to European traffic was renewed in 1899
and again in 1902, but the new European pools increased the
percentage of the annual gross receipts going to the Mexican
Railway and the Interoceanic Railroad from 69 to 79.4 per cent
and proportionately reduced the share allotted to the American
lines.[56] The system for handling traffic from the United States
was renewed in 1899 but was canceled by the Central and
National lines in 1902. The Interoceanic and Mexican companies continued their agreement to charge uniform rates for
domestic traffic carried to competitive stations, and similar
arrangements were made in 1902 for the American traffic
coming into Veracruz.[57]

The pooling and rate-fixing policies may have prevented
some of the Big Four from falling into bankruptcy, but they
could not produce a financial miracle. The American-owned
Central and National lines did not pay dividends during the
years 1892-1902, and when the reorganizational complexities of
the British Interoceanic Railroad are untangled it is clear that
the same was true of that company.[58] The Mexican Railway
was able to return small yearly profits to its first preference
holders and a half-year 4 per cent dividend to second preference
shareholders in 1897. The ordinary shareholders received
nothing.

The record of the Mexican Railway's gross earnings during
this period illumines an important problem. In 1891, the year
before the pools were instituted, the line's gross receipts were
3.90 million pesos,[59] about 1.12 million pesos less than the 5.02

[54] Compare *SAJ*, XLVI (Jan. 21, 1889), 68, with *ibid.*, XL (Jan. 11, 1896), 48-49.
[55] Consul Chapman, memorandum, June 18, 1897, FO 50, Vol. 515.
[56] *MF*, XXIX (Nov. 14, 1896), 177-78; *SAJ*, XLI (Nov. 7, 1896), 508-9; *ibid.*, XLVI (May 13, 1899), 539.
[57] *SAJ*, LV (Dec. 12, 1903), 571-72.
[58] See Table 6, p. 59.
[59] See the semi-annual reports of the Mexican Railway Company, 1891-1902. An accessible published source is *Economist*, LIX (Aug. 24, 1901), 1279.

million pesos earned by the railroad in its most profitable year. The gross earnings of the Mexican were 2.9 million pesos in 1894, and then moved upward to 3.3 million pesos in 1896, 4.1 million pesos in 1898, and 4.4 million pesos in 1900. One would not imagine, given these figures, that the railroad carried more passengers and freight from 1892 to 1900 than at any time during its history, but such was the case.[60] The increase, unfortunately, was not great enough to compensate for the lower rates, especially on freight, that were forced on the Mexican Railway and the other companies by competitive conditions after 1892. It was not until 1902 that the Mexican was able to announce that the year's gross receipts, 5.3 million pesos, were the highest ever earned by the railway.

Irritated investors in the Mexican Railway found that the situation was made less palatable by the knowledge that the gross receipts during the years 1892-1902, judged by gross revenues in the 1880's, should have produced higher dividends than actually were paid. In 1882, when the company's gross revenues were 5.02 million pesos, full dividends were paid on the 8 and 6 per cent preference shares and 14 ½ per cent on the ordinary shares. In 1902 a slightly higher gross revenue brought 2½ per cent dividends for first preference shareholders but no returns for second preference or ordinary shareholders. In 1890 gross receipts of 3.7 million pesos resulted in the payment of small dividends for ordinary shareholders and 8 and 6 per cent semi-annual returns for the preference holders. Ten years later a gross revenue of 4.4 million pesos produced no returns for the second preference and ordinary shareholders and a 6.7 per cent dividend for the year for first preference shareholders.[61] The answer lay, of course, in the Mexican Railway's net sterling receipts. Despite an increase in gross receipts, the company's net profits in sterling were, for example, £158,000 less in 1902 than in 1892.[62] The Mexican Railway's working costs, particularly for labor, increased during the decade and this accounts in part for the lower net profits.[63] More im-

[60] Semi-annual reports of the Mexican Railway Company.
[61] Above, Tables 4 and 8, pp. 35 and 140.
[62] *Economist*, LX (Nov. 8, 1902), 1884-85.
[63] Evidence of the increased costs is found in *SAJ*, XLVI (May 13, 1899), 539; *ibid.*, LII (Nov. 15, 1902), 550; and the summary in *ibid.*, LIV (Dec. 12, 1903), 571.

portant was the fact that the price of an ounce of silver, in 1892 over 35 per cent lower than in 1876, continued to fall until in 1902 it was worth less than one-half its 1876 value.[64] The Mexican's directors emphasized that this was disastrous for an enterprise that had to pay most of its debts and dividends outside Mexico, and occasionally the board offered evidence to prove that the silver crisis was a major reason for the company's small returns.[65] The *South American Journal* preferred to discuss overcapitalization, high construction costs, and sorry management in advising its readers to stay clear of Mexican Railway shares, but the editor admitted that the declining value of silver was also an important problem.[66]

Investors and directors associated with the Interoceanic Railroad joined mourners from the Mexican Railway at the bier of cheap silver from 1892 to 1902. "The real trouble with this company," wrote the Chairman of the Interoceanic when he announced a reorganization to obtain more cash in 1896, "has been the fall in the price of silver."[67] The Interoceanic followed the Mexican's lead in publicizing the deplorable effects of the declining value of silver, but the concern also was burdened with other afflictions.[68] The road faced the fundamental difficulty of having a low annual gross revenue. The Interoceanic was nearly twice as long as the Mexican Railway in 1892 and almost two and one-half times longer in 1902; yet the Interoceanic's gross earnings were lower than the Mexican Railway's gross receipts every year from 1892 to 1902.[69] The line was greeted by economic depression and keen competition for the available traffic when it was opened in the early 1890's. The length of the line and the inability of the Interoceanic locomotive drivers to keep their trains on the track kept the company's

[64] *Ibid.* (Dec. 12, 1903), 571; table in Pletcher, *JEH*, XVIII, 38.

[65] Many reports on the advantages and disadvantages of the fall in the price of silver were written by the British diplomatic staff during this period. See GBDCR, MS No. 302, *Report on the Effect of the Depreciation of Silver on Mexico* (London, 1892). Also see *ibid.*, AS No. 3262, *Report for the Year 1903 on the Trade and Commerce of the Consular District of Vera Cruz* (London, 1904). Comments on the crisis are found in St. John to Rosebery, No. 1 Commercial, April 3, 1893, FO 50, Vol. 489; St. John to Rosebery, No. 31 Diplomatic, July 7, 1893, FO 50 Vol. 488; Consul Stronge to Salisbury, No. 49, Dec. 21, 1897, FO 50, Vol. 508.

[66] *SAJ*, LIV (July 18, 1903), 58.

[67] *Ibid.*, XL (April 10, 1896), 179, 182.

[68] See the figures and comments in *ibid.*, LIV (Jan. 17, 1903), 66; *ibid.* (Dec. 12, 1903), 571; *ibid.*, LVI (Dec. 10, 1904), 632, 636.

[69] File No. 26575, balance sheets for the years 1892-1903.

working costs high and cut the net revenues available for
dividends. The silver muddle was only one of a list of ailments.

The Mexican Railway and the Interoceanic Railroad, 1903-1910

The system of pooling traffic and traffic receipts made in
1902 was halted in 1903, resumed in 1905, and was still used
with slight modification by the British and American lines
serving Mexico City in 1910.[70]   But to understand the records
of the Mexican and Interoceanic companies in the late Díaz
period particular attention also must be given to certain
economic and social changes in the conditions under which the
companies operated in Mexico after 1902. These changes
included the modernization of Veracruz by British capital and
technology, Mexico's adoption of the gold standard, the organization of the National Railways of Mexico by the Díaz
government, and the startling expansion in the value of the
Republic's trade.

Porfirio Díaz considered throwing the weight of his government behind a project to improve Veracruz and its harbor in
the 1880's.   He was then anxious to counterbalance the influence of the American lines in the North by increasing the
amount of foreign goods entering Veracruz.[71]   The project was
postponed until 1895, when Díaz offered a £3,000,000 contract
for the construction of breakwaters, piers, and ancillary harbor
works to Weetman Dickinson Pearson, a British contractor
who at the age of forty presided over a firm employing nineteen
thousand men.[72]   His association with the President began in
1889 when Díaz interrupted the Briton's work on the Hudson
River tunnel to ask that he come to Mexico City to undertake
the draining of the valley of Mexico. The mountains that
surrounded the valley enclosed the capital in a basin over seven
thousand feet above sea level, and a modern, efficient canal

---

[70] The pooling arrangements are discussed in *SAJ*, LIV (Dec. 12, 1903), 571-72;
ibid., LXII (Feb. 16, 1907), 180; *ibid.*, LXVIII (April 23, 1910), 465.
[71] Baker to Salisbury, No. 8 Commercial, April 19, 1887, FO 50, Vol. 461.
[72] J. H. Spender, *Weetman Pearson, First Viscount Cowdray, 1856-1927* (London,
1930), Appendix.

Table 6. Dividends paid on selected shares and debentures of the Interoceanic Railroad, 1892-1910[a]

Year	5 per cent (10£) first prefer. (per cent)	4 per cent (10£) second prefer. (issued in 1896) (per cent)	7 per cent (10£) cumulative preference (per cent)	7 per cent "B" debentures (10£) (per cent)	4½ per cent 2nd debenture (10£) issued end of 1910 (per cent)
1892	Nil	—	Nil	Nil	—
1893	Nil	—	Nil	Nil	—
1894	Nil	—	Nil	Nil	—
1895	Nil	—	Nil	Nil	—
1896	Nil	Nil	Nil	Nil	—
1897	Nil	Nil	Nil	Nil	—
1898	Nil	Nil	Nil	Nil	—
1899	Nil	Nil	Nil	Nil	—
1900	Nil	Nil	Nil	Nil	—
1901	Nil	Nil	Nil	Nil	—
1902	Nil	Nil	Nil	Nil	—
1903	Nil	Nil	Nil	Nil	—
1904	Nil	Nil	Nil	Nil	—
1905	Nil	Nil	Nil	6	—
1906	Nil	Nil	2	4½	—
1907	Nil	Nil	Nil	7	—
1908	Nil	Nil	Nil	7	—
1909	5	4	?[b]	7	—
1910	5	4	?[c]	7	—

[a] F. C. Mathieson and Sons, I, IX; File No. 26575, Vol. F; Stock Exchange Year-Book, 1892-1911.
[b] Figures not available.   [c] Ibid.

was needed to carry off the occasional high waters and constant sewage in the area.[73]

Pearson's competent handling of a problem that had plagued Mexican leaders for centuries and his rapport with the Díaz family made him the logical choice to tackle the work at Veracruz. The job lasted from 1895 to 1902. Most of the laborers were hired in Veracruz but a number of Irish navvies signed contracts in England and were transported to the Republic at Pearson's expense. Electric lights and pure water, innovations at the port in 1895, were provided for the crews; and with few exceptions the relations of management and labor were excellent.[74] The Pearson gangs constructed a breakwater enclosing an area 2,500 by 900 meters, deepened the harbor to at least 8.5 meters at all points, and built jetties for unloading ships of all sizes.[75] Finally, 250 acres along the two-mile waterfront were reclaimed for use as the site of railroad sidings, storage sheds, public buildings, and parks. On March 6, 1902, Pearson, Díaz, members of the Cabinet, and a light cruiser sent by the Admiralty at Pearson's request attended the inauguration ceremonies.

The changes at Veracruz were important, but they could not compete in British circles in 1902 and 1903 with rumors that the Mexican government intended to halt the extreme fluctuations in the value of silver.[76] The government had studied the silver issue in the 1880's and 1890's but always hesitated to act. Many monetary experts long insisted that the advantages of dropping bimetallism for Mexico's foreign trade, her budget, and for certain types of enterprise in the country would be outweighed by the ruin devolving on certain segments of the economy.[77] The Minister of Finance, José Limantour, and his advisers, were more concerned by 1904 with the dangers of

[73] *Ibid.*, pp. 87-97, for a summary of the problems encountered. Also see Deny's memorandum, July 8, 1889, FO 50, Vol. 469; *TR*, Aug. 21, 1889.

[74] Chapman to Salisbury, March 16, 1898, FO 50, Vol. 515; H. Churchill to Salisbury, April 7, 1898, FO 50, Vol. 516. Also see Ricardo Rodríquez, *Historia auténtica de la administración del Sr. Gral Porfirio Díaz*, II (México, 1904), p. 259.

[75] The pamphlet issued by Weetman Pearson to commemorate the opening of the port works was enclosed in George Greville (British Minister in Mexico) to Lord Lansdowne (Foreign Secretary), No. 24 Diplomatic, April 3, 1902, FO 50, Vol. 527. The title is "1902: Vera Cruz Port Works—Descriptive Memoir of the Great Undertaking Which is Today Being Inaugurated."

[76] *SAJ*, LIV (Jan. 31, 1903), 117.

[77] Pletcher, *JEH*, XVIII, 52.

clinging to bimetallism. In September they sent a bill to Congress designed to place the nation on the gold standard. The law that went into effect in early 1905 did not lift the silver peso to levels that older investors in the railway companies recalled with nostalgia, but at least its value was relatively stable until the end of the Díaz era. The price of one ounce of silver in London from 1905 through 1910 averaged 24.2d.[78] The quotation on Mexican railroad shares began to rise in London as soon as the news of Limantour's action was published.[79]

While Limantour pressed for the reform of the nation's currency, he also began the consolidation of Mexico's railway system under government control. His plans for the National Railways took form in a period when Mexico's international trade was rapidly expanding. In 1900 the value of the Republic's imports and exports was 291,029,000 pesos; in 1910-11 the figure was almost 500,000,000 pesos.[80] Limantour and the *científicos* around Díaz believed after 1900 that a merger of the large railroads by American capitalists was imminent. The Minister of Finance intended to prevent the formation of such a combination or trust, and in 1903 the placing of £1,000,000 in second debentures shares of the Interoceanic Railroad on the public market gave him the opening he needed.[81] Limantour took up the entire issue, and his purchase, added to the block of shares held by President Díaz, his Cabinet, and the Banco Nacional de México, gave the Mexican government control of 47½ per cent of the company's capital.[82] During the next three years the Díaz administration obtained control of the Interoceanic Railroad, as well as the Mexican National and the Mexican Central. In 1909 British owners of the Mexican Southern leased their railway to the Interoceanic company and

[78] The semi-annual reports issued by the Mexican Railway Company continued to devote a column to the price of silver during the year.

[79] *SAJ*, LVI (April 30, 1904), 451.

[80] Howard F. Cline, *The United States and Mexico* (Cambridge, 1953), p. 354. The reader must remember that the basis for Mexican trade data was changed in 1903-4. Records for that and subsequent years are not strictly comparable with periods before 1903-4.

[81] A partial bibliography on the subject may be found in Powell, pp. 174-78; also see *The Mexican Year Book 1909-10* (México, 1910), pp. 287-88. *SAJ*, LVI (Jan. 16, 1904), 61.

[82] GBDCR, AS No. 3262; Henry Bamford Parkes, *A History of Mexico* (Cambridge, 1938), p. 301.

the entire system was unified under a venture, the National
Railways of Mexico, in which the government owned over
half of the shares.[83]

This is the sizable mold—the pooling arrangements, the
improvements of Veracruz, the flight from bimetallism, the
nationalization of the railroads, and the swelling trade statistics
—into which the records of the Mexican Railway and the
Interoceanic Railroad from 1903 to 1910 must be placed for
examination. The above developments stemmed in some measure from the very existence of the railroads and, although no
accurate measurement can be made, each affected the progress
of the Mexican and Interoceanic companies.

The Mexican Railway's gross earnings in 1902 were, as we
have seen, 5.3 million pesos. This figure climbed slowly but
ballooned in 1906 to 7.1 million pesos, 8.1 million pesos in 1907,
and 8.4 million pesos in 1910.[84] The Mexican line carried over
one million passengers in 1910 compared to 912,000 in 1902,
while 75 per cent more freight measured by tonnage was hauled
in 1910 than in 1902.[85] The greatest proportion of the larger
traffic receipts came from carrying goods originating outside
Mexico. Most of this foreign traffic—coal, dry goods, hardware, machinery, and liquor—was carried to Mexico City, but
the increasing amount of imports unloaded at intermediate
stations suggests a widening of the rural as well as the urban
market in the closing years of the Díaz epoch.[86]

The expansion of the gross revenues and the stabilization
of silver offset the highest working costs in the history of the
line and enabled the Mexican Railway to improve its dividend
record. In 1906 the first preference shareholders received their
first full 8 per cent dividend since June, 1891. They also received 8 per cent returns in 1907, 1908, and 1910. In December,

[83] File No. 28880, III; Powell, p. 177.
[84] *SAJ*, LXII (April 27, 1907), 462; *SAJ*, LXX (Feb. 4, 1911), 139; MRC, *Report
... for the Half-Year Ended June 30, 1907* (London, 1907); *ibid., Report ... for the
Half-Year Ended December 31, 1907.*
[85] Figures for the last years of the Díaz era are found in *SAJ*, LXIX (Oct. 15, 1910),
433-34; *ibid.,* LXX (Feb. 4, 1911), 139. These should be compared with the statistics
in México, Secretaría de Hacienda, *Exposición de la secretaría de hacienda de los estados
unidos mexicanos de 15 de enero de 1879 sobre la condición actual de México* (México,
1879).
[86] The sections titled "Tonnage carried to and from each station" in the Mexican
Railway Company reports give this information. See, for example, MRC, *Report ...
for the Half-Year Ended December 31, 1908* (London, 1909).

1906, the second preference shareholders earned their first dividend since 1897; in the period July-December, 1910, they received a full 6 per cent return on their shares. When the ordinary shareholders earned a dividend in 1910 it marked the end of an eighteen-year drought.

The Interoceanic Railroad's balance sheets after 1902 are difficult to interpret. The line became involved with Limantour's nationalization plans after 1903, and its revenues and expenditures were interlaced with the activities of other companies from that year until the Revolution. The financial reports were made more complicated in 1909 when the Interoceanic added the Mexican Southern to its organization. The Interoceanic's length spurted to 878 miles, and no attempt was made to separate the earnings of the two lines in the financial statements issued in 1910 or 1911. The company's gross receipts were approximately 6.4 million pesos in 1905-6, a new high for the enterprise, 7.8 million pesos in 1909-10, and 8.6 million pesos in 1910-11.[87] It was during this span that the Interoceanic, as shown in Table 6, returned its first dividends to holders of preference shares in the company.

Other British railway activity in Mexico, 1885-1910

The two Veracruz-Mexico City lines, together with the Mexican Southern Railway, were the only important British railroads built through the efforts of a limited company. Two other limited ventures, the Coahuila & Zacatecas Railroad and the Michoacan Mining and Railroad Company, were constructed by parent mining concerns to link their camps to the Mexican National Railroad.[88] Another mining enterprise, the Palmarejo Company, laid fifteen miles of track from its mines in Parral, Chihuahua, to the Chinipas River, where a smelter treated the company's ore.[89] Five other limited concerns were registered in London and then withdrawn by the directors

[87] *SAJ*, LXII (Feb. 16, 1907); *ibid.*, LXX (Jan. 7, 1911), 3; *ibid.*, LXXI (Nov. 11, 1911), 573.
[88] See Map 3, p. 37; Appendix, Table B.
[89] *Ibid.*; also see CRO, File No. 27579, Mexican Mineral Railway.

before any shares were placed on the market, while the promoters of the Pachuca, Zacultipan, and Tampico Railway returned the capital received in 1890 after they failed to get their expected concession from the Díaz government.

Such an early collapse would have saved Londoner George Hume and those who invested in the Mexican Pacific Railway both energy and capital. Hume purchased a concession to construct a railroad from Tonala, near the Gulf of Tehuantepec, northward to Tuxtla, the capital of Chiapas, from George Wilson of New York for £89,493 in November 1888.[90] Hume eventually hoped to connect his railway with other roads in Guatemala and the Isthmus of Tehuantepec, but his concession was revoked in the mid-1890's by the Díaz government because no work had been done on the project. Hume doubted the legality of this action, demanded £1,714,050 in damages from the Mexican government, and asked the British Foreign Office to press his case. The Office refused to intervene, informing Hume that the company was to settle disputes with the Mexican authorities in the courts of the Republic.[91]

Britons purchased three railways after they were built by capitalists and engineers from other countries and organized their operations under the limited-company system. The Mexican Eastern from Marcos to Teziutlán was taken over from native owners in 1901 and became part of the Interoceanic Railroad. The thirty-mile Torres to Prietas, Sonora line was purchased from Yankee speculators who in 1910 convinced British investors of the copper, gold, silver, and timber potentialities of the coastal district. The earliest sale of a foreign-built road to Britishers was carried off by Robert R. Symon, an American who was active in various Mexican enterprises after the middle of the nineteenth century. Symon dreamed of a web of railroads in western Mexico, but in 1890 the main evidence of this dream, the Altata-Culiacán railway in Sinaloa, was on the brink of bankruptcy.[92] Symon's Mexican partners pulled out of the concern, but Symon was able to convince Sir

[90] CRO, File No. 27725, Mexican Pacific Railway.
[91] The case may be traced in Secretary, Mexican Pacific Railway, to Rosebery, June 5, 1891, FO 50, Vol. 494; Consul Trench to Lord Kimberley (Foreign Secretary), No. 25 Diplomatic, July 4, 1894, FO 50, Vol. 494; Salisbury to Sir Francis Dering (British Minister to Mexico), Jan. 30, 1896, FO 50, Vol. 502.
[92] Powell, p. 131 n. 9; CRO, File No. 32279, Western Railway of Mexico.

Edward Cassell, representing five British brokers, that the road would prosper when the state was developed economically. After Cassell and his friends put their capital into the railway it was used for twenty years by a mint at Culiacán to transport its bullion to Altata. It also was employed by the British-owned Anglo-Mexican Mining Company to bring equipment and Chinese labor to their Culiacán site.[93] The railroad seldom showed any profits and shortly before the fall of the Díaz government Sir Edward informed the board of directors that "conditions in the state of business have not yet improved."[94]

British capital turned up at times in railway companies organized in countries outside Great Britain. The Mexican Central and Mexican National were examples of such interests. Britons had a minor part in the grandiose schemes of American promoter Arthur E. Stilwell to link the coast of Sinaloa with Kansas City, a plan that flickered out in the dead-end railroad that shot northeast from Topolabampo.[95] A small amount of sterling also was invested in the Mexican North-Western Railway Company, a Canadian enterprise that in 1910 bought American-owned railways running from Ciudad Juárez to Terrazas and from Chihuahua to Temósachic.[96] Fred Stark Pearson, a New York engineer who had developed public-utility and dam projects in Brazil and Peru, was President of the Canadian venture.[97] Pearson, no relation to Weetman Pearson, began his program to exploit the lumber, mining, and cattle opportunities of northern Chihuahua by establishing the town of Pearson for laborers and officials of the company and their families.

Far to the south, near the port of Salina Cruz, another town named Pearson stood in 1910 as a sort of monument to the best example of British capital and engineering skill in a non-British company. During the nineteenth century many attempts

[93] The history of the Anglo-Mexican Mining Company is examined in chap. iv.
[94] File No. 32279.
[95] The line is traced on Map 3, p. 37; also see *Anglo-American and Mexican Mining Guide*, X (Jan. 30, 1907), 1; George Greville (British Minister to Mexico) to Lansdowne, No. 14 Commercial, Aug. 16, 1902, FO 50, Vol. 528; Rippy, *Latin America and the Industrial Age*, pp. 152-65.
[96] Mexican North-Western Railway Company, *First Annual Report for the Year Ending December 31, 1910* (no place of publication). The report is in the Library of Congress, Washington, D. C.
[97] *The Dictionary of American Biography* (New York, 1920).

were made to build a communications system across the Isthmus of Tehuantepec, but it was not until 1894 that a single-track, rickety railway, a product of international finance and engineering, was completed from Salina Cruz to Coatzacoalcos.[98] Delfín Sánchez, a promoter of the Interoceanic Railroad, and Chandos Stanhope, an Englishman who was a director in three British concerns in Mexico, were among those who raised money to construct the line. They were connected with a line that had the distinction of being one of the worst railways in the world. It was impossible to carry heavy loads on unballasted track or over wooden bridges that rotted under the stifling heat and torrential rains. The passengers who were willing to ignore the record of derailments and to brave the chances of contracting smallpox and yellow fever at the port cities, puttered along in swaying cars that occasionally reached a speed of thirteen to fifteen miles an hour.

Porfirio Díaz asked Weetman Pearson in 1896 to put the Tehuantepec railroad and the ports in working order, but other commitments, among them the Veracruz job, prevented Pearson from joining the President in the government-organized Tehuantepec Railroad Company until 1899.[99] The nominal capital of the enterprise was then set at 5 million pesos, half of which was supplied by Pearson's company in London. Contracts signed in 1899, 1902, and 1904 promised Pearson 37 per cent of the railroad's net profits for five years and a larger percentage of the earnings after that date. All accounts were to be handled by the Mexicans and no construction or repair work could be carried out until the blueprints were submitted to a council appointed by the President.[100]

Weetman Pearson grappled with an assortment of problems in Tehuantepec. The Isthmus region supplied little of the construction materials or labor that he needed. Pearson requested aid from the Foreign Office, explaining the advantages

[98] Spender, pp. 110-22; GBDCR, MS No. 658, *Report on the Mexican Isthmus (Tehuantepec) Railway* (London, 1908); *México*, Secretaría de Comunicaciones y Obras Públicas, *Ferrocarril nacional de Tehuantepec* (México, 1908).

[99] The original request was noted in Dering to Salisbury, No. 9 Commercial Confidential, March 31, 1896, FO 50, Vol. 304.

[100] México, Ministerio de Comunicaciones y Obras Públicas, *Contrato celebrado entre Francisco Mena . . . en representación del ejecutivo de la unión y el Señor John B. Body, represente de Pearson and Son, Limited* (México, 1902); *The Mexican Year Book, 1909-10*, pp. 305-6; GBDCR, MS No. 658.

of a short-cut from Europe to the Far East. The Foreign Office immediately established a vice-consulate at Salina Cruz, expedited the departure from London of doctors and workmen bound for the Pearson camp, and instructed its representatives in Jamaica to act as intermediaries when Pearson's representative arrived to hire workers.[101] Pearson attempted to provide stores, homes, and clubhouses for his crews but many were unable to stand the malaria, bad food, and backbreaking work demanded by the contractor as the price of this comfort.[102]

The Tehuantepec Railroad was officially opened for coast-to-coast traffic on January 27, 1907. Pearson, Díaz, their sons, and the usual top-hatted group of minor functionaries rode on two trains along the 170-mile route to Salina Cruz. There Díaz praised the efficiency of his British friend, inspected the city's widened streets and large public squares, and pulled the handle of a giant crane that lifted a bag of Hawaiian sugar and dropped it into one of the company's new boxcars.[103]

The success of the Tehuantepec line depended mainly on how much sugar and other general traffic it could draw from the steamship companies that sailed from New York and Europe to the Far East. Pearson signed contracts with the British Leyland-Harrison Line, the Cuban Line, and the American-Hawaiian Steamship Company before the railway was finished. His most important agreement was with the Hawaiian-American venture, an enterprise in which he held a large number of shares. The New York office agreed to abandon its route from Hawaii to New York via the Straits of Magellan in favor of the Isthmus route. Before 1910 other companies were leaving goods at Coatzacoalcos and picking them up at the western terminus for shipment to Tokyo and Vancouver.[104] Traffic also was often taken from a midway point on the railway to Vera-cruz on two narrow gauge lines and on steamboats that were

[101] Chapman to Salisbury, No. 3 Consular, March 31, 1898, FO 50, Vol. 515; enclosure in Consul Jerome to Salisbury, No. 35 Consular, Oct. 6, 1900, FO 50, Vol. 522; Chapman to Salisbury, No. 4 Commercial, June 20, 1900, FO 50, Vol. 522.

[102] *Modern Mexico*, XVIII (March, 1905), 31-32.

[103] Spender, p. 120; other details in the newspaper clippings enclosed in United States, Mexican Despatches, David Thompson to Elihu Root (Secretary of State), No. 243, Oct. 8, 1906, Vol. 180.

[104] *The Mexican Year Book*, 1909-10, p. 304.

purchased by Díaz and Pearson in 1900.[105] Díaz kept the Tehuantepec Railroad under Mexican control, but he allowed the connecting system to be placed under Pearson's jurisdiction at the end of 1900. Pearson combined the steamer service and the two railways into one venture, the Vera Cruz (Mexico) Railway Limited, and distributed most of the shares among his family and executives in the Pearson and Son Company.[106]

The Tehuantepec Railroad Company operated less than five years before Díaz was overthrown. The freight handled by the line increased from 361,735 tons in 1907 to 856,000 tons in 1911, but this plus the passenger travel was not enough to bring any dividends to investors.[107]

* * * * * *

When Porfirio Díaz began his first presidential term Mexico had less than 400 miles of railways.[108] This figure was nearly 3,700 miles in 1885, and when the dictator left the country in 1911 Mexico had 16,000 miles of track. Between 1885 and the end of 1910 Britons formed sixteen limited companies to build or buy railroads in Mexico.[109] Four lines were constructed and their length, added to that of the Mexican Railway, brought the total miles built by British limited ventures to about 1,400 miles. Britons were, moreover, associated with the operations of at least 3,000 additional miles of railroads whose activities were not initiated under the aegis of the limited company system.

It is difficult to measure the amount of British sterling in Mexican railroads at any time, and after the formation of the National Railways of Mexico the task borders on the impossible. The tendency of British companies to issue large amounts of shares as fully paid, and the failure of the holding companies organized by American railway concerns to list the home country of their investors, creates the basic problem. The figure of £8,500,000 is an accurate estimate for 1890. By 1900 over £11,000,000 was invested in limited companies and by Decem-

---

[105] GBDCR, AS No. 2539, *Report for the Years 1898, 1899, and part of 1900 on the Trade and Commerce of Vera Cruz* (London, 1900).

[106] CRO, File No. 66525, Vera Cruz (Mexico) Railways.

[107] Spender, p. 119.

[108] There are almost as many figures as authors. Different figures are, for example, presented in Powell, p. 1; GBDCR, AS No. 3429, *Report for the Year 1904 on the Consular District of Mexico* (London, 1905). Also see the sources listed in J. Fred Rippy, *The United States and Mexico* (New York, 1931), p. 312.

[109] Appendix, Table B.

ber, 1910, about £14,500,000 was placed in the companies. At least another £20,000,000 was invested in shares and bonds of American and Mexican companies.[110]

The Mexican Railway, Interoceanic Railroad, and, to a lesser extent, the Mexican Southern and the Tehuantepec lines were the key railways in which British engineering talent and money were involved before 1911. None of these lines waged vigorous promotional campaigns to attract British capital after 1885, nor was it necessary for them to do so. The Mexican Railway's shares were distributed before that date, and Weetman Pearson and President Díaz had no wish to pull the public into their Tehuantepec concern. The Interoceanic and Southern roads issued prospectuses, but shares were taken up before other promotional devices were needed.

The railways were not all affected by the same problems. The Tehuantepec concern faced the most trying construction situation but it did not have to endure many of the handicaps that beset the limited companies. There was not enough regular passenger or freight traffic, given the internal problems of the companies, the factor of competition, and the decisive drawback of cheap silver to produce dividends for many investors either in the Mexican Railway from 1885 to 1902 or the Interoceanic enterprise from 1892 to 1902. The Mexican Railway's ordinary dividends from 1888 to 1891 were paid when the line hauled equipment for the Interoceanic and the Southern, itself later affected by overcapitalization, skimpy traffic, and the fluctuating peso. There was not sufficient traffic to support four lines when the Interoceanic joined the Mexican Railway, Mexican Central, and Mexican National in serving the capital. The pooling system was an admission of this fact. The Interoceanic and the Mexican Railway were in better financial condition after 1902, but the pools remained as a crutch that none of the large railways was willing to abandon completely.

Whatever the problems at hand, the Foreign Office did not choose to interfere in the relations of the British companies and the Mexican government. This was made clear in the handling by the Office of the Mexican Railway's attempt to prevent the completion of the Interoceanic line and its refusal to consider

[110] *SAJ*, LXVI (Feb. 27, 1909), 242-43, gives the figure of £37,000,000, but this estimate is too high.

George Hume's case in 1894. Weetman Pearson was able to extract assistance from the Foreign Office and the Admiralty, but this aid did not involve the British government in any argument with the Díaz administration on behalf of the prominent Briton.

It has been said that the investors in the American railroads in Mexico may have regretted ever having heard of the country. Many British shareholders perhaps experienced the same emotions, although the Mexican Railway and the Mexican Southern yielded higher average annual returns than the other lines. Regardless of the returns to investors, the railroads helped to stimulate some agricultural production by the large farmers and industrial development, to increase the mobility of the population, and to boost the trade of the Republic. Mexico was still an underdeveloped area when Díaz was deposed, but in the final analysis the nation may have profited more from the railroads before 1911 than did the men whose capital and engineering skill built them.

4. The Mining Story, 1885-1910

The British Golf Club at the El Oro Mining and Railway Company, north of Mexico City, probably did not have a layout comparable to that of the better courses in England, and it undoubtedly was difficult to re-create the tone of the London season on the adjoining polo grounds owned by the enterprise.[1] But the golf course and polo field, whatever their inadequacies, could at least boast a rather exclusive clientele—the staff of one of the few profitable British mining companies in the Republic during the era of Porfirio Díaz. The El Oro venture was one of 210 British limited mining companies organized to work in Mexico from 1885 to 1910.[2] The paid-up capital of these companies was £2,760,835 in 1891, £3,790,319 in 1900, and £4,522,755 in 1910. These totals included shares issued fully paid to investors and to vendors. The amount subscribed in cash did not exceed two-thirds of the total paid-in capital.[3] Fifty-seven of the 210 companies actually mined ore in Mexico and 15 of these returned dividends; only three of the companies managed to pay these dividends for more than five years.[4]

A psychologist would have trouble unraveling all the motives that induced Britons to expend their energy on Mexican mining. The possibility of a fabulous strike always draws investors like a magnet to mining enterprise, but Mexico's

[1] *Modern Mexico*, XVI (Nov., 1903), 30-31.
[2] See Appendix, Table C, for a list of the companies and the paid-up capital in each concern.
[3] This conclusion follows a careful study of the company records.
[4] See Table 7, p. 72.

Table 7. *British dividend mining companies, 1885-1910*

Name of company	Average paid-up capital during dividend period £	Average dividends on yearly basis
United Mexican Mining Company	1,295,220	1885-1887: 1.25 per cent
Anglo-Mexican Mining Company	374,250	1889-1897: 10.6 per cent
Silver Queen United	230,000	1885: 5 per cent
Pinos Altos Bullion Company	175,000	1886-1889: 10 per cent
Quintera Mining Company	52,000	1898-1907: 14.8 per cent
Chiapas Mining Company	96,853	1896-1897: 10 per cent
New Guadalcazar Quicksilver Mines	123,000	1892: 5 per cent
Grand Central Mining Company	250,000	1896-1899: 18.7 per cent
Mesquital Mines	25,000	1900-1901: 18.75 per cent
El Oro Mining and Railway Company	891,038 before 1900; 1,147,000 after 1903	1900-1910: 12.5 per cent
Esperanza	455,000	1904-1910: 68.8 per cent
Dolores	70,000	1907-1908: 12.75 per cent
Mexico Mines of El Oro	180,000	1908-1910: 46.6 per cent
Palmarejo and Mexican Gold fields	625,748	1904-1905: 15 per cent
Mazapil Copper Company[a]	—	—

Total Companies   15

[a] Figures for this company are not available, but for comments on its dividend position, see *MJ*, LXXXV (May 1, 1909), 550. Source for table: *Mining Manual* (London, 1885-1911); *Stock Exchange Ten-Year Record of Prices and Dividends*, I, IX (London, 1907, 1915).

political stability, the presence of British diplomats in the country after August, 1884, the enactment of legislation favorable to foreign miners, and the publicizing of the Mexican mining industry in England also help to explain the formation of a large number of companies.

The traditional picture of Mexico as a lawless and violent nation governed by scoundrels or dullards gradually was replaced in the writing of many English observers with a more optimistic view before the renewal of diplomatic relations. The *Mining Journal* struck this note in late 1883 when it informed those with money to invest that they now could have "the fullest confidence in Mexico and Her Government."[5] Articles in English weeklies advised Britons to share in the tranquil Porfirian future by acquiring mines before Americans picked off the best bargains. Life and property were secure in the Republic, wrote the *Pall Mall Gazette, Mining World,* and *Mining Journal,* and the only sensible course of action was to get into the field while the prices were low.[6]

The restoration of diplomatic relations offered further encouragement to British capitalists. It was comforting to know that your company's requests would be considered by British representatives. Can you recommend a lawyer to handle our affairs? Would you send us a copy of the mining laws? Can you speed the shipment of tools from Veracruz? How can we halt the strikes of native workers at our mine? Will you press the investigation of a murder case in which our company is involved?[7] Sir Spenser St. John once suggested that the best

[5] *MJ,* LIII (Oct. 27, 1883), 1249.

[6] The *Pall Mall Gazette's* statement is quoted in *ibid.,* LIV (April 19, 1884), Supplement. Also see *ibid.,* LIII (Sept. 8, 1883), 1049; *MW,* XXVI (Feb. 2, 1884), 110.

[7] British diplomatic records were open for inspection to Dec. 31, 1902 during the preparation of this volume. Many requests for diplomatic assistance may be found in these papers. See Trojes Mining and Smelting Company to Lord Iddlesleigh (Foreign Secretary), Oct. 20, 1886, FO 50, Vol. 457; Baker to Iddesleigh, No. 1 Commercial, Oct. 26, 1886, FO 50, Vol. 457; Secretary, United Mexican Company to Carden, Public Record Office, London, Foreign Office Archives, Consular Despatches, Mexico, Series 203, Vol. 116; El Refugio Company to Carden, Aug. 16, 1892, Public Record Office, London, Foreign Office Archives, Consular Despatches, Mexico, Series 204, Vol. 138; La Trinidad Company, various letters in FO 50, Vols. 465, 468; Mesquital Company to Bland, Sept. 20, 1892, FO 50, Vol. 483; Bland to Salisbury, No. 48 Diplomatic, Sept. 28, 1892, FO 50, Vol. 483; Santa Rosalia Company to Carden, June 7, 1895, FO 50, Vol. 496; Greville to Lansdowne, No. 39 Diplomatic, Aug. 27, 1901, FO 50, Vol. 524. Reference to murder cases may be found in Carden to Salisbury, No. 9 Consular, July 17, 1891, FO 50, Vol. 479; T. Sanderson (Foreign Office) to Jefferis, Sept. 8, 1891, FO 50, Vol. 480; Dering to Salisbury, June 5, 1899, FO 50, Vol. 517.

way for a company to get all the help it needed without calling on the consular service was to bribe the chief authority in the district where it was located.[8] This may have been done on occasion, but there also is evidence that British diplomats aided many companies after 1884 by making what Consul Carden called "private and friendly" visits to Mexican leaders. Carden himself tried to avoid interfering in company-government matters, but he was willing to use his influence with Mexican friends after an enterprise had aired its grievances in court.[9]

Mexican mining received more publicity in England than any other kind of enterprise in the Republic. Changes in the nation's mining code that simplified the procedure for registering titles, made ownership dependent only on the payment of a Federal tax, and lowered import duties on machinery, were reported in the press.[10] The leading trade journals in London, as well as the Foreign Office, published informative and objective articles on the Mexican mining industry. Edward Halse of the *Mining Journal* examined each state and its potentialities in a series of technical studies published in 1895.[11] In 1898 Halse again went into Mexico to gather information, this time on gold mining. After explaining that gold fever was nothing new in the Republic, he discussed the high cost of mining average gold sites and warned that expert advice should be sought before any purchases were made.[12] The Foreign Office concurred and, while admitting that great mineral wealth existed in Mexico, reminded Britons that profits were never made unless huge sums of money were available for development work.[13]

More eloquent, if less authoritative, information was supplied by Englishmen and Mexicans who wished to promote the

[8] St. John to Sanderson, May 4, 1889, FO 50, Vol. 468.
[9] Carden Report, April 29, 1897, Public Record Office, London, Foreign Office Archives, Consular Dispatches, Mexico, Series 205, Vol. 42.
[10] *Economist*, XL (Dec. 2, 1882), 1493; *MJ*, LVII (Jan. 22, 1887), 114-15; *ibid.*, LXVI (Dec. 5, 1896), 1539; *ibid.*, LXXVI (July 2, 1904), 5; *Mexican Mining Journal*, VI (Nov., 1908), 9.
[11] See, for example, Edward Halse, "Deep Mining in Mexico," *MJ*, LXV (July 6, 1895), 766, 810.
[12] Edward Halse, "Gold Mining in Mexico," *MJ*, LXVIII (Dec. 10, 1898), 1394. Other technical articles may be found in *Mexican Mining Journal*, VI (March, 1908), 20; *MM*, I (Sept.-Dec., 1909), 224.
[13] GBDCR, AS No. 3112, *Report for the Year 1902 on the Trade of Mexico* (London, 1903).

sale of Mexican mines. This group tirelessly bombarded the public with copy that stressed the profits that could be made in Mexico without mentioning the less halcyonic side of the coin. Company prospectuses were issued but other methods also were used. One writer who called himself "Observer" put the spotlight on Mexico in 1884:

> What chance have our English mines of competing with the extraordinary mines of that country? What must their ores consist of when it appears from undoubted authority that they were so rich as to be worked with men hauling water, refuse, and ore on their backs? The columns of the *Mining Journal* have shown the extraordinary riches of Mexican mines, and now that they are being thrown open to the world they have become a matter of serious import to England.[14]

James Jefferis, a British subject who had lived in Mexico for twenty-five years, explained that there was no need for heavy capital outlays; he personally knew men with practically no money who had made "thousands and millions" in Mexican mining.[15] Jefferis insisted that Englishmen were popular in Mexico and consequently that most Mexicans preferred to do business with capitalists from London, Birmingham, and Manchester. Another writer who penned a lengthy piece under the banner "Mexico—the Marvelous Mining Country," finished his article by quoting Cecil Rhodes:

> In my opinion the richest mining countries in the world are Mexico, Peru, and Bolivia, especially Mexico. And while Providence has cast my lot in the opposite section of the globe, I am not blind to the consensus of opinion . . . that Mexico will one day furnish the gold, silver, copper, and precious stones that will build the empires of tomorrow and make the future cities of this world veritable New Jerusalems.[16]

Articles in the *London Evening Standard, Sunday Sun,* and *Daily Express* in the early 1900's printed similar appraisals of Mexico.[17] E. W. Toye, writing in the *Anglo-American and Mexican Mining Guide,* pointed to the character of the Mexican President as proof that mining investors would find a favorable reception in the Republic:

[14] *MJ*, LIV (May 24, 1884), 613.
[15] *Ibid.*, LVII (Feb. 5, 1887), 157.
[16] *Anglo-Colorado and Mexican Mining Guide*, VIII (Jan. 28, 1905), 2-4.
[17] Quoted in *ibid.* (Oct. 31, 1905), p. 147.

. . . I can recall no man within my memory . . . worthy to be
placed on so lofty a pedestal as the President of Mexico. Such is my
estimate of President Díaz and such my reading of history that I
hesitate not to compare him favorably with the conquerors of old—
even the Alexanders and the Caesars, William the Norman, or to
come nearer, the Great Napoleon.[18]

Could mining investments possibly be unsafe in such a country?
A group of Britons at the Stock Exchange evidently thought
not, for in 1907 they reprinted and circulated an article in *The
Financier* entitled "Marvelous Mexico." Important sections
in bold type noted that mines in Guadalajara were yielding
phenomenal riches at 300 feet under the stimulus of modern
equipment. The article called on Englishmen to form corporations of "absolutely first-class people" who could explain the
wonders of mining to the public.[19]

The Mexican Information Bureau, established by Díaz in
London in 1900, was another important cog in the promotional
wheel. Manuel Barriga, the head of the Bureau, stated that
its purpose was to acquaint Britons with the natural resources
of the Republic, a fact that could hardly escape the person who
entered the Bureau's suite of offices.[20] Jars containing samples
of minerals from Mexico were placed around the room. Maps
of Mexico hung on the walls and brochures containing pictures
of mining camps could be enjoyed while the visitor waited for
Señor Barriga. Barriga's main theme was that Mexican mining
had been underestimated in England. Britons, for example,
seemed convinced that the available labor force was inefficient.
According to Barriga this was untrue:

> The natives like the occupation—they are accustomed to mining,
> and take what you English would call a "sporting interest" in the
> results—so that whatever other difficulties the management of Mexi-
> can companies may have to deal with, there is certainly no labor
> difficulty.[21]

The mineowners could pay the peon $0.50 a day compared to
$3.00 in the United States, and he could pay him with the cheap
peso. There was plenty of copper, lead, and other minerals in
most mines; these could be sold abroad for gold, thus overcoming

[18] *Ibid.*, XIII (Sept. 28, 1910), 137.
[19] *The Financier* (London), Oct. 10, 1907.
[20] *MJ*, LXXVI (Oct. 1, 1904), 326.
[21] *Ibid.*

the handicap of the silver problem. Barriga usually ended his interviews and his written material with a touch of flattery:

The Government is particularly anxious to enlist English interest in the development of the mines for . . . the Englishman does anything he takes up thoroughly, and what we want is English capital— capital for providing proper machinery, capital for working the deposits in a miner-like manner, and not pushing the eyes out of the mine.[22]

Some of Barriga's statements could have been analyzed and perhaps refuted, but no questions or retorts appeared in the major mining magazines. The British investor rarely found any articles on Mexican mining that were permeated with skepticism. *The Mexican Financier* believed that trying to stem the flood of mining enterprises was useless and perhaps unwise when the capital was available for export. In any case, Britons were gullible and they would be victimized; it was as simple as that.[23] The editor might have added that the mining mania was kept alive by the undeniable fact that a small number of limited companies working in Mexico earned profits and paid dividends.

The dividend mining companies

A cursory examination suffices for nearly one-half of the fifteen limited concerns that paid dividends after the Anglo-Mexican diplomatic breach was closed. The Quintera Mining Company that averaged annual returns of 14.8 per cent on a capital of £52,000 between 1898 and 1907 was registered in London, but it was controlled by Baron Emile Erlanger and a few French bankers.[24] German capitalists from Bremen gradually assumed control of the United Mexican Mining Company

[22] *Ibid.* Other Barriga articles may be found in *ibid.* (Oct. 8, 1904), p. 352; *ibid.*, LXXVII (April 22, 1905), 432; *ibid.*, LXXXIII (Feb. 22, 1908), 216.

[23] *MF*, XV (Jan. 25, 1890), 422-23.

[24] Reports of annual meetings, etc., of companies listed on the Stock Exchange were deposited in the Stock Exchange Library in London. Much of the information contained in these reports was published in the *Mining Journal* and other British financial magazines. These journals have been cited in this chapter. As in previous chapters, considerable material from the Company Record Office in Bush House also has been used.

after 1884, and only a few Britons shared in the dividends of 1.2
per cent in 1885, 1886, 1887.[25] The directors of the Silver
Queen United venture started operations in 1885 in Los Bronces,
Sonora, by predicting that dividends of 100 per cent might be
paid when the mines were worked at top efficiency. A dividend
of 5 per cent on a paid-in capital of £115,000 was returned to
investors in November, 1885, but two years later the company's
funds and ore both ran out.[26] The Chiapas Mining Company
was the only limited dividend concern south of Mexico City.
The crushing and concentrating of ore began in 1892, and in
1896 and 1897 the company announced dividends of 10 per cent
for the 181 shareholders in London and Paris. The mines were
sold to Mexican speculators in 1904 just after the ore production was reduced to a trickle.[27] The directors of the Guadalcazar
Quicksilver Mines in San Luis Potosí unloaded their mine on
American promoters after investors received one 5 per cent
dividend in 1892. This action was hastened by the refusal of
the peons in the locale to work in the main tunnel after hearing
stories that it was known in Mexican lore as "dead men's
cave."[28] The Mazapil Copper Company of Saltillo, Coahuila,
was a paying concern after 1896, but it was more concerned
with smelting ore belonging to other companies than in mining
activities of its own.[29] The same was true of the Grand Central
Mining Company, located southeast of Los Bronces in Sonora.[30]

The Anglo-Mexican Mining Company

Two companies that were organized before the signing of
the Preliminary Agreement, the Anglo-Mexican Mining Company and the Pinos Altos Company, became dividend enterprises
after 1884. When the former venture was registered in 1883 its

[25] New York capitalists purchased the property in 1905. See CRO, Files No. 2744,
48932, and 58533 to follow the reconstructions and changes in name; AAMMG, VIII
(Nov. 30, 1905), 165.
[26] A copy of the prospectus may be found in *MW*, XXIX (Oct. 3, 1885), 10; CRO,
File No. 21101, Silver Queen United.
[27] CRO, File No. 28782, Chiapas Mining Company.
[28] *MW*, XLV (Nov. 4, 1893), 631-33; *MJ*, LXX (Nov. 24, 1900), 1422.
[29] *MJ*, LXXXV (May 1, 1909), 550.
[30] CRO, File No. 49058, Grand Central Mining Company. The company's activities are examined in *MJ*, LXVII (Dec. 11, 1897), 1465; *ibid.*, LXVIII (Nov. 12, 1898).
276; *ibid.*, LXX (Nov. 10, 1900), 1362.

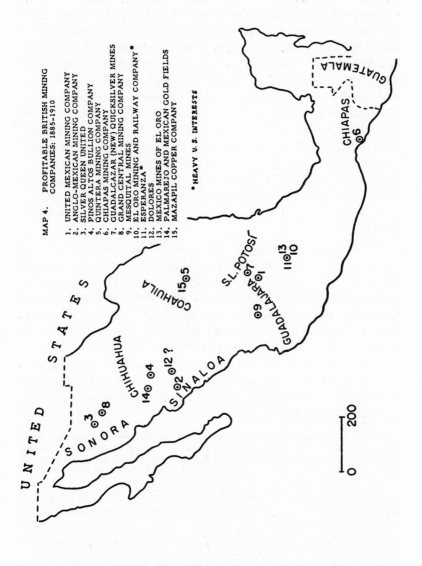

MAP 4.   PROFITABLE BRITISH MINING
COMPANIES: 1885-1910

1. UNITED MEXICAN MINING COMPANY
2. ANGLO-MEXICAN MINING COMPANY
3. SILVER QUEEN UNITED
4. PINOS ALTOS BULLION COMPANY
5. QUINTERA MINING COMPANY
6. CHIAPAS MINING COMPANY
7. GUADALCAZAR (NEW) QUICKSILVER MINES
8. GRAND CENTRAL MINING COMPANY
9. MESQUITAL MINES
10. EL ORO MINING AND RAILWAY COMPANY *
11. ESPERANZA*
12. DOLORES
13. MEXICO MINES OF EL ORO
14. PALMAREJO AND MEXICAN GOLD FIELDS
15. MAZAPIL COPPER COMPANY

*HEAVY U.S. INTERESTS

backers included a baronet, a member of Parliament, and civil engineers who had mined for silver in various Latin American countries.[31] On August 30 George Hopkins, the chairman of the company, and George Gibbs, an important shareholder in the Mexican Railway Company, purchased mines near Culiacán, Sinaloa, from American owners for £175,000 in cash and £105,000 in shares of the Anglo-Mexican concern.[32] Hopkins and the seven Britons who held the majority of company shares did not open the mines until the re-election of Díaz in 1884 provided the feeling of security that they demanded. Hopkins then quickly built a small electrical plant at the mine, persuaded the Mexican government to string telegraph lines from the mine to the city of Culiacán, and experimented with a new but unannounced method of treating ore that ultimately produced 8 to 9 per cent more metal than the directors had believed possible.[33]

The company's progress was impeded by a lack of Mexican laborers, a constant problem for other British mining concerns in northern Mexico.[34] In 1886 Hopkins signed a contract with a Hong Kong firm to transport Chinese coolies to Mazatlán and Guaymas and then to the mining camp.[35] The project was bungled in its early stage and when the Chinese arrived in Mazatlán from San Francisco in October, 1886, no agent from the company was on hand to meet them. A few Chinese violated their contracts and left for cities in Sonora and northern Sinaloa; the rest were housed and fed at the expense of the city

[31] *Ibid.*, LIV (Jan. 12, 1884), 45.

[32] File No. 18783.

[33] Most of the company's bullion was sent to San Francisco and Omaha. Some British companies shipped their ore to Wales and Hamburg; most sent it to Kansas City and St. Louis. See *MW*, XXXVI (May 4, 1889), 771-72; *MJ*, LVII (May 21, 1887), 642; *ibid.* (Dec. 24, 1887), 1554; Anglo-Mexican Company to Denys, April 13, 1889, FO 204, Vol. 207; *Mining Investor* (Feb., 1910), p. 36.

[34] Evidence of this may be found in Edmund Harvey (La Trinidad) to Denys, March 28, 1889, FO 204, Vol. 207; D. Baker to St. John, May 28, 1891, FO 204, Vol. 217; *MJ*, LXXVI (Oct. 1, 1904), 326; *ibid.* (Oct. 8, 1904), 352; *Mexican Mining Journal*, VI, (July, 1908), 19.

[35] British officials at Hong Kong attempted to stop this emigration; see México, Secretaría de Relaciones Exteriores, *Correspondencia diplomática cambiada entre el gobierno de los estados unidos mexicanos y los de varias potencias extranjeras desde el 30 de junio de 1881 a 30 de junio de 1886*, IV (México, 1887), Numero 2, pp. 602-3. Coolie labor had been used in Mexico before Hopkins signed his contract; see St. John to Granville, No. 14, March 19, 1884, FO 50, Vol. 445.

until a representative arrived to take them to the mine.[36] Chairman Hopkins reported in 1889 that two hundred Chinese lived and worked at the British camp.[37]

When the Anglo-Mexican Company paid its first dividend of 30 per cent in 1889 on a paid-in capital of £370,000, the major credit for the returns was given to George Hopkins. Additional gold and silver mines were obtained in the early 1890's. From 1890 to 1897 investors earned average dividends of 10.6 per cent a year. The ore then began to give out, and in 1900 Hopkins instructed his resident manager to sell the venture's equipment, pay the workers that remained in Culiacán, and leave the mines. The fate of the Chinese laborers was not discussed in the company's final report, but an American consul advised Washington in July, 1900, that coolies were streaming north to Sonora with the idea of crossing into the United States.[38]

The Pinos Altos Company

The Pinos Altos Company of Cusihuiriachic, Chihuahua, was the only other British mining company organized before 1884 to pay dividends for more than two successive years after the renewal of diplomatic relations. The military coterie that dominated the company spent £140,000 to open the mines in 1884 and 1885. This sapped the entire capital. The enterprise was able to begin mining two years later after the acquisition of more money, the appointment of a new general manager, and a reshuffling of the board of directors.[39] Machinery for drilling, hoisting, and amalgamating the ore was shipped from Chicago and carried by pack mules from Chihuahua to Pinos Altos. This was imported duty free, as was the salt, charcoal, cord wood, and coal brought from the United States. By terms of the concession granted by Díaz, federal troops accompanied the

[36] *TR*, Oct. 14, 1886. United States, Consular Despatches, Mazatlán, E. Kelton to Department of State, Sept. 18, 1889, Vol. 5.

[37] The activities of the Chinese laborers may be traced in *MJ*, LVII (Jan. 1, 1887), 23; *MW*, XXXVI (May 4, 1889), 771-72; *Mining Record*, I (Jan. 3, 1890), 4.

[38] United States, Consular Despatches, Mazatlán, L. Kaiser to Thomas Cridler (Assistant Secretary of State), July 10, 1890, Vol. 6.

[39] File No. 13015-19462. For an excellent report on the mine, see H. Waithman to Denys, March 27, 1889, FO 204, Vol. 207.

supply and bullion trains. Bandits, it seemed, sometimes were a nuisance.[40]

The Pinos Altos concern, like the Anglo-Mexican Company, complained that it could not hire enough miners, but the shortage was probably not acute. The possibility of bringing in Chinese workers was vetoed in London, and the same negative reply was given a plan to pay Mexican laborers more than the going rate. The company opened a general store in Pinos Altos that provided supplies for the entire community of two thousand persons. The directors believed that the low prices at the store helped to draw labor to the town.[41] The resident manager never missed an opportunity to augment his working crews. When Díaz sent troops to the region in 1888 to crush a reported revolutionary uprising, the company provided the soldiers with food and then temporarily employed them as miners at less than the regular wage scale.[42]

The company paid dividends of 10 per cent from 1886 through 1889 on a paid-up capital of £250,000. Four men, including the chairman, held three-fifths of the shares. The company, unfortunately, attempted to press its good fortune too far. In 1892 the directors borrowed heavily from the South American and Mexican Company, a loan agency in London, to open up what appeared to be a promising vein. It produced nothing but worthless ore and in 1893 the Pinos Altos venture was placed in the hands of a receiver. The South American concern later attempted to reopen the mines, but fires, cave-ins, and eventual bankruptcy culminated in the seizure of the property by a bank in Mexico City.[43]

The Palmarejo Mining Company
Palmarejo and Mexican Gold Fields

Chihuahua also was the site of the Palmarejo mines, a series of lodes that in 1886 belonged to a self-styled American mining engineer, Edgar Applegarth. The spring season and Mr. Applegarth arrived in London at almost the same time in 1886. He

[40] *MJ*, LIX (May 19, 1889), 559.
[41] *Ibid.*, LVII (May 21, 1887), 627.
[42] Waithman to Denys, March 27, 1889, FO 204, Vol. 207.
[43] *MJ*, LXV (July 6, 1895), 797; File No. 38126.

convinced a group of West End bankers that the mines were potential bonanzas. They paid the American £200,000 in cash for the sixty-square-mile concession.[44] On July 31 the Palmarejo Mining Company was registered in London with an authorized capital of £400,000. Applegarth was given 30,000 shares to complete the sale on the eve of his departure to Chihuahua as the company's manager.

The mines were located on the western edge of the state near the town of Palmarejo, a spot that never appeared on most maps. It was the home of most of the 1,000 to 1,200 men who worked at the neighboring mines.[45] These miners used the adit system—a horizontal passage entering the mine from the surface. British mining engineers, technologically speaking, usually followed the pace set by their American counterparts in Mexico; the men who accompanied Applegarth from London were no exceptions. The richest yields from the mines in the 1880's were reduced by the old and tedious patio process that amalgamated mercury with the ore. In 1890 a crushing mill and smelting furnace were erected on the banks of the Chinipas River, about fifteen miles from the main operation, and a conduit seven feet wide and five feet deep was installed to bring water to the mine. When the improvements were completed the two areas were linked by a narrow-gauge railroad.

The cost of the project, over £200,000, unleashed a flurry of criticism at the Palmarejo's office in London. Shareholders periodically had expressed disgust with the management of the company,[46] and their tempers were not improved in 1892 and 1893 by articles published in the *Mining World*. Did shareholders know that Applegarth had done a good job of ruining mines in Nevada before he switched to Mexican promotions? Did they realize that the Palmarejo mines were rejected by American financiers just before they were sold in London? Another editorial suggested that the Palmarejo company was a "wretched sink" into which Britons unwisely had thrown their money.[47]

The floating of more Palmarejo shares and mortgage deben-

[44] *MW*, XLIII (Sept. 10, 1892), n. p.
[45] *MJ*, LVII (Nov. 27, 1886), 1101; *ibid.*, LXXVII (June 3, 1905), 599.
[46] Early criticism may be found in *ibid.*, LVIII (Jan. 28, 1888), 95.
[47] *MW*, LXIV (March 25, 1893), 478.

tures on the market, a deepening debt, and finally the writing off of capital highlighted the next five years. In 1898 the directors decided to windup and reorganize under the name "Palmarejo and Mexican Gold Fields."[48] The new enterprise was able to pay dividends in 1904 and 1905 under the management of E. H. Oxnam, an English-born engineer who had lived most of his life in Latin America. Oxnam reduced the company's debts and gained working capital by selling portions of the Palmarejo property to other mining concerns. He then restricted his mining operations to a small area and, abandoning the patio method, used a cyanide process to reduce the company's ore.[49]

The Palmarejo's success was short-lived. The search for more gold and silver after 1905 went on whenever the directors were able to find a shareholder willing to take the risk of opening new veins. Money was borrowed for machines, labor, and salaries, and when the company's 1910 balance sheet showed a debt of £20,000, an American mining magazine advised shareholders to admit their failure and get out of the country. Oxnam and his associates were nothing if not tenacious. The Díaz regime was on shaky ground when they announced that a power station was being built at Palmarejo, and that telephone lines, electric lights, and a new water tunnel from the Chinipas River were to be installed within a few months. The project was being worked out in London when Francisco Madero entered Mexico City in June, 1911.

Mesquital Mines

The Mesquital Mines, in Juchipila, Zacatecas, a village sixty miles from Guajalajara, was owned in the early 1800's by a wealthy Spanish bureaucrat who fled the country on the eve of the independence movement.[50] The lodes were worked by Mexican wildcat miners and local companies for the next fifty years. In September, 1885, the mines were placed on sale for £12,500 by Juchipila owners through advertisements in various Mexico City newspapers. Ralph Archbold, the agent of Lon-

[48] CRO, File No. 57939, Palmarejo and Mexican Gold Fields.
[49] *MW*, LXVIII (June 3, 1905), 698-99.
[50] SEL, Prospectus for the Mesquital Del Oro Mining Company.

don speculators who were buying up property all over the world, purchased the twenty-three mines and registered the Mesquital Del Oro Mining Company on September 19, 1885.[51] "PROFITS OF £7,000 A MONTH ASSURED" read the prospectus. Within a year £20,000 had been subscribed by 129 shareholders.[52] Fifteen mining engineers, accountants, and foremen sailed from England in 1886 to supervise the 500 Mexican workers at Juchipila.[53] They managed the mine for ten discouraging years. The quality and quantity of ore did not measure up to expectations. Influenza and smallpox hit the British staff. This was followed by a series of robberies at the camp office and the attempted murder of the resident manager, Captain Charles Harvey, by drunken miners.[54] The last episode resulted in Sir Spenser St. John calling on the Mexican Minister of Foreign Affairs to ask politely that steps be taken to apprehend and sentence the thieves and the would-be assassins. This visit became necessary when St. John learned that the local police chief was helping to dispose of the stolen property.[55]

The Mesquital group understandably lost interest in their Mexican venture after these experiences. In 1896 the directors drew up and signed an agreement with Frederick Hawdon and Walter Maclachlan, two British promoters whose careers illustrate an important new trend in British mining in Mexico. Maclachlan and Hawdon agreed to manage the company in return for a portion of the Mesquital's shares. The enterprise began to show a profit in a year, although it was 1900 and 1901 before dividends of 29 and 12 per cent were returned on a capital of £25,000.[56] By 1901 the Mesquital concern represented only a small portion of the Maclachlan-Hawdon mining empire. The duo had organized mining companies to exploit property in Santa Barbara, Hidalgo, Parral, Chihuahua, and

[51] CRO, File No. 21604, Mesquital Del Oro Mining Company.
[52] *Ibid.*
[53] *MW*, XXXIV (May 26, 1888), 767; *MJ*, LVIII (May 26, 1888), 591; Archbold to Rosebery, Sept. 27, 1892, FO 50, Vol. 486.
[54] *MW*, XLII (June 25, 1892), 947; Hervey to Bland, Sept. 20, 1892, FO 50, Vol. 483; Archbold to Bland, Sept. 27, 1892, FO 50, Vol. 486.
[55] The knife wielder was caught and given a short sentence. St. John was not satisfied with the sentence but there is no indication that his protest made any impression on the state government; see Archbold to Rosebery, April 7, 1893, FO 50, Vol. 491.
[56] See Table 7, p. 72. The company was reconstructed three times; see Files No. 81172, 90556, 105691.

northern San Luis Potosí.[57] After they gained control of the
Mesquital company, the promoters placed the entire cluster of
enterprises under the management of the Mexican Mines
Selection Syndicate. Maclachlan and Hawdon served as directors in all the subsidiary ventures.[58]

The Mesquital mine was played out after its profitable burst
in 1900 and 1901. It remained part of a growing network of
mining companies during the remaining years of the Díaz administration. Maclachlan traveled extensively in the Republic
after 1901 to ferret out likely sites for three syndicates in which
he and his partner held large interests. Only the Mesquital
mine was a dividend property before the Revolution.[59]

Joint enterprise: The El Oro Mining and Railway Company and Esperanza Limited

The most profitable mining companies in Mexico in which
British capital was heavily invested were products of American,
French, and German, as well as British, managerial and promotional skill. Few mining companies have had more prominent
men in the world of finance connected with their activities than
the El Oro enterprise and Esperanza Limited. The history of
the El Oro venture stretched back to the 1700's.[60] A British
company worked the one and one-quarter square mile area
from 1815 to 1830, but the mines then lay idle for nearly forty
years. The American Mining Company, a concern organized
under the laws of West Virginia, purchased the mine property

[57] CRO, File No. 62510, Consolidated Copper Company; CRO, File No. 73385,
Diaz, Limited; CRO, File No. 73383, Beckman Mines; *MJ*, LXXIII (May 23, 1903),
627.

[58] A large number of limited companies were organized after 1888 to buy, sell, or
promote mining property in Mexico. Only a small number were active concerns.
Among those listed in the Company Registration Office were: CRO, File No. 26554,
Mexican Loan and Agency Company; CRO, File No. 26698, Mexican Mortgage,
Trust, and Agency Company; CRO, File No. 31552, Mexico City Property Syndicate;
CRO, File No. 86425, Mexican and General Syndicate; CRO, File No. 100795, Union
Syndicate of London and Mexico. Some of the important syndicates are discussed in
this chapter.

[59] In April, 1903, Maclachlan and Hawdon became involved in what proved after
the Díaz period to be one of Britain's most profitable holdings in Mexico; see CRO,
File No. 77075, San Francisco Del Oro Mining Company; *Mining Investor*, I (Oct.,
1909), 31.

[60] *The Mexican Year Book, 1908* (México, 1909), pp. 479-81; CRO, File No. 63105,
El Oro Mining and Railway Company, especially Articles and Memorandum of Association.

in 1894 from Mexican owners. The Americans were unable to make the mine pay, mainly because the equipment and methods they used could not cope with low grade ores.[61]

Britons became interested in the El Oro property in 1899. The Exploration Company, organized soon after Díaz took office in 1876, was part owner of mining concerns in Australia, Africa, the United States, and South America when its board of directors, which included the Baring and Rothschild families, picked the El Oro mine as a potentially profitable investment.[62]

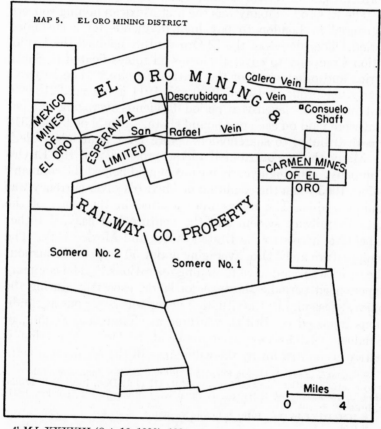

MAP 5.   EL ORO MINING DISTRICT

[61] *MJ*, XXXVIII (Oct. 16, 1909), 109.
[62] CRO, File No. 29924, Exploration Company; *MJ*, LXXI (April 6, 1901), 413; *AAMMG*, IX (Feb. 26, 1906), 23.

The other capitalists from England, France, Germany, and the United States who held executive positions in the company readily agreed, and in July, 1899, the mine and the small railway belonging to the American company were purchased for £820,084 in cash and £65,988 in shares of the company registered in London on July 27. Five countries were represented in the list of 370 shareholders who paid out £859,012 in cash for shares during the El Oro Mining and Railway Company's first year in business. The Exploration Company held 89,660 shares. An additional 75,000 were controlled by Francis Baring and Lord Nathan Meyer Rothschild under their own names.[63]

The El Oro Company was the first Mexican mining concern registered in London to pay high dividends for a sustained period. The success of the El Oro venture enabled the Exploration Company to cover its losses on mines floated in South Africa and other parts of the British Empire.[64] The El Oro's yearly net profits between 1900 and 1911 averaged £210,000, and during the eleven-year period dividends averaging 12.5 per cent were paid on each one pound share. A total of £1,353,312 was distributed to shareholders before Díaz went into exile.[65]

Many things contributed to the prosperity of the El Oro Company. The high yearly output of gold helped the company before 1905 when the condition of Mexico's silver currency was undependable. The mines were located in the heart of the nation's railway system and the venture had easy, if rather expensive, access to the United States and Mexico City. The temperature at El Oro, averaging about 50 degrees throughout the year, was conducive to mining operations.[66] The company experienced periodic shortages of labor, especially during the harvest season, but the situation never was as serious as conditions reported by British ventures in Chihuahua, Sonora, or Sinaloa. Strikes were uncommon at El Oro, a fact that is partly accounted for by the willingness of the Mexican govern-

---

[63] Summary of shareholders in Files No. 63105 and 29924. Summaries of the company's early operations may be found in *MM*, III (July-Dec., 1910), 289; *Mining Manual, 1900* (London, 1901), pp. 71-72; *Mining Manual, 1903* (London, 1904), p. 1012.
[64] *MM*, III (July-Dec., 1910), 289; File No. 63105.
[65] *Ibid.*
[66] W. E. Hindry, "Esperanza Mine, El Oro Mexico," *MM*, I (Sept.-Oct., 1909), 131, has information on the climate.

ment to suppress any outbreaks of violence at the mine.[67] Relations between the company and the Díaz regime were excellent, and only once did the El Oro directors ask the Foreign Office to approach the Mexican government in their behalf.[68] The company, unlike many limited concerns in Mexico, was willing and able to spend lavishly for machinery, general improvements, and an efficient managerial staff. Rawlinson Bayliss, the British manager at El Oro, was an outstanding example of the thoroughness displayed by the company directors in selecting its supervisors. Bayliss believed that even the best mines in Mexico seldom produced high-grade ore. They usually had been worked by many miners; unless a new company had plenty of capital and was prepared to absorb temporary losses, it should keep out of the Mexican morass. Bayliss' philosophy was put into action in 1904 when, following a dip in the profits, he closed the mine for twelve months while new mills and stamping equipment were erected.[69] A subsidiary lumber company also was formed to provide fuel for the company. At the same time Bayliss began to direct the installation of electrical power on a scale never before attempted by any British mining company. In 1905 the Mexican Light and Power Company, an English-Canadian venture guided by Dr. Fred Stark Pearson, a graduate of Tufts and later the President of the North-Western Railway Company, agreed to provide electric energy to the El Oro Company, other mines in the district, and to parts of the Federal District.[70] The source of this power was a hydroelectric plant built by F. S. Pearson's company in Necaxa, about 176 miles southeast of El Oro. The cost of stringing lines to the camp and installing motors in many of the machines was more than £20,000.[71] When the job was finally completed the appraisal of most observers was summed up in *Moody's Magazine:*

[67] *MJ,* LXXXIII (Feb. 15, 1908), 205.

[68] A company employee was held without trial on a murder charge; Greville to Lansdowne, No. 39 Diplomatic, July 18, 1901, FO 50, Vol. 524; Greville to Lansdowne, No. 47 Diplomatic, Aug. 27, 1901, FO 50, Vol. 524.

[69] *AAMMG,* XII (March 31, 1909), 43; *MM,* III (July-Dec., 1910), 289; *Mining Investor,* I (Nov., 1909), 21-22.

[70] The career of F. S. Pearson is studied more fully in chapts. iii and vi.

[71] *MW,* LXVII (Oct. 29, 1904), 521-22, made this estimate. It is difficult to tell from the balance sheets, File No. 63105, exactly how much was spent.

There have been few aids to industrial development in the world's history that have meant as much to the happiness and prosperity of a great region as the recently discovered . . . source of power which the . . . mines of El Oro . . . and the Federal District so sadly needed.[72]

Esperanza

Among the other mines served by electric power from Necaxa before Díaz was overthrown was Esperanza Limited. The mine, which can be located on maps 4 and 5, was discovered in 1890 by August Sahlberg, a Norwegian who came to Mexico after years of fruitless wandering in the mining areas of the western United States.[73] Sahlberg, backed by wealthy Mexicans, organized the Bumerango and Anexas Mining Company and for ten years was able to pull out large amounts of gold from the mine. In 1903 he sold the property to John Hays Hammond, representing the Guggenheim family of New York, for £450,000.[74] The Guggenheim-Hammond interests decided to secure part of their working capital in Britain, the plan being to develop the Esperanza mine through a British limited company in which they would control the largest block of shares.

The task of organizing Esperanza was given to Weetman Pearson, an old hand at Mexican enterprise, and Robert J. Price, a member of Parliament who at one time was chairman of forty-five mining companies in Canada, Rhodesia, Africa, and Mexico.[75] Price and Pearson had been interested in Mexican mines for ten years when they were approached by the Guggenheim group. Two syndicates, the Mexican Gold and Silver Recovery Company and the Venture Corporation, were at the apex of the Pearson and Price organization that held the controlling interest in mines in at least six Mexican states before 1900.[76] It was the Venture Corporation that carried out the

---

[72] Quoted in *AAMMG*, XIII (June 29, 1910), 87.
[73] Hindry, *MM*, I, 131.
[74] *Ibid.*, *AAMMG*, XII (March 31, 1909), 43.
[75] *Ibid.*

[76] A Pearson-Price syndicate controlled the Mexico Mines of El Oro, later one of the British dividend companies, until 1904, when it was sold to the El Oro Mining and Railway Company. Price was made a director in the company and Pearson was given 38,000 of the Mexico Mines's 180,000 shares. See CRO, File No. 82292, Mexico Mines of El Oro; Map 4, p. 79; Map 5, p. 87. Price and Pearson controlled companies that held mining property in Australia, Tasmania, Montana, Colorado, Maine, California, and Russia; see *AAMMG*, X (April 27, 1901), 51.

registration of Esperanza Limited in London and expedited the sale and distribution of 127,947 of the company's 455,000 shares.[77] The installation of new stamping equipment from the United States, a cyanide plant to treat the ore, and electrical power from Necaxa, helped to increase the average daily production of the Esperanza mine almost 400 per cent from 1903 to 1910.[78] The yearly value of the gold extracted never exceeded £194,000 until the Guggenheim-British group took over the mine. Under the new owners the totals never fell below £320,000.[79] In 1906 the company paid out a dividend of 160 per cent and from 1904 through 1910 investors received annual average returns of 68.8 per cent.

About 3,200 native workers drew wages from the company when the mines were running at full capacity.[80] Most were residents of the district but some were brought from Zacatecas and Pachuca by the British and American staff. Few of the imported workers did their jobs in a satisfactory manner. The company found that its advertisements too often lured only a conglomeration of shiftless peons. Many reported for work until they had a few pesos and then left the camp for a long liquor binge. Others saved enough to visit friends in distant villages and ended by making their vacation a permanent one. Excessive absenteeism was combated by paying the miners at the end of each day rather than on Saturday. If a worker received his wages at the end of the week the mine usually operated on short time on Monday, but if a daily wage was handed out this amount was spent or lost in gambling by the next morning. Under the new scheme, as one writer explained it, the native was "more likely to be in a fit state for work."[81] The company also began to pay part of its labor on a piece-work basis and to hand out a bonus to those who appeared regularly for work.

---

[77] CRO, File No. 78725, The Venture Corporation.
[78] The yearly balance sheets are found in CRO, File No. 78724, Esperanza Limited. The production reports also are in the SEL. See "Cyanide Practice at Esperanza," *MM*, III (July-Dec., 1910), 298.
[79] Hindry, *MM*, I, 131.
[80] *Ibid.*
[81] *Ibid.*

The blueprint for success—and failure

There obviously was no fixed formula that a company could
follow to insure profitable operations in Mexico. The dividend
mines all had sufficient ore stocks but beyond that the picture
is not clear. The most prosperous concerns mined gold. This
was important in a country that was enmeshed in the coils of
an unstable currency until 1905. These same bonanza concerns
had the backing of men who could spend enough money to make
the mines pay if they were going to pay at all. This was
certainly true in the case of the Esperanza and El Oro companies.
The choosing of a manager who was willing to experiment with
new methods and who could gather and hold a labor force while
keeping costs at a reasonable level often was important.
George Hopkins, E. H. Oxnam, and Rawlinson Bayliss were
good examples, although economy was not stressed at El Oro as
it was elsewhere. The availability of electric power, railroad
facilities, a temperate climate, and the backing of the Díaz
regime in labor-management relations assuredly did not hurt
the dividend record of the most important companies, but some
concerns earned sizable profits without enjoying all of these
advantages.

Most experts assumed that only a few companies could make
profits; others felt that too many companies failed because
Britons displayed a lack of common sense. It was charged that
Britons selected their mines without seeing them and later were
shocked to discover that the mines were worked out and had
long been known as worthless property.[82] Critics of British
mining believed that Americans selected their mines more
carefully, a doubtful proposition, but one that regularly appeared in the *Mining World*. Investors in the United States, it
was said, had greater opportunities to make money from mines
in their own country. They were apt to verify carefully the
claims set forth in prospectuses by ambitious promoters of
Mexican enterprises. On the other hand, the *Mining Journal*
and the *Mining Magazine* took the stand that British investors,
particularly in the late Díaz period, were overly cautious in
selecting their mines. A large amount of ore had to be in sight,

[82] Foreign Office report on Mexican Mining, Dec. 5, 1889, FO 50, Vol. 469.

and even if the mine looked promising the British buyer would offer such a low price that the owners refused to sell.[83]

Many of the men who managed the British companies were incompetent. These "miners" got their jobs because they knew the chairman or an influential shareholder. They arrived in Mexico without being able to speak Spanish, ignorant of local customs and labor conditions, and devoid of any mining experience.[84] Men who were wise in the ways of African or Australian mining sometimes came to the Republic when the boom flagged in those countries, but this group was prone to using machines and techniques that were suited to the Rand or Kalgoorlie rather than Mexico.[85]

The companies that worked for lengthy periods between 1885 and 1911 without getting any results discussed this problem in the annual meetings. Many collapsed for the basic reason that they had no ore in their mines.[86] At least one was pressed into Chancery Court by shareholders who claimed that the mine outlined in the prospectus did not exist.[87] The paucity of labor and the frequency of strikes ruined other companies.[88] A few concerns spent all their capital on opening up the mine and had to give up when shareholders refused to subscribe further funds.[89] Some found that the public would not take up their shares when they were first offered on the market. The Mexican Santa Barbara Company folded in this manner in 1887 when the *Mining Journal* told Britons, especially "widows, clergymen, and all those of limited income" to put their money in the Post Office Savings Bank rather than in the Santa Barbara venture.[90] It must also be remembered that fewer than one-half of the companies registered in London ever went to allotment. In some instances property could not be ob-

---

[83] *MJ*, LXXXVI (Aug. 11, 1909), 197; W. A. Prichard, "Looking for Mines in Mexico," *MM*, I (Nov., 1909), 205.

[84] *MJ*, LXXVIII (March 11, 1905), 260; *ibid.* (Sept. 16, 1905), 301.

[85] *Ibid.* (March 11, 1905), 260.

[86] See, for example, File No. 52209; *MJ*, LXVIII (June 25, 1898), 736.

[87] The directors of Panuco Copper barely escaped prosecu ion; *MJ*, LXX (March 31, 1900), 389; *ibid.*, LXXI (Feb. 2, 1901), 143; *ibid.* (March 16, 1901), 315.

[88] Labor troubles may be traced in St. John to Salisbury, No. 25, July 22, 1886, FO 50, Vol. 453; St. John to Salisbury, No. 3 Diplomatic, Feb. 6, 1889, FO 50, Vol. 468; Foreign Secretary to Greville, No. 12 Commercial, Sept. 28, 1901, FO 50, Vol. 525.

[89] *MM*, III (July-Dec., 1910), 292.

[90] *MJ*, LVII (April 30, 1887), 536. Also see CRO, File No. 25942, New San Acasio and Freehold Land Company; CRO, File No. 81311, North Dolores.

tained; in other cases the organizers may have shifted their
interests to other types of business after the concern was
registered.   Many of the reasons for withdrawing from the
mining contest before any shares were put up for distribution
will never be known.

* * * *

Britons invested in Mexico's mines with an eagerness that
they did not display in getting into any other form of Mexican
enterprise. While the total investment of pounds sterling in
mining was exceeded by the amount of capital in Mexican railways, the number of mining enterprises organized in London
between 1885 and 1910 was almost three times greater than the
companies formed to work in all other fields attracting British
capital.   During the years 1885-1910 there was only one
twelve-month period when no Mexican mining ventures were
registered in England.   Publicity and promotional pressure
kept up a steady interest in Mexico, but it is impossible to
ascertain what amount of prodding really was needed to pull
capital into the mining orbit.

The list of problems encountered by the active ventures
does not need to be recited again; the Foreign Office handled
the questions that came to its attention as it did those presented
by the railway companies.   No official protests were sent to the
presidential palace from the British Crown, but the unofficial
help that was extended usually satisfied the companies concerned.   One problem that did not bring forth cries of anguish
from the mining directors as it did from those in the railway
ventures was the decline in the value of silver. This was partly
because the most profitable companies, and thus the ones that
received the most attention in the journals, concentrated on
mining gold.   For other companies the payment of wages and
the purchase of supplies in Mexico with the cheap peso, the
increased extraction of lead, copper, zinc, and gold that could be
sold in Europe for gold and used to buy needed imports, and the
changes in Mexico's mining laws that cut expenses all created a
situation where the fall of silver was seldom mentioned in company reports from 1885 to 1905. The silver crisis was one of the
few possibilities that was dismissed when Britons attempted to
explain why so many of their Mexican companies collapsed.

The proportion of concerns that succumbed was high, but the proportion in this highly speculative type of enterprise also was great in other areas where British capital was invested before 1911.[91] The number of actual dividend companies also was low; yet the British record was no worse than that compiled by other foreign companies in Mexico.[92] Neither this fact nor the knowledge that they had provided jobs for Mexican workers, brought low grade deposits of ore into exploitation by their modern methods, contributed taxes to the national treasury, supplied traffic to the railways, or fattened the pocketbooks of untold brokers, machine manufacturers, or promoters, could have given many investors much pleasure. The enthusiasm of the late 1880's and early 1900's had waned by the time Díaz left Mexico, but the *Mining Magazine* reminded its subscribers that they still could play for big stakes.[93] More good mines were being placed on sale; improvements in the field of metallurgy were becoming available; the use of electrical power was increasing; and railroads were reaching out to remote sectors of the country. It was a familiar refrain but one that was bound to attract investors who believed that there always was a chance of another El Oro or Esperanza.

[91] See the author's "British Investments in Latin-American and African Mines: A Study in Contrasts," *IAEA*, VI (Spring, 1953), 29-38.

[92] American mining companies are treated in Pletcher, *JEH*, XVIII, 48-49.

[93] *MM*, I (Nov., 1909), 205.

5. *A Disastrous Adventure in Real Estate and Rubber*

When the editor of a London financial weekly noticed the increasing number of land and colonization companies being organized in the late 1880's, he advised parents with an eye to the future to prepare their sons to be liquidators of such enterprises since "there will be, by and by, so many to wind-up that extra hands will be required to perform the task."[1] If the writer was alive in 1910 he may have counted himself something of a prophet, at least where Mexican ventures were concerned.

British investors organized thirty-two limited companies to colonize large tracts, cultivate rubber trees, grow tobacco, coffee, sugar cane, cotton, and raise cattle and horses in Mexico between 1885 and the end of 1910.[2] The total property owned

[1] *MJ*, LIX (Feb. 23, 1889), 229.

[2] The term "real estate" in this chapter includes land which Britons acquired for colonization, farming, and ranching. The complete list of companies may be found in the Appendix, Table D. Britons seldom operated outside the limited company system and British holdings in American enterprises never were large. The four active ranch companies (see Map 6, p. 98) waged no promotional campaigns in England. London journals seldom contained news of their activities; none acquired a quotation on the Stock Exchange; and there is no evidence that any paid a dividend. The Highland Land and Livestock Company, a Scottish concern, has been placed on Map 6. The English companies purchased their land from American and Mexican owners, and all but the Guerrero (Mexican) Land Syndicate, breeding horses valued at £24,000 in 1910, disposed of their property before the Revolution. See Consul Trench to Kimberley, No. 3 Consular, April 25, 1894, FO 50, Vol. 492; Carden to Salisbury, Oct. 27, 1895, FO 50, Vol. 500; *SAJ*, XXXII (Feb. 4, 1888), 7; *Modern Mexico*, XIV (Nov. 1902), 42; *ibid.*, XV (July, 1903), 35-36; International Bureau of the American Republics, eds., *Mexico* (Washington, D. C., 1904), pp. 214-15. British interests in coffee, tobacco, sugar cane, and cotton were not important. Three companies planning to produce these crops in southern Mexico gave up because of a lack of capital. The Cotton Estates of Tlahualilo Company in Mapimi, Durango, was ruined when the Mexican

by the companies covered almost 41,000 square miles.[3] The paid-up capital of the companies was £3,367,158 in 1890, £3,259,873 in 1900, and £3,658,053 at the end of 1910.[4] However, only £473,000 in cash was received for shares in the enterprises.[5] None of the ranching or agricultural companies was important, and less than one-half of any of the concerns attempted to work in Mexico. Three-fourths of the total sterling was placed in ventures active in Lower California, but British investors also contributed to companies controlling one million acres in Chiapas and Durango and smaller areas in Chihuahua, Oaxaca, Coahuila, Sonora, Veracruz, and San Luis Potosí.[6] Almost all their efforts in Mexico ended in failure. Few Britons migrated to the Republic; only two of the companies returned dividends; and many of those remaining in business in 1910 were selling sections of their concessions to recoup heavy losses.

The British excursion into these fields must be examined within the framework of Díaz' land policies. The dictator and his *científicos*, guided by their belief in progress through industrialization and immigration, accelerated the process of dividing Mexico into immense principalities. Laws passed in 1883 and 1894 granted concessions to survey land in the Republic. Two-thirds of the surveyed land was to revert to the Mexican nation. One-third was kept by the examiners and, in fact, they usually were allowed to purchase the remainder at a low price. One authority has estimated that Díaz virtually handed over 134,000,000 acres to individuals and to land companies controlled mainly by foreigners.[7] In 1910, partly as a result of this policy, almost 50 per cent of the Republic's rural population lived surrounded by large estates and probably less than 5 per cent of the populace owned land.[8]

partners absconded with most of the company's money in 1899. Also see GBDCR, MS No. 393, *Report on the Cultivation of Coffee in Mexico* (London, 1896); Dering to Salisbury, No. 6 Confidential, July 24, 1899, FO 50, Vol. 518; Greville to Lansdowne, No. 4 Commercial, July 24, 1901, FO 204, Vol. 284; enclosure in Greville to Lansdowne, No. 5 Commercial, March 29, 1902, FO 50, Vol. 528.

[3] *Ibid.*
[4] Appendix, Table D.
[5] The figure is derived from the company reports.
[6] Map 6, p. 98.
[7] Eyler N. Simpson, *The Ejido, Mexico's Way Out* (Chapel Hill, 1937), pp. 27-28.
[8] Simpson, pp. 36-37.

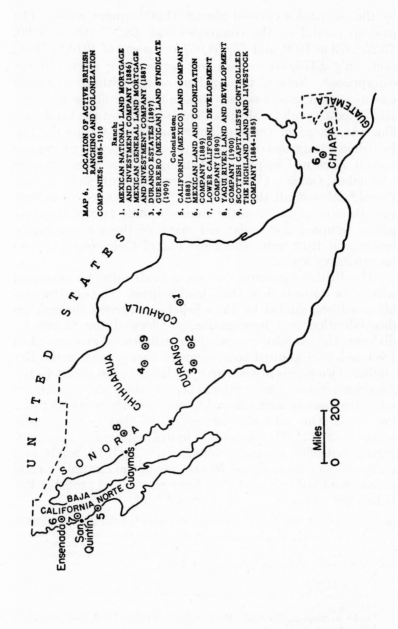

MAP 6. LOCATION OF ACTIVE BRITISH RANCHING AND COLONIZATION COMPANIES: 1885-1910

Ranch:
1. MEXICAN NATIONAL LAND MORTGAGE AND INVESTMENT COMPANY (1886)
2. MEXICAN GENERAL LAND MORTGAGE AND INVESTMENT COMPANY (1887)
3. DURANGO ESTATES (1897)
4. GUERRERO (MEXICAN) LAND SYNDICATE (1909)

Colonization:
5. CALIFORNIA (MEXICO) LAND COMPANY (1888)
6. MEXICAN LAND AND COLONIZATION COMPANY (1889)
7. LOWER CALIFORNIA DEVELOPMENT COMPANY (1890)
8. YAQUI RIVER LAND AND DEVELOPMENT COMPANY (1900)
9. SCOTTISH CAPITALISTS CONTROLLED THE HIGHLAND LAND AND LIVESTOCK COMPANY (1884-1885)

Englishmen began to evince interest in acquiring Mexican land for colonization and farming when it became apparent that diplomatic relations between the two countries would be renewed. Shortly after the Preliminary Agreement was signed in August, 1884, Lionel Carden outlined Díaz' land program to his superiors in London.[9] One of Carden's associates in Mexico, George Jenner, published a report outlining the opportunities for British capital under the new scheme. After reminding his readers that Britons were known as pioneers in backward countries, Jenner explained that large plots of land in northern Mexico could be purchased for $0.35 (Mex.) to $0.50 (Mex.) an acre. An ideal climate, low taxes, and the proximity of the markets and railways of the United States offered an excellent base for profitable enterprise.[10] No attempt was made to relate the fall in the price of silver to the opportunities for investment, and Jenner did not, of course, mention the unfortunate record of previous attempts in this type of enterprise in the northern states.[11]

The Foreign Office soon began to receive numerous letters asking for information on conditions in Mexico. One Briton asked how he might purchase an estate from the Mexican government. Another wanted a summary of Mexican citizenship laws for those who registered land titles in the Republic. A third wished to know if rice could be grown on a ranch he was planning to purchase.[12]

In January, 1889, Sir Edward Jenkinson, a secretary to the Lord Lieutenant in Ireland, told the Foreign Office that he was leaving for Mexico to acquire more than 20,000,000 acres in Lower California for a group of British investors.[13] Jenkinson left England with an official letter of introduction and in May, 1889, announced the formation of the Mexican Land and

---

[9] Carden to Salisbury, Sept. 25, 1885, FO 50, Vol. 448.

[10] GBDCR, Commercial No. 18, *Report on Investments for British Capital in Mexico* (London, 1886).

[11] Charles Nordhoff, *Peninsular California* (New York, 1888), pp. 22, 25-32; Hubert Howe Bancroft, *History of the North Mexican States and Texas*, II (San Francisco, 1889), 727-28.

[12] A. A. Dance to Foreign Secretary, Feb. 16, 1887, FO 50, Vol. 463; Charles Phillips (acting consul, Mexico City) to Blair Robertson, July 2, 1888, FO 203, Vol. 109. Also see St. John to Salisbury, No. 16, Diplomatic Confidential, May 4, 1888, FO 50, Vol. 465.

[13] Jenkinson to Pauncefote, Jan. 10, 1889, FO 50, Vol. 472; Salisbury to St. John, Jan. 12, 1889, FO 50, Vol. 479.

Colonization Company. This enterprise proved to be the largest and most controversial of the British colonization concerns.[14] The company's property in Lower California, Chiapas, and Sonora was purchased from American and Mexican interests who decided to give up after years of disheartening operations. George Sisson, a Michigan attorney, Louis Hüller, a naturalized United States citizen, and some Mexican financiers formed the International Company of Mexico in the early 1880's to exploit a government grant of 14,602,620 acres in Sonora, Lower California, two islands off the western coast of the peninsula, and over 340,000 acres in Chiapas.[15] Sisson hoped to establish a steamer service along the coast, construct a network of railroads in northwestern Mexico, build hotels at Ensenada, and string telegraph lines from there to the United States. He also had plans to someday build a university in Lower California.[16]

Land was offered for sale to American and European colonists in 1886 over the objections of Mexican nationalists who pictured the venture as part of a plan by the United States to annex Mexican border areas.[17] In the first rush of enthusiasm over three thousand Central Europeans, Norwegians, and Americans may have come to Lower California, but they were lured by gold rather than any desire to establish permanent homes.[18] The exodus began when alluvial deposits gave out three feet below the surface. A shortage of wood and water in the Ensenada district added to the company's problems, and by 1889 only nine hundred of the original emigrants remained in

[14] CRO, File No. 28841, The Mexican Land and Colonization Company. Reference must be made to the 4,000,000 acre tract in Lower California purchased from the Mexican government by the California (Mexico) Land Company. The Company was registered in London in 1888, but Britons held only 3,500 of the concern's 55,640 one pound shares. The remainder were controlled by bankers in Paris. These bankers probably were responsible for a 7 per cent dividend paid in 1890 to promote the company. Its concession was revoked by the Mexican government because of a failure to develop the property. See Carden to Salisbury, No. 1 Commercial, May 23, 1890, FO 50, Vol. 475; Slaughter and May (solicitors) to Lansdowne, Feb. 11, 1901, FO 50, Vol. 526; CRO, File No. 26608, California (Mexico) Land Company.

[15] File No. 28841.

[16] México, Secretario de Fomento, *Exposición que hace el secretario de fomento sobre la colonización de la Baja California* (México, 1887), pp. 95-99, for the original contract. Also see File No. 28841.

[17] *La Novedades*, Nov. 28, 1886; *El Tiempo*, Nov. 28, 1886, quoted in México, Secretario de Fomento, *Exposición . . . sobre la colonización de la Baja California*, pp. 1-9.

[18] Report by Denys, Dec. 5, 1889, FO 50, Vol. 469; also see United States, Consular Letters, Matamoros, Werner Sutton to Assistant Secretary of State, No. 558, March 15, 1889, Vol. 23. Waiters and telegraphers, among others, had rushed from Ensenada to prospect for gold.

Lower California.[19] In April of that year, having spent
£600,000 to promote their company, Sisson and Hüller decided
to abandon the project.[20]

A complex arrangement transferring the property to Sir
Edward Jenkinson was made on April 4, 1889. Sisson and
Hüller sold their holdings to the Mexican Land and Colonization Company; others in the International enterprise exchanged
their shares for shares in the British concern. The new company's share capital of £3,100,000 in 1889 was divided among
four hundred shareholders, including the River Plate Trust
Company, the Bankers' Investment Trust Corporation of
London, two members of the House of Commons, and American
capitalist J. Pierpont Morgan.[21] The Mexican Land and Colonization Company took over approximately 15,000,000 acres
from the International Company and also acquired an additional 3,000,000 acres in Chiapas from the Mexican government
for the token price of 6,000 pesos in bonds of the Consolidated
National Debt.[22] The company was to settle nine hundred
colonists on the Chiapas property within ten years. It was to
forfeit a 100 peso Mexican government bond for every colonist
under that figure. Settlers were exempted from federal taxes
for a decade and could import machinery without paying duty
for the same period.[23]

The company's board of directors appointed Jenkinson
General Manager in Mexico with offices in Ensenada. His
contract was for five years at an annual salary of £2,000. After
obtaining a clear title in the Mexican courts to the lands held by
the company, Jenkinson formulated a plan for dividing and
selling sections of the property.[24] The first important sale was
made in 1890 when a group in the Mexican Land and Colonization Company headed by A. P. Allsopp purchased 400,000 acres
surrounding the port town of San Quintin from the parent

[19] *Ibid.*

[20] St. John to Mr. Jervoise, Private, Nov. 28, 1889, FO 50, Vol. 468.

[21] File No. 28841.

[22] Simpson, p. 28; also see CRO, File No. 86790, Land Company of Chiapas; Map 6,
p. 98, for location of the Chiapas property. This area was later sold to the Land Company of Chiapas. The records of the company contain the best brief summary of the
concession's history.

[23] *Ibid.*, SEL, Prospectus for the Mexican Land and Colonization Company.

[24] St. John to Jervoise, Private, Nov. 28, 1889, FO 50, Vol. 468; St. John to Salisbury, June 11, 1890, FO 50, Vol. 474; Salisbury to Carden, No. 1 Commercial, June 13,
1890, FO 50, Vol. 475.

concern.[25] The price was £30,000 in cash and £100,000 in shares in Allsopp's enterprise, the Lower California Development Company. Allsopp obtained permission from the Mexican authorities to institute a mail service from San Quintin to Ensenada and up the coast to San Diego. He and the directors hoped this service would keep the concern solvent until settlers came to the peninsula.[26]

The Mexican Land and Colonization Company and the Lower California Development Company almost collapsed during the next three years. The economic crisis of 1890 and the panic of 1893 helped to halt the flow of whatever British capital might have been available to develop Lower California. It further was apparent by 1893 that not many Britons and other Europeans were going to migrate to Mexico. The Foreign Office, in fact, discouraged emigration to the Republic during this period. Lionel Carden informed prospective settlers that a man with ample capital, a knowledge of Spanish, and the proper introductions had only a fair chance of success in the country. He urged artists, doctors, house painters, and un-skilled laborers, among others, to remain in England.[27] Most of the 2,500 Britons in Mexico in the early 1890's were in the Federal District, Chihuahua, Pachuca, Guanajuato, and Coahuila. There were but 135 Britons in Sonora and Lower California and only 10 settlers from England had been attracted to the Mexican Land Company's property in Chiapas.[28] Lionel Carden felt that only one Briton in Ensenada was qualified to serve as vice-consul in that district.[29]

Relations between the British companies and the Mexican government grew tense after 1890. On April 12, 1892, Charles Anthony, a California engineer, publicly accused the Mexican Land and Colonization Company of being an agent of the

[25] CRO, File No. 32395, Lower California Development Company.
[26] *Ibid.*
[27] Lord Lister (Foreign Office) to St. John, Feb. 13, 1892, FO 50, Vol. 487. GBDCR, AS No. 2464, *Report on the Trade and Agriculture of Sonora* (London, 1900); Carden to W. Williamson, March 4, 1891, FO 203, Vol. 114; Carden to R. Angier, March 31, 1891, FO 203, Vol. 114; Carden to M. Taylor, April 10, 1893, FO 203, Vol. 119.
[28] Estimates of the number of foreigners in Mexico are found in St. John to Salis-bury, July 1, 1891, FO 50, Vol. 477; Carden, Report on Britons in Guanajuato, Duran-go, and Coahuila, Aug. 16, 1893, FO 204, Vol. 219; GBDCR, AS No. 3888, *Report for the Year 1906 on the Trade and Commerce of Mexico* (London, 1907); W. J. Forsyth to Carden, Feb. 11, 1892, FO 203, Vol. 116.
[29] Carden to Salisbury, Oct. 27, 1895, FO 50, Vol. 500.

British government in Ensenada.[30] The British skeleton crew living in the city was there to draw maps of the western coastline in preparation for a filibuster raid from San Diego across the border. This raid would lead to interference by the British Navy to protect British subjects and to seize San Quintin. The port then would be turned over to the Admiralty. The British Minister in Mexico City promptly denied the existence of a plot, explaining that no coaling station in Mexico was worth the loss of Mexican friendship or the rancor of the United States.[31] In the House of Commons a representative from the Admiralty announced that his department had no interest in San Quintin, if only because "of the impossibility of fortifying and holding a position in the mainland in the presence of the forces and resources of American Continental Nations, at such a distance from the mother country."[32]

More trouble for the British concerns came in the form of a letter to President Díaz from the Governor of Lower California in early May, 1892.[33] Governor Luis Torres wrote that J. A. Drought, a director of the Lower California Development Company, recently had suggested that the Governor assist his company in bringing Lower California under the control of the United States.[34] British property values would increase, debts could be erased, and Torres would be rewarded for his help. Torres also implicated Sir Edward Jenkinson in the plot. Jenkinson and Drought promptly were summoned to Díaz' office in the capital for a conference.[35] Jenkinson was exonerated but Drought was not allowed to get off so easily. He had visited San Diego and had been seen with Americans known to be part of a small annexationist party.[36] Drought admitted meeting with Governor Torres, although he denied that any-

[30] *The Times* (London), April 12, 1892. The story also was printed in *The Mexican Financier* and the *New York Herald*.
[31] St. John to Salisbury, April 14, 1892, FO 50, Vol. 483; Sanderson to St. John, April 15, 1892, Vol. 483.
[32] Evan MacGregor (Admiralty) to Salisbury, FO 50, Vol. 486.
[33] Report of the letter was made in Mariscal to St. John, Private, May 19, 1892, FO 50, Vol. 484.
[34] Reactions in the Foreign Office may be found in St. John to Salisbury, No. 8 Consular, Feb. 25, 1892, FO 50, Vol. 484; Lister to Salisbury, May 2, 1892, FO 50, Vol. 484.
[35] *Ibid.*
[36] St. John to Salisbury, No. 14 Confidential, April 13, 1892, FO 50, Vol. 484.

thing irregular had been suggested.[37]   Sir Spenser St. John, the British Minister, was convinced that Drought and others in the Lower California concern were guilty of the charge. St. John and Lord Salisbury insisted, however, that the case should be handled by the Mexican government.[38]   On May 27 Mexico's Minister of Foreign Affairs informed St. John that the Lower California company had to be "reorganized" if it expected to remain in the government's favor.[39]   The company evidently recognized the subtle hint. When Drought handed his resignation to the directors and left for England, President Díaz immediately said that the affair was closed.[40]   Probably no one familiar with the fracas was surprised when the Lower California enterprise soon announced that it was reselling its property to the Mexican Land and Colonization Company and closing its offices in Mexico.

During the years just studied representatives of the Mexican Land and Colonization Company returned to England, and plans for appointing a Briton as vice-consul in Ensenada were canceled.[41]   The annexation incidents, world-wide economic problems, and the collapse of the colonization plans impelled the company to reappraise its policy.   When the Mexican Land concern reopened the Ensenada office in June, 1894, its aim was to dispose of the company's lands in large chunks as quickly as possible and pull out of Mexico.   Directors maintained that the antagonism toward the company generated during the early 1890's forced this action.[42]

The company's first sale under this new policy was made in Sonora in 1900.   No attempt had been made to exploit this section of the company's property after it was acquired in 1889, mainly because southern Sonora was kept in an uneasy condi-

[37] Drought to Salisbury, May 20, 1892, FO 50, Vol. 484.
[38] See Salisbury's note on reverse side of Lister to Salisbury, May 2, 1893, FO 50, Vol. 484; Salisbury to Drought, May 27, 1892, FO 50, Vol. 487.
[39] St. John to Salisbury, May 20, 1892, FO 50, Vol. 484.
[40] Bland to Salisbury, No. 19 Commercial, Aug. 19, 1892, FO 50, Vol. 484.
[41] Secretary, Mexican Land and Colonization Company to Rosebery, June 14, 1894, FO 50, Vol. 494.
[42] There were manifestations of anti-British sentiment after the Drought episode. When the manager of the Mexican Land concern was suggested as a suitable candidate for the job of vice-consul in Ensenada in 1894, the Mexican government rejected him in terms that suggested the diplomatic imbroglio had not been forgotten. See Carden to Rosebery, No. 10 Consular, July 14, 1894, FO 50, Vol. 493.

tion by Yaqui Indian raids and government reprisals.[43] By 1900 thousands of the Indians had been killed or transported to distant states by government order.[44] This helped to open the way for the sale of the land in Sonora. On July 31, 1900, Francis Pavy and Edgar Welles of New York purchased 87,000 acres between Agua Caliente and the Yaqui River from the Mexican Land venture for £40,000 in cash and an unannounced number of shares in Pavy's London-registered Yaqui River Land and Development Company.[45] The company prospectus extolled the virtues of the Sonora area. The Sonora Railway's terminus at Guaymas brought transportation facilities to the company's doorstep, and when irrigation canals were dug in the area a brisk trade in produce such as oranges and tomatoes would be developed with the United States.[46]

While Francis Pavy attempted to parlay his Sonora purchase into a going concern, the Mexican Land and Colonization Company continued to press its primary objective. The company had been unable to raise enough capital or enthusiasm to develop its 4,000,000 acre tract in Chiapas. When the almost universal interest in rubber gained momentum after 1900, the company was able to find a buyer for the entire Chiapas property.[47] In 1905 Weetman Pearson and Captain Buchanan Scott, both involved in other British enterprises in Mexico, and eager to exploit an area reported to contain more than 3,000,000 wild rubber trees, joined with friends of President Díaz to purchase the Chiapas acreage from the Mexican Land and Colonization Company.[48] Pearson's new enterprise paid £170,000 in cash and £30,000 in company shares to the Mexican Land concern for the property.[49] Pearson registered the Land company of Chiapas in London and began to promote the venture

[43] Pletcher, *IAEA*, I, 41-42; Robert H. Murray, "Mexico and the Yaquis," *Sunset Magazine*, XXIV (1910), 624, quoted in Pletcher, *IAEA*, I, 42.

[44] *Ibid.*

[45] Company Record Office, File No. 66430, Yaqui River Land and Development Company; see Map 6, p. 98.

[46] SEL, Prospectus for the Yaqui River Land and Development Company; Pletcher, *IAEA*, I, 41-42; File No. 66438.

[47] Rippy, *Latin America and the Industrial Age*, p. 178. The standard work on the rubber industry is Howard and Ralph Wolf, *Rubber, A Story of Glory and Greed* (New York, 1936).

[48] CRO, File No. 86790, Land Company of Chiapas.

[49] *Ibid.*

with his customary vigor.[50]

The Mexican Land and Colonization Company used the cash payments received for the Sonora and Chiapas concession to pay off debts incurred since the company's registration in 1889. The directors continued to manage the steamer service operating from Ensenada, a third-rate hotel in the city, and a few mining operations around San Quintin.[51] These efforts were designed to reduce the liabilities of the company; hope of profit or of colonization on the peninsula had been forgotten. When the balance sheet for 1910 valued the company's assets at £2,920,473, one financial journal called the summary "a ridiculous and terrible document," challenged the figure as obviously being too high, called attention to the venture's "bad record," and noted that only three shareholders attended the annual meeting in November.[52]

If the records of the companies organized by Francis Pavy and Weetman Pearson are accurate, the Mexican Land and Colonization Company was fortunate to have sold its property at any price. There was little response in London when Pavy attempted to draw British capital into his Yaqui enterprise. The refusal of the Foreign Office to encourage Britons to invest their sterling in Sonoran companies, much less to emigrate to the state, may have been a factor in the ruination of Pavy's plans.[53] The Yaqui River Land and Development Company was still on the Registrar's list of active concerns in 1910, but the truth was that nothing had been accomplished on the property since its purchase.

Weetman Pearson made a wrong guess concerning the Mexican *castilloas* rubber tree, a mistake that was made by investors in the United States and, to a lesser extent, by those in Great Britain. Pearson's Land Company of Chiapas was one of six limited concerns organized during the Díaz era to tap the rubber trees native to southern Mexico.[54] Since nearly two hundred American companies frantically and usually unsuccessfully plunged into the Mexican rubber boom before 1911, Britons were lucky to have escaped the *castilloas* fever.

[50] SEL, Prospectus for the Land Company of Chiapas.
[51] File No. 28841, II, summary of capital and shares, 1907.
[52] *AAMMG*, XIII (Nov. 30, 1910), 172.
[53] GBDCR, AS No. 2464.
[54] Appendix, Table D.

The origins of investment sprees often are difficult to uncover, but an article published in both the *India Rubber World* and *Two Republics* shortly after the American State Department called on its consuls for reports on the rubber situation in 1890 typified the approach of the promoters. Matías Romero, a politician and diplomat whose opinions on the Mexican Railway appeared earlier in this volume, saw no reason why 450 acres of land having 100,000 rubber trees could not bring a judicious owner a net profit of $25,000 in six or seven years.[55] According to Romero, thousands of wild *castilloas* trees with trunks measuring 78 inches in diameter were growing on the borders of Chiapas in low, damp lands under temperatures ideal for the cultivation of rubber. Profits also could be earned from side crops such as cotton and corn until the trees were ready for tapping. To Romero's statements were added a plethora of news items and advertisements in the *Mexican Herald, Modern Mexico*, and the *India Rubber World*, as well as the encouragement of Sir Thomas Lipton and Collis P. Huntington, two men known for their financial acumen.[56]

The first two British rubber concerns in Mexico received concessions near San Juan Bautista in northern Chiapas and in Pochutla, Oaxaca, from the Mexican government in 1890 and 1892.[57] The Chiapas group raised only £4,380 in four years and forfeited its grant in 1894. The other venture, the Anglo-Mexican Planting and Trading Corporation, answered inquiries in 1897 by saying that while their land in Pochutla "was now uncultivated," it abounded in rubber trees, had bottom land suitable for rice and sugar, and was blessed with an excellent harbor.[58] Unfortunately, none of these advantages could be utilized with the £7 taken by the company for shares before giving up its concession in 1897.

The Foreign Office used the example of the Pochutla fiasco to explain to prospective rubber barons that at least £10,000 was needed to start a plantation. One British consul admitted that certain competent persons believed that selling rubber

[55] *TR*, April 30, 1892. Also see Rippy, *Latin America and the Industrial Age*, p. 166.
[56] Rippy, *Latin America and the Industrial Age*, p. 169.
[57] CRO, File No. 32230, Mexican Estates and Trading Syndicate; *ibid.*, File No. 37841, Anglo-Mexican Planting and Trading Corporation.
[58] A summary of the report was made in Carden to John Martin and Company, Miscellaneous No. 1, Jan. 7, 1897, FO 203, Vol. 129.

would prove a lucrative business, but he insisted that the experimental nature of most enterprises made them a hazardous investment.[59] Lionel Carden advised two London companies to send out experts to examine property being considered as a site for a rubber estate since swindles were common.[60]

Weetman Pearson had more than the minimum amount of capital suggested by the Foreign Office, and he was not a man to buy property until it had been thoroughly examined. Between 1905 and 1910 he and his friends collected £87,608 from British investors.[61] A small trained staff was sent to Tapachula, Chiapas, at a yearly cost of £6,000; native labor was hired to tend the plantation; and almost £21,000 was spent to prepare the estate for the day when the trees could be tapped.[62] The company was still waiting when Díaz fled from the Revolution, but Pearson had admitted the collapse of his enterprise in 1908. By then many rubber men were convinced that the *castilloas* trees would not yield enough rubber to cover the cost of establishing most plantations. The competition of British and Dutch producers in the Far East and the announced development of what apparently was a superior species of rubber shrub in other sections of Mexico completed the bleak outlook presented to investors at the company's annual meeting in 1910.

W. D. Pearson was not the last Briton to try his luck with the *castilloas* tree. In 1907 a company that originally planned to operate in Chile instead purchased 20,000 acres in Veracruz from a Mexican promoter in the capital of the state.[63] Two hundred peons were employed to clear land and plant 34,000 large trees on the Mano Marques estate in 1908.[64] Machinery was brought from England and plans were made to augment the rubber bonanza by establishing a trade in rice, cotton, and coffee. It was possible, according to the managing director, that gold would also be found on the property. The exploitation of the property and the capital reserves of the company came to an end at the same time in 1910. None of the concern's trees

[59] Consul Stronge to Martin, Feb. 16, 1898, FO 204, Vol. 266.
[60] Carden to J. Bennett Brothers, Miscellaneous No. 60, May 12, 1897, FO 203, Vol. 129; Carden to A. Evans, June 15, 1897, FO 203, Vol. 129.
[61] See the balance sheet for 1910 in File No. 86790.
[62] *Ibid.*
[63] CRO, File No. 79239, Chilean Exploration and Development Syndicate.
[64] *AAMMG*, XI (Jan. 31, 1908), 11-12.

were ready for tapping and directors were preparing a request for further contributions when news of the Revolution reached London.[65]

Only one limited rubber company seemed to have a future in 1910. German capitalists and scientists began to experiment with the guayule rubber shrub in northern Mexico in the early 1900's.[66] In 1909, following their researches in Saltillo, Coahuila, and in San Luis Potosí near the Mexico National Railway, the Germans were able to produce 2,181,277 pounds of crude rubber from the guayule shrub.[67] It was decided to expand operations by raising capital through a British limited company. A syndicate in London was given the job of registering the Guayule Rubber Company on April 6, 1910. The £248,468 that was subscribed for shares within a few months came mainly from banking houses in Berlin, Paris, and London. The company announced a dividend of 5 per cent on its capital in December, 1910, an announcement that gave it uniqueness among limited rubber concerns.[68]

*   *   *   *   *

Britons in the banking, shipping, or machine supply business and those who went out to supervise or manage the limited companies may have profited from the dabblings of their countrymen in the enterprises described. The man who risked his capital in these companies as an investor rarely received any returns for his trouble. The British ventures, with one exception, were not ruined by chicanery; it is impossible to explain the over-all picture on this basis. The Mexican Land and Colonization Company, larger than all the other concerns combined in terms of capital and numbers of shareholders, did not enjoy harmonious relations with the Mexican government,

---

[65] File No. 79239; *SEYB*, 1911 (London, 1912). The story of the San Cristobal (Mexico) Rubber, Tobacco, and Estates Company follows almost the same pattern. See CRO, File No. 104031.

[66] SEL, Prospectus for the Guayule Rubber Company; CRO, File No. 108932, Guayule Rubber Company.

[67] *Ibid.*

[68] *SEYB, 1911* (London, 1912). Articles summarizing the experiments on the guayule shrub are found in *India Rubber World*, XXXVIII (Sept. 1, 1908), 395-96; *ibid.*, XXXIX (Oct. 1, 1908), 21. The Guayule Rubber Company paid dividends before World War I. The *castilloas* tree is discussed in *ibid.*, XLII (Sept. 1, 1910), 410. The number of British rubber ventures declined rapidly after 1910. By 1925 Britons had less than £300,000 invested in rubber companies in Mexico.

suffered through the economic vicissitudes of the early 1890's, and owned property that held no attraction for European colonists. Other companies were unable to raise enough capital in Britain to begin operations in Mexico. Some were registered in London at precisely the time when the money market was tight and never got beyond the directors' table. This was true of some of the rubber companies, but even without this problem Weetman Pearson and others were victims of the failure of the *castilloas* experiment. The importance of many factors cannot be measured. The Foreign Office sensibly refused to portray Mexico in terms that would lure Britons to the Republic. The examination and selection of land by some companies may have been done in haphazard fashion. Perhaps the American dollar picked off the more attractive ranch and farm sites. Finally, one wonders how vigorously the British companies really worked to make their properties pay dividends. Were first-rate managers and technicians sent to Mexico to handle company affairs? To how many Britons was the investment in Mexican enterprise a sideline from which one could retreat quickly if the profits did not begin to appear in a few months?

The fact that eleven British companies were listed at the Company Registration Office in 1910 was misleading. Only two ventures were active in the Republic. The Mexican Land and Colonization Company was a dying concern, as was Francis Pavy's Yaqui enterprise and Weetman Pearson's rubber venture. Two others had passed the time limit for sending in annual reports and soon were to be removed from the Register. Two more were registered in November and December, 1910, and had not as yet raised any capital. The future of another company was being settled in the Mexico City courts. Two rubber companies whose directors did not choose to believe the bad news printed in the *India Rubber World* were hopefully awaiting the maturation of their rubber trees. While they waited other Britons were showing considerable interest in three relatively new types of enterprise in the Republic: public utilities, factories, and petroleum.

6. Some British Investments in the later Díaz Period:
Utilities, Factories, and Petroleum

An advertisement in the *Mexican Herald* on November 10, 1910, entitled "Breakfast for Two Cooked on the Table," depicted a man and his wife in Mexico City eating their morning meal.[1] The caption announced that it no longer was necessary to prepare meals in a hot oven. One could now purchase an "Electric Toaster Stove," and the power to run it, from the Mexican Light and Power Company, a concern in which English capital played an important role. During the morning meal the young couple possibly used salt produced at a British factory. Later in the day they may have ridden on tramways built with the aid of British pounds. The señor may have been employed by a Mexico City company which distributed oil that was uncovered and exploited by a British enterprise. And on the way home in the afternoon he may have puffed on a cigar turned out by a British firm in Veracruz.

In the later years of the Díaz era the dawn of the electrical age, Mexico's drive for industrial development, and the world demand for petroleum and rubber furnished Britons with outlets for their capital and technological abilities. It has been convenient to consider Britain's unfortunate excursion into the rubber business in a previous chapter; by 1911 the pound sterling was involved in one limited company, a venture conceived and controlled by Germans.

[1] *Mexican Herald*, Nov. 9, 1910.

Utilities

Anglo-Mexican diplomatic relations had been broken for sixteen years when H. H. Gibbs and William Barrón, associated with the Mexican Railway Company, received a concession from the Mexican government to supply the capital with 600 gas lights and 1,200 electric lights.[2] Barrón, Gibbs, six other members of the Antony Gibbs family, Augustus Sillem, and J. C. Hayne, all connected with the Mexican Railway, combined to organize the Mexican Gas and Electric Light Company. They allotted the share capital of the company, £100,000 in £20 shares, to themselves.[3] The concession stated that if the government decided to revamp or enlarge the lighting system after the Gibbs-Barrón concern completed their contract, the Mexican Gas and Electric Light Company was to be given the first opportunity to reject or accept the job.[4]

In 1885 the company sent engineers to Mexico City to plan the lighting of the northern districts. No private homes were to be served by the British concern. The gas lights were shipped from England and installed before Christmas in 1885. The installation of the electric lights proceeded at the same time.[5] The energy for this part of the project was supplied by steam boilers from Colchester, England, operating from a small generating plant that was built at San Lazaro, near the Interoceanic Railroad's main station.

Thomas Braniff, the general manager of the Mexican Railway Company, was appointed to the same job with the Mexican Gas and Electric Light Company in 1891.[6] Braniff was in Mexico City in April, 1896, when the city council issued a brochure asking for bids on a 9,000-horsepower generating plant at suburban Nonoalco.[7] This announcement touched off a lengthy controversy between the company and the city govern-

[2] CRO, File No. 18223, Mexican Gas and Electric Light Company; Corporation of Foreign Bondholders, *Annual Report, 1891* (London, 1892). For a list of the public utility companies in which British capital was invested, see Appendix, Table F.
[3] File No. 18223.
[4] Dering to Salisbury, No. 11 Commercial, May 1, 1900, FO 50, Vol. 521.
[5] File No. 18223.
[6] Dering to Salisbury, No. 11 Commercial, May 1, 1900, FO 50, Vol. 521.
[7] A copy of the brochure, "City Council of Mexico, Tender for the Lighting of Mexico City," may be found in FO 50, Vol. 505.

ment. Alban Gibbs, a company director, told the British Foreign Secretary that the Mexican Gas and Light concern rejected the job in 1896 because the board did not believe that the type of incandescent bulb then available could furnish the amount of light specified in the council's pamphlet.[8] The council, having fulfilled the terms of the original concession, offered the contract to the German firm of Siemens and Halske.[9] It was immediately accepted, but when the contract was published the manager of the Mexican Gas company claimed that modifications had been made in the contract subsequent to its rejection by the British company. He insisted that the contract would have been acceptable had the directors seen the changes.[10] The council dismissed this claim and further roused the company's ire by requesting that it stand the cost of removing the gas light fixtures so that they might be replaced with Siemens and Halske electric lights.[11] The Mexican Gas and Electric Light Company ignored four letters and the fixtures were removed at city expense. For a time it appeared that the council might publicly parade its anger by asking the company to dispose of its electric light plant at San Lazaro, but Sir Henry Dering, the British Minister, persuaded the city fathers to allow the company to maintain its plant and, in fact, to increase its service.[12] Within two years the company laid over a hundred miles of underground cable in Mexico City and doubled the total capacity of the Lazaro plant.[13]

The Siemens-Halske company carried out its contract in Mexico City with the help of a new British limited enterprise, the Mexican Electric Works, organized in 1897.[14] The building of the electrical plant at Nonoalco was only part of the $3,500,000 contract. Seven hundred electric lights were installed in key municipal offices, 400 at important street crossings, and facilities were readied for supplying at least 30,000 private homes

[8] Gibbs to Foreign Secretary, April 25, 1900, FO 50, Vol. 523.
[9] *SAJ*, XLIII (Aug. 28, 1897), 235.
[10] Gibbs to Foreign Secretary, April 25, 1900, FO 50, Vol. 523.
[11] Dering to Salisbury, No. 11 Commercial, May 1, 1900, FO 50, Vol. 521.
[12] *Ibid.*
[13] GBDCR, AS No. 2951, *Report for the Year 1902 on the Trade and Commerce of Mexico* (London, 1903); GBDCR, AS No. 3285, *Report for 1903 on the Consular District of Mexico* (London, 1904); GBDCR, AS No. 3429.
[14] CRO, File No. 52281, Mexican Electric Works.

with electricity.[15]   German engineers and English capital combined with what the company directors termed "hundreds of men" to complete the job in 1900.

The electrical power facilities of the Mexican Electric Works were not completed when the company paid its first dividend in 1898. From that year until 1903 the venture returned annual average dividends of 6.7 per cent on a paid-up capital of £400,000.[16]   In 1903 the company's Nonoalco plant was purchased by the Mexican Light and Power Company, incorporated under Canadian laws with a capital of $12,000,000.[17]   Britons held approximately one-half of the shares. The remainder were controlled by capitalists in the United States and Canada. The board of directors included men from each of these countries, but its best known member was Dr. Fred Stark Pearson, later president of the company and a man who, as we have seen, was interested in railway and mining enterprise during the Díaz period.   Pearson served as consulting engineer for the company that built Boston's first electric railway system and in 1896 helped to construct trolley lines in New York City. A few years later his private power company supplied Toronto with electricity from Niagara Falls.   Dr. Pearson's first Latin American effort was in São Paulo, Brazil, where he supervised the installation of electric lights.[18]

Fred Pearson's plans for the Mexican Light and Power Company went beyond the acquisition of the Nonoalco plant. Under his personal direction the company in 1903 began the construction of a 144-foot-high dam at the junction of the Necaxa and Tenango rivers, 92 miles from Mexico City, in the state of Puebla. A permanent town large enough to house many of the company's 6,000 workers was built near the site of the dam.[19] The town boasted a health department, commissary, cabins and bunkhouses, and a stable of riding horses for the employees.[20] After three villages in the area were evacuated, the crews created an artificial lake with a capacity of ten billion

[15] *SAJ*, XLIII (Aug. 28, 1897), 235.
[16] *SEYB, 1903* (London, 1904).
[17] *Ibid.*
[18] F. S. Pearson's career is sketched in the *Dictionary of American Biography* (New York, 1920).
[19] *Modern Mexico*, XX (April, 1906), 14-15, 17, 19-20, 45; GBDCR, AS No. 3429.
[20] *Modern Mexico*, XX (April, 1906), 23-24.

gallons[21] and constructed six small storage dams to contain the reservoir. The system ran smoothly until 1909 when the clay and limestone on the top of the main Necaxa dam poured down the face of the structure after a torrential rain. The dam was repaired at a cost of £50,000.[22]

The Necaxa station served two major areas. Double transmission lines carried the power generated by 60,000-volt-capacity turbines to Mexico City and to the mining area around El Oro.[23] The El Oro undertaking was financed in part by an issue of an additional 2,400,000 pesos in company shares. A portion of this issue also was used to buy out the company's competitors, the Mexican Electric Works and the pioneer Mexican Gas and Electric Light Company.[24] Segments of the Mexican press expressed the fear that the electric rates would be increased but their apprehensions were dissipated when Pearson announced that the charges per kilowatt hour would be cut to $0.15—a reduction of 50 per cent—on January 1, 1906.

The Mexican Light and Power Company's policy of absorption ultimately was extended to the tramway system in Mexico City. In 1876 the Compañía de Ferrocarriles del Distrito Federal de México, supported by German capital, operated a few cars pulled by mules and twenty-five miles of steam-driven trams in the capital.[25] In April 1898 twenty-seven investors in London and Paris organized the Mexico Electric Tramways to acquire these lines in Mexico City.[26] The investors, many of them members of Parliament and retired naval officers with no past experience in Mexican ventures, capitalized the concern at £1,000,000 and over £608,000 was paid in by 1900. A controlling interest in the Compañía de Ferrocarriles then was purchased from Wehrner Beit and Company of Berlin.[27]

[21] GBDCR, AS No. 3429. Colonel George Goethels, famous for his work on the Panama Canal, visited the Necaxa dam in 1909 to study construction problems, see *Economist*, LXIX (Oct. 16, 1909), 761-62; *MM*, III (July-Dec., 1910), 375. The Necaxa project was operated by a subsidiary of the Mexican Light and Power Company, the Mexican Electric Company, organized on July 25, 1905; see Appendix, Table F.

[22] *Ibid.* (Oct. 2, 1909), 642-43; *Economist*, LXIX (Sept. 11, 1909), 509-10.

[23] *MJ*, LXXVIII (Oct. 2, 1905), 438.

[24] File No. 18223, especially summaries for 1908 and 1910, and the letter dissolving the company in 1911.

[25] Different estimates on the mileage may be found in CRO, File No. 56932, Mexico Electric Tramways; *SEYB, 1908* (London, 1909).

[26] File No. 56932.

[27] *Ibid.*

The Mexico Electric Tramways venture assigned Canadian engineer A. E. Worswick and over 2,000 engineers and laborers the job of electrifying and extending Mexico City's streetcar system. A power plant capable of generating extra energy during the rush-hour traffic was built. Six hundred coaches, including special funeral cars, were ordered from J. C. Brill of Philadelphia.[28] The company inaugurated its service on January 15, 1900, although the entire 190-mile route was not ready for another year. Ignacio Mariscal; Worswick; Díaz' son; Chandos Stanhope, the line's manager; and Joaquín Casasús, a Mexican economist and a member of the Mexico Electric Tramway's board of directors, were present at the ceremony in 1900. The trams quickly became one of the main attractions in Mexico City. Crowds of small boys became exhausted chasing the coaches while their elders pushed and shoved for seats on the top of the double decker cars that traversed a ten-mile stretch from the center of the capital to San Angel.[29] In 1901 over 26,000,000 fares were paid on the electrified line, 28,285,044 in 1902, and 48,000,000 in 1905.[30]

Many of the company's board of directors in London were satisfied with the management of the capital's tram system in the early 1900's, but their opinion was not shared by *El Ferrocarrilero*, a newspaper in Mexico City. From July to December, 1905, this newspaper unleashed a series of diatribes against the Mexico Electric Tramways or, as the editor chose to call it, "El Ferrocarril Homicida."[31] The line had a poor safety record mainly because the rails in certain sections of the city were unsafe. The waiting stations, when they existed at all, were a disgrace. Passengers usually waited in the sun or rain for trains that seemed never to arrive. It was, of course, difficult to tell whether a train was on schedule since the clocks set up by the company around the city plazas all kept different time. The passenger had little hope of arriving at his destination

---

[28] Spender, p. 205; GBDCR, AS No. 2951; *Modern Mexico*, VII (July, 1899), 6; *ibid.*, XIV (Jan., 1903), 46-47.

[29] *Modern Mexico*, VIII (March, 1900), 5-6; *ibid.*, IX (July, 1900), 7; also see México, Secretaría de Comunicaciones y Obras Públicas, *Memoria por el secretario de estado y del despacho de comunicaciones y obras públicas Leandro Fernández corresponde al período transcurrido del 1° de julio de 1902 a 30 de junio de 1903* (México, 1904), p. 153.

[30] GBDCR, AS No. 2951; *AAMMG*, IX (Oct. 31, 1906), 150.

[31] *El Ferrocarrilero*, July 14, 1905.

without long delay even after he finally stepped into a coach. Power failures and split cables were common. *El Ferro-carrilero* also complained that the company exploited its employees. The editor admitted that the caliber of the conductors and engineers who swore at the passengers or pocketed part of the money taken in for the lottery that the company operated each month, was not the highest, but this might be prevented if workers were paid at 1905 rather than 1895 rates.[32]

Most of the company's original investors had pulled out of the concern before *El Ferrocarrilero* launched its attack. Between 1898, when the Mexico Electric Tramways was organized, and October, 1905, they sold approximately 75 per cent of their shares to capitalists in Toronto, Canada.[33] A company was formed in Toronto to take over the streetcar line owned by the Mexico Electric Tramways. The president of the new venture, which called itself the Mexican Tramways Company, omitting the word "Electric" used by its predecessor, was Dr. Fred Stark Pearson.[34] One-fourth of the company's capital, or about £1,770,197 in shares, was held by English investors when Díaz began his last term of office. By the end of 1909 both the Mexican Tramways Company and the Mexican Light and Power Company were controlled by the same investors.[35] The joint venture thus held a near monopoly of the electrical utility field in the Federal District. In 1909 Mexican Tramways earned enough profits to provide investors with dividends of 6 per cent. In 1910 the return was 6.5 per cent.[36] During the same period the Mexican Light and Power Company earned profits that produced dividends of 4 per cent a year.[37]

British interests in electrical utilities extended outside the Federal District and Necaxa. By the end of 1910 four cities south of the capital were enjoying small-scale service as a result of English, Canadian, and American enterprise. Weetman Pearson, Fred Pearson, and directors of the Mexican Light and

[32] Articles and editorials may be found in *ibid.*, July 7, 1905; *ibid.*, Aug. 11, 1905, *ibid.*, Sept. 22, 1905; *ibid.*, Sept. 25, 1905; *ibid.*, Sept. 29, 1905; *ibid.*, Oct. 27, 1905; *ibid.*; Nov. 3, 1905; *ibid.*, Dec. 8, 1905.

[33] *AAMMG*, IX (Oct. 31, 1906), 150.

[34] A list of directors may be found in *SEYB, 1910* (London, 1911).

[35] See supplementary information added to File No. 56932 in 1911.

[36] F. C. Mathieson, IX; *SEYB, 1911* (London, 1912).

[37] *Ibid.*

Power Company and the Mexican Tramways were the outstanding figures in the story of electric power service in Veracruz,
Puebla, Orizaba, and Córdoba.

Weetman Pearson's construction company was completing
the harbor works in Veracruz in 1901 when he accepted a
contract to provide the city with a pure water and sewerage
system, electrify the six-mile-long animal-powered tram system,
and install 300 arc lights and 335 incandescent lights in the
downtown district.[38] Settling tanks and a filter station were
built at Tejar, nine miles from Veracruz on the Jampa River.
The water was pumped into a reservoir above Veracruz and
then carried into the city. The project was important from the
standpoint of health, but it also meant that residents could
draw 225 liters of water per head each day rather than the
previous high of 47 liters.[39] The Pearson crews also laid about
35 miles of clay piping beneath the city and connected it with a
main tube that took the city's sewage out to sea.

In 1906 the British contractor was ready to begin installing
the electrical works outlined in the contract. He hired A. E.
Worswick, who had just finished the electrification of the
Mexico City streetcar system, as his chief engineer. A sub-
sidiary concern, the Vera Cruz Electric Light, Power, and
Traction Company, was then formed to handle the job. Or-
dinary shares totaling £350,000 were issued fully-paid to
Weetman's son Harold and other members of the family, J. B.
Body, an executive in the Pearson enterprises, and Canadians
Dr. Samuel Machew, John MacDonald, and Robert Bird.
W. D. Pearson, Vincent Yorke, chairman of the Mexican Railway Company, and H. C. Waters, a director of the London
Bank of Mexico and South America, joined Bird on the company's board of directors.[40] Lights were installed along many
of the city's main promenades and in a number of stores and
private homes between 1906 and 1910. The streetcar system
was opened just before the Revolution.[41]

Weetman Pearson became interested in buying and then

[38] Spender, p. 107; CRO, File No. 89686, Vera Cruz Electric Light, Power, and
Traction Company.
[39] Spender, pp. 107-8.
[40] File No. 89686; Appendix, Table F.
[41] Spender, p. 109; GBDCR, AS No. 4021, *Report for the Year 1907 on the Trade and
Commerce of the Consular District of Vera Cruz* (London, 1908).

enlarging electric power stations in the Puebla-Orizaba area in 1906. He undoubtedly wanted to supply his burlap sack factory in Orizaba with electric power, but this was only part of his scheme. An American concern, the El Portzuelo Light and Power Company of Chicago, owned a small power house near Puebla. On January 27, 1906, Weetman Pearson, Samuel Machew, Robert Bird, and John MacDonald organized the Anglo-Mexican Electric Company for the purpose of acquiring this and other installations.[42] By July, 1907, the Anglo-Mexican venture had bought not only the Puebla station but also Mexican-owned power plants in Córdoba and Orizaba and an animal tram system in the latter city.[43] The money for the purchases was raised by the issuance of £450,000 in debentures in London. On July 1 the entire system was placed under the management of a company that Weetman Pearson registered in Toronto. Three directors of the Mexican Light and Power-Mexican Tramway ventures, including Fred Stark Pearson, were invited to sit on the board of directors of the Puebla Tramway Light and Power Company.[44] The company operated at a slight loss each year from 1908 to 1910 and no dividends were issued.

Weetman Pearson's mental blueprints for electrification projects in northern Mexico failed to materialize before 1911.[45] English engineers did, however, assist a Canadian company in Monterrey in the early 1900's.[46] Mackenzie, Mann, and Company of Toronto purchased and enlarged the electric light works and tramway system built in 1890 by German technicians. The Canadians constructed a waterworks plant capable of delivering ten billion gallons a day to the city and a sewerage system complete with septic tanks and cement conduits. Mackenzie then organized the Monterrey Electric Tramways and Power Company to consolidate his holdings. Vice-consul Stanford in Monterrey said in 1906 that the money spent by the company in the city for wages and materials was a "vital factor" in the economic life of the area.[47] He attributed the 100 per cent rise

[42] CRO, File No. 87403, Anglo-Mexican Electric Company.
[43] *Ibid.*
[44] *Ibid.*
[45] Spender, p. 206; *MM*, II (Jan., 1910), 28.
[46] GBDCR, AS No. 3888.
[47] *Ibid.*

in real estate prices in Monterrey to the influence of the water-works, sewerage, and streetcar system.

Factories

Few Britons were attracted by the idea of risking their capital in limited companies organized to build or buy factories in Mexico, and only three of the eleven ventures formed for this purpose were of any importance.[48] The Santa Gertrudis Jute Mill Company did not mark the first attempt by a British concern to erect or purchase an industrial plant during the Díaz administration, but it was their first successful venture.[49] Weetman Pearson and his son-in-law, Thomas Kinnell, believed that a factory making burlap sacks from the fiber of the jute plant would find a market for its product among the tobacco, sugar cane, and cotton growers of southeastern Mexico. Pearson based his optimism on information he received in interviews with various Mexican estate owners and members of Díaz' inner circle—José Limantour, Ignacio Mariscal, Romero Rubio, and others. The factory was built on the outskirts of Orizaba in 1893. The Santa Gertrudis concern was listed at the Company Record Office in London as a private enterprise.[50] Most of the business was handled by Kinnell from his large home in Orizaba where Pearson, President Díaz, the Governor of Vera-cruz, and various local personages frequently gathered as house guests.[51] The company's paid-up capital was set at £152,730 by 1910. The shares were divided unequally among twenty shareholders, including Pearson and his wife, Annie; Samuel Machew and John MacDonald; the Kinnell family; and Guillermo Escandón, a rancher and son of the man who transferred

[48] See Appendix, Table G.   English money was also invested in the Linen Company of Mexico and the San Rafael and Anexas Paper Company, both incorporated in Mexico.   John B. Body was vice-president of the first concern in 1910, and Thomas Braniff held the same office in the Anexas venture.

[49] CRO, File No. 38820, Santa Gertrudis Jute Mill Company.   For a list of the three unsuccessful ventures that preceded the formation of the Santa Gertrudis concern, see Appendix, Table G.

[50] File No. 38820.

[51] Comments on the social life in Orizaba and elsewhere where Weetman Pearson carried on business may be found in Spender, pp. 107, 205.

the concession for building the Mexican Railway to British financiers in 1868.[52] From 1894 through 1910 shareholders received annual average dividends of 9.4 per cent. In 1909 and 1910 the company's net receipts exceeded £10,000.[53]

Lionel and Herbert Pinto, tobacco sellers in London, planned in 1890 to build sawmills in Mexico and to manufacture cigar boxes for export traders.[54] This scheme collapsed, but in 1898 the Pintos decided to enter the Mexican cigar business on a grand scale. They purchased the property of Francisco Rendon, a tobacco grower in Veracruz, for £200,000.[55] Rendon's estates consisted of tobacco fields in Ozomacin, Oaxaca, warehouses in Veracruz, and four cigar-making plants in St. Andres, Teziutlán, and Jalapa, Veracruz. A sawmill in San Carlos, near the port city, manufactured the cigar boxes. The operation provided jobs for four hundred Mexican laborers.

The Pinto company was a private concern in which the two Londoners and a few cronies that included John MacDonald, a partner of Weetman Pearson, held the entire share capital. The first balance sheet issued by the L. and H. Pinto Company in 1899 was an impressive document. The company was able to pay 7 per cent dividends on its £87,123 in preference shares and 5 per cent on its £128,000 in ordinary shares.[56] Preference shares also were paid in 1899 and 1900 but these were the last returns before 1911. The enterprise never recovered from hurricane winds and rain that destroyed its tobacco crop on the Oaxaca plantation in 1898 and 1899. Company property in Oaxaca was sold in 1908 and by 1910 the two factories, sawmill, and the warehouses also were placed on the market.

The third limited venture operating a factory in the later Díaz era was the Salinas of Mexico Company, organized in 1906 by Adrian Chamier, a director of the Mexican Southern Railway; George Houghton of the Interoceanic Railroad; and Chandos Stanhope, at one time the manager of the Mexico

[52] Lord Ritchie of Dundee, Scotland, Sir Clarendon Hyde, a director in W. D. Pearson's Vera Cruz Terminal venture, and the Whitehall Securities Company of London also were important shareholders; see File No. 38820.

[53] *Ibid.*, balance sheet, 1910.

[54] CRO, File No. 32749, Anglo-Mexican Saw Mills.

[55] CRO, File No. 54109, L. and H. Pinto.

[56] *Ibid.* It is possible that much of the company's profits came from the business activities of the Pinto brothers in London.

Electric Tramways.[57] The Salinas company purchased 100,000 acres of "salt producing land" a few miles north of San Luis Potosí from a French owner for £110,000 in cash and shares in the Salinas concern. Luis Errazu of Paris had supplied buyers in Mexico City with 33,000 tons of salt a year for twelve years prior to the sale in 1906.[58] Errazu employed thirty-five Mexicans who hoisted the salt from six lagoons, ran it through an evaporating plant, and packed the salt in bags for shipment. Between 1902 and 1906 Errazu's enterprise earned over 1,000,000 pesos.[59] By 1906 the supply of salt was being drained so rapidly that buyers were threatening to go to companies located on the coast for their needs. Errazu believed that about £30,000 was needed to open up new salt deposits in ten lagoons and to modernize some of the evaporating processes. Chamier and his friends joined Errazu in promoting the sale of £200,000 in debentures in England during 1906. The company's prospectus indicated that dividends of 15 per cent a year could be expected.[60] The money from the sale in England was used to import eight new dredgers, open up eight lagoons, and build a small battery-driven generating plant. The Salinas venture shipped 41,000 tons of salt to Mexico City in 1908, 53,000 tons in 1909, and 55,000 tons in 1910.[61] This was not enough to earn profits for the company or dividends for the investors before 1911.

Petroleum

The first British consular report on petroleum deposits in Mexico was written in 1887,[62] but eleven years elapsed before the organization of the first British company to drill for oil in the Republic. In 1898 George Jeffrey, one of the early prospectors in the Peruvian oil fields, obtained a lease on oil lands a

---

[57] *Directory of Directors, 1907, 1910*; CRO, File No. 88222, Salinas of Mexico.
[58] File No. 88222; SEL, Prospectus for the Salinas of Mexico.
[59] *Ibid.*
[60] *Ibid.*
[61] File No. 88222, balance sheets.
[62] GBDCR, MS No. 66, *Report on the Mines and Minerals of the State of Vera Cruz, 1887* (London, 1887).

mile from Pánuco, a town southwest of Tampico.[63] The property was close to a navigable river and there was an ample supply of firewood. Fresh water necessary in the drilling operations was found only one mile from the main derricks.[64] Jeffrey arrived from Peru in September to examine the lease. Rotary drills were ordered from Chicago and drillers and unskilled laborers were hired at a cost of £150 a month. Jeffrey's total monthly expenses, exclusive of the purchase price for the machinery, were £475.[65] Over £4,000 was spent in development operations before the Oil Fields of Mexico venture began to drill in 1900. Jeffrey was able to sell enough oil to buyers on Mexico's east coast before 1911 to remain in business, but the company could not earn enough to warrant the payment of any dividends.

Jeffrey had just begun to drill in Pánuco when Weetman Pearson arrived in Laredo, Texas, in April, 1901, to find an oil boom in the making. During the next five years Pearson received oil concessions covering 600,000 acres in Veracruz, Tabasco, Campeche, and Chiapas from the Mexican government.[66] He planned to put £1,500,000 in the oil business and then withdraw if profits were not in sight withn a few years. W. D. Pearson's first wells were sunk in 1901 at San Cristóbal, Veracruz, twenty miles north of the Tehuantepec Railway. By 1905 he was ready to invest £500,000 in a refinery and storage center at nearby Minatitlán, and a year later six-inch pipelines linked the center and the Cristóbal drilling area. Pearson estimated that after the Mexican market was supplied he would still have 250,000 barrels to send to Europe and the United States each year.[67]

The ubiquitous Briton was confident enough of success in 1906 to make an agreement promising to supply oil to the C. T. Bowring Company, a large London concern. The signing of the contract was badly timed. Oil pools in San Cristóbal began to

[63] CRO, File No. 55665, Oil Fields of Mexico; see Appendix, Table E, for a list of the petroleum companies.

[64] A general article on the early industry in Sydney A. R. Skertchly, "Oil in Mexico," *MM*, III (July–Dec., 1910), 283.

[65] File No. 55665.

[66] Spender, pp. 149, 152. A survey of the Republic's petroleum deposits and a study of the need for the product in the early 1900's is found in *Mexican Herald*, April 2, 1902; *MJ*, LXXIV (July 26, 1902), 1037.

[67] Spender, pp. 152, 154.

give out in 1907, and Pearson was forced to buy oil from George Jeffrey's Oil Fields of Mexico Company in order to keep the Bowring contract. Jeffrey had expanded his Pánuco efforts to include drilling about fifty-four miles inland from Tuxpan on the Gulf coast. Pearson promised to connect this area, Furbero, to Tuxpan by a narrow-gauge railway and a pipeline if Jeffrey would cut the price of the oil. Pearson was playing for time until his own wells came in, an expensive game that had cost him over £1,000,000 by the end of 1907.[68]

Pearson's problems multiplied rapidly. Topographical difficulties hindered the laying of the Tuxpan-Furbero pipeline, and when it was finished Pearson and Jeffrey discovered that the Furbero fields could not supply Pearson with even the minimum amounts of oil that he needed. Pearson then made temporary agreements with Texas companies to supply him with enough oil to keep the Minatitlán refinery open and to honor the commitments he had made in the United States and England. Meanwhile, on July 4, 1908, Pearson's drillers struck oil at the Dos Bocas well on the banks of Lake Temiahua, north of Tuxpan. The pressure from the strike obliterated the derrick and the four-inch drill pipe. The oil somehow was ignited and a column of flame over a thousand feet high shot out from the well. The Dos Bocas fire raged for fifty-eight days and when the conflagration was brought under control the well had turned to hot salt water.[69]

Pearson viewed the loss as only a temporary setback. Oil was soon found in the Temiahua district at 115 feet, and in May 1910 Pearson consolidated his petroleum interests in the Mexican Eagle Oil Company.[70] The company was registered in Mexico and Pearson did not reveal the list of shareholders who received 21,000,000 pesos in fully-paid Mexican Eagle shares. A clue was offered by the presence on the board of directors of Porfirio Díaz, J. B. Body, Guillermo Escandón, and Pearson himself.[71] Preferred shares having a par value of 8,500,000 pesos were sold in Britain through the London City and Midland Bank.

[68] *Ibid.*, pp. 153-154, 157.
[69] Chester E. Bowles, *The Petroleum Industry* (Kansas City, 1921) p. 40, has a vivid description of the fire.
[70] *SEYB, 1911* (London, 1912).
[71] *Ibid.*

Seven months after the company was formed a Pearson well pumping 100,000 barrels a day was brought in east of Tamaihua.[72] This so-called Potrero gusher established the Mexican Eagle Company as a major oil producer in Mexico. It also ushered in the last phases of an oil war between Pearson and American oil capitalists that began in 1904. In that year the Standard Oil Company and the Mexican Fuel Oil Company, dominated by Henry Clay Pierce and Edward Doheny, began drilling wells in Ebano, west of Tampico.[73] When Pearson announced his intention of entering the Mexican retail oil trade in direct competition with Pierce in particular, the American naturally viewed Pearson as an interloper. Their struggle had become open and bitter by 1908:

> Everybody in the least degree interested in Mexican oil knows of the Pearson and Waters-Pierce war, and how the Waters-Pierce organs dwell on the lack of oil in the Pearson camp, the . . . white elephantism of the Pearson Minatitlan refinery, and the general foolishness of the Pearson ideas, the Pearson engineers, and the Pearson ambitions; simultaneously, the solid nature of the Waters-Pierce undertaking in all its bearings is indicated.[74]

By 1910 Pearson had forty railway tank cars hauling his oil to various points in Mexico. Probably 25 per cent of the Republic's retail lubricating trade was in his hands, but as prices tumbled in the heat of the oil war he was forced to take severe losses.[75] Pierce, of course, hoped that the competition would force Pearson out of business. It was the opening of the Potrero well that put Weetman Pearson back into the fray with renewed vigor at the end of 1910.

* * * *

The first active utility concerns, factories, and oil companies in which English capital was invested were, with one exception, organized after 1890. Most of the utility companies and two of the three manufacturing ventures managed to earn profits and return dividends at some time during their years of operation before 1911. The petroleum business was then still in its

---

[72] Spender, p. 160.
[73] *MJ*, LXXVI (Nov. 19, 1904), 505.
[74] *Ibid.*, LXXIV (June 4, 1910), 711.
[75] Spender, p. 166.

embryo stage. A close relationship often existed between the utility, factory, and petroleum companies since many Britons controlled large blocks of shares or held directorships in each of the three types of enterprise. These companies seldom attempted to draw the British public into their activities. Most of the concerns were closed corporations of financiers, their families, friends, and business associates. But when shares and debentures did appear on the market, these names seemed to have a magical effect on sales.

The effect of the fall of silver on railway and other facets of British enterprise has been examined in this volume. It was not a significant factor in the activities of the companies just described, although until the legislation of 1905 was passed the utility companies may have suffered from the poor exchange rate. Weetman Pearson's burlap sack factory and the Pinto brothers' tobacco enterprise may have been aided before 1905 by the falling peso. Both purchased all their supplies in Mexico and paid their Mexican workers with cheap silver. The petroleum boom began after the price of silver was stabilized. The industry later proved so durable that even a relapse into a chaotic currency situation could not ruin its prosperity.

There were, however, other problems. Weetman Pearson's favored position gained him the oil concessions he wanted, but it did not protect him from the normal hazards involved in opening up oil wells or the competition of American companies. The problem of competition, at least after the troubles of the Mexican Gas and Electric Light Company were solved, did not often affect the utility concerns, either because they were the only active ventures in an area, or because they attained a monopoly status before a competitive situation developed. These same utility companies did encounter technological puzzles in building dams, laying cable, and maintaining steady service. On only one occasion did any of the companies call on the British legation for assistance.

In 1880 there were no electric light companies or electrified tramways in Mexico. Twenty years later Englishmen were involved in the operation of at least two-thirds of the 265 miles of tramways in Mexico City and in most of the tramway systems outside the capital. They were important shareholders in the Mexican Light and Power Company, which served Mexico City and one of the most important mining centers in the country. Outside this district the entire lighting facilities of Veracruz were erected by Weetman Pearson as part of a larger public works projects, and Pearson also provided sections of four other cities with electric lights. Englishmen and Canadians purchased a German lighting plant in Monterrey and were planning to enlarge Pachuca's lighting system at the end of 1910.[76] The Díaz period was one of brisk activity in the public-utility field, but it must be remembered that thirty years after Díaz left Mexico, less than 2 per cent of the communities in the Republic had electrical service.[77] Contemporary statistics delineating industrial expansion in Mexico are likely to be misleading, but it is obvious that the over-all English role in Mexico's factory development before 1911 was small.[78] American oil men were responsible for most of Mexico's production of 12,000,000 barrels of oil in 1911; W. D. Pearson's fortune in petroleum lay in the future when Díaz left the country to go into exile.[79]

[76] GBDCR, AS No. 4215, *Report for the Year 1908 on the Trade and Commerce of the Consular District of Tampico* (London, 1909); *MM*, III (July-Dec., 1910), 283; Rippy, *Latin America and the Industrial Age*, pp. 208-9.

[77] Frank Tannenbaum, *Mexico: The Struggle for Bread and Peace* (New York, 1950), p. 216.

[78] In 1876 there were about 70 cotton factories in Mexico, 127 in 1899, and 139 in 1909. In the early 1900's Mexico had 482 tobacco factories; 2,196 small establishments producing candy and chocolate; 2 large jute sack factories; 9 iron and steel works; and at least one government-controlled meat packing house. See GBDCR, AS No. 2546, *Report for the Year 1899 on the Trade and Commerce of Mexico* (London, 1900); Chester L. Jones, *Mexico and Its Reconstruction* (New York, 1922), p. 179. The number of employees or the size of the factories is not given in these sources.

[79] Bowles, p. 49.

7. The Loss of British Commercial Pre-eminence

British merchants controlled about one-half of Mexico's small import trade shortly after the Latin American country won its independence.[1] The value of British imports remained almost stationary for the next forty-five years, but a slight decline occurred after the break in diplomatic relations.[2] The total value of all Mexican imports in 1876 was 29,000,000 pesos, almost 35 per cent of this figure coming from Britain, 25.8 per cent from the United States, and 13.1 per cent from Germany.[3] The most important item in the list of goods sent from Britain was cotton manufactures, followed in order of value by linen goods, iron, chinaware, machinery, silk manufactures, and woolen goods. Chambers of Commerce from fifty-two cities in Britain directed the attention of the Foreign Office to these statistics in December, 1876, urging that the resumption of diplomatic accord was essential if Britain was to maintain her favored position.[4] Their letter heralded the opening of a contest

[1] Jones, pp. 194-98. Britain was far more interested in Mexico as a market for British goods than as a source of raw materials. My analysis is concerned with the story of British exports to Mexico. An examination of Mexican exports to Britain strengthens my thesis regarding the relative decline of Britain in the Mexican trade pattern. British consular reports reveal that Britain received 39 per cent of Mexico's exports by value in 1876, the United States 37.5 per cent, and Germany 4.6 per cent. In 1910 almost 75 per cent of Mexico's exports went to the United States, 14 per cent to Britain, and 7 per cent to Germany.

[2] Mexican trade statistics during this period had their limitations. It is impossible in most tables to determine what percentage of the imports from the United States include goods from Europe and Canada that were reshipped from ports in the United States. Also the terms "England" and "United Kingdom" are often used indiscriminately.

[3] Antonio Cubas, *Mexico in 1876* (Mexico, 1877), pp. 30-32.

[4] Memorial to Derby, Dec. 12, 1876, FO 50, Vol. 437.

for commercial hegemony that was an important adjunct of the scramble for pre-eminence in the field of capital investment. The contest also represented an important chapter in the almost world-wide struggle for markets between the United States, Germany, and Great Britain before World War I.

In April, 1883, while negotiations for a restoration of diplomatic relations continued, the Foreign Office was informed that the annual value of exports from the United States to Mexico then exceeded the amount supplied by Britain, and, according to one Englishman: "The commercial influence of the U. S. A. is being so rapidly extended that it bids fair before long, unless some stimulus and encouragement is given to British commerce there, to drive it out altogether."[5] When the United States signed a trade agreement with Mexico in 1883 Lord Edmund Fitzmaurice reminded his colleagues at the Foreign Office that Britain previously had shown only mild interest in restoring relations with Mexico: "Now, however, it is . . . a matter of considerable commercial importance to Great Britain . . . owing to an evident intention on the part of the United States to exclude Great Britain from Mexican markets."[6] Sir Spenser St. John upheld this view a year later when he was in the Republic to discuss the renewal of diplomatic relations. St. John felt that the Mexican government's willingness to insert a most-favored nation clause in the document restoring relations stemmed from Mexican fears that the United States might otherwise monopolize the trade of the Republic. He also believed that the United States hoped to create so many economic links between the two countries that Mexico eventually would be absorbed by her northern neighbor.[7]

British reports on Mexican trade were published soon after the restoration of Anglo-Mexican relations in August, 1884. These contained conflicting statistical data, but it was clear that Britain's proportionate share of Mexico's import trade had declined since 1876, whereas the share provided by the United States had increased.[8] Consul Lionel Carden warned in 1885:

[5] Renshaw to Foreign Secretary, April 4, 1883, FO 50, Vol. 443.

[6] Fitzmaurice memorandum respecting the renewal of diplomatic relations with Mexico, No. 1 Domestic Various, March 23, 1883, FO 50, Vol. 443.

[7] St. John to Greville, No. 1 Confidential, Dec. 17, 1884, FO 50, Vol. 446.

[8] Kohzevar, pp. 157, 167; Great Britain, Foreign Office, Commercial No. 18, *Report on British Trade with Mexico to 1885* (London, 1886).

... the American ratio is pushing higher and before long their enterprise will become absolute. It remains to be proved whether the British commercial world is content to submit quietly and without an effort to being driven from a market which though insignificant ... today, is unquestionably destined ere long ... to be one of the most important, if not THE most important of the Spanish-American Republics.[9]

Mexican trade rapidly increased during the next twenty-five years. Her imports jumped in value to 133,020,170 pesos in 1900, four and one-half times greater than the figure for 1876.[10] However, Britain had become relatively less important in the market, supplying 17 per cent of Mexico's imports in 1900. The United States provided 51.1 per cent of the imports, while Germany's share was approximately 11.5 per cent of the total.[11] During the last year of the Díaz regime the value of the Republic's imports reached 205,874,000 pesos. The United States by then provided 55.5 per cent of the imports by value, Germany 12.8 per cent, and Great Britain 11.4 per cent.[12] The absolute value of British exports to Mexico had more than doubled between 1876 and the end of 1910, but this rate of expansion was far slower than that of her two competitors.

German competition most startled the British staff in Mexico. The Foreign Office was warned of an impending German drive for Mexican trade in 1886, but it was the late 1890's before much attention was given to German incursions.[13] During the ten-year period after 1896 Germany pushed ahead of Britain in providing Mexico with steel rails and bars, lime, cement, coal, and iron and steel wire.[14] The hardware trade, safely in British hands when Díaz began his first term, was almost entirely controlled by Germany in 1906.[15]

---

[9] Great Britain, Foreign Office, Commercial No. 18, *Report on British Trade with Mexico to 1885.*

[10] Howard Cline, *The United States and Mexico*, p. 354.

[11] *The Mexican Year-Book, 1909-10* (London, 1910), pp. 129-32.

[12] GBDCR, AS No. 4742, *Report for the Year 1910 on the Trade of Mexico* (London, 1911), GBDCR, AS No. 4976, *Report for the Year 1911 on the Trade of Mexico* (London, 1912).

[13] Consul Strachen to Rosebery, No. 3, June 8, 1886, FO 204, Vol. 193; GBDCR, AS No. 2527, *Report for the Year 1899 on the Trade and Commerce of Mexico* (London, 1900).

[14] GBDCR, MS No. 662, *Memorandum on Imports from the United Kingdom and Germany* (London, 1907).

[15] Britain failed to exploit Mexican demands for electrical supplies. By 1906 almost 50 per cent of Mexico's light bulbs were made in Germany. See GBDCR, AS No. 3888.

German competition, American domination of the market, the turgescence of Mexican industry, and a demand for new products after 1876 all were reflected in the type of British goods and manufactures sent to the Republic in the latter half of the Díaz era. Textiles remained the most important single item that Mexico received from Britain, but with the expansion of Mexico's home cotton industry the demand for British textiles steadily contracted.[16] Textiles were followed in order of value by machinery, although Britain supplied only one-tenth of Mexico's imports under this heading.[17] Galvanized iron sheets, hemp and jute sacks, and caustic soda were included on the list of major British items arriving in the country. Chemical imports were minor items, but Britain was the main source of supply.[18]

Numerous attempts were made to analyze Britain's inability to maintain her proportionate share of Mexico's import trade. Many observers believed that this situation was inevitable since Mexico, from the point of view of British commerce, was not "on the main line."[19] Sir Spenser St. John complained that British firms sent only their worst ships to Mexico. These were unsafe, slow, and lacked proper sanitary facilities.[20] Consuls attempted to publicize the advantages of operating freight lines from Liverpool and other ports to Mexico, but only two concerns provided regular service to the Republic in the early 1900's.[21] The existence of a network of railroads in Mexico, some of which connected Mexico City to points on the northern border after the building spree of the 1880's, furnished additional ammunition for those who stressed the main-line theory. Lionel Carden emphasized the effect of the railways on United States-Mexican commercial relations in 1885, and in the same year economist Edward Kohzevar showed that customs receipts at the northern ports were rising swiftly under

[16] *Ibid.*, AS No. 3503, *Report for the Year 1904 on the Trade and Commerce of the Consular District of Vera Cruz* (London, 1905); *ibid.*, MS No. 662; Jones, p. 200.
[17] GBDCR, AS No. 3262; *ibid.*, MS No. 662.
[18] *Ibid.*, AS No. 3502; *ibid.*, AS No. 4472; *ibid.*, AS No. 4976.
[19] *Ibid.*, AS No. 2951.
[20] St. John to Salisbury, No. 1 Commercial, Feb. 17, 1887, FO 50, Vol. 468.
[21] Chapman to Salisbury, No. 4 Commercial Confidential, April 5, 1898, FO 50, Vol. 515; Dering to Salisbury, No. 6 Commercial, March 27, 1899, FO 50, Vol. 518.

the influence of the new railroads.[22] Britons agreed that the location of Mexican railways gave a tremendous commercial advantage to the United States.

Many Britons pointed to the long diplomatic drought, fluctuations in the price of silver, and Mexico's tariff regulations as key factors in the changing pattern of Anglo-Mexican trade relations. After the withdrawal of the British diplomats in 1867 English commercial houses, "once so numerous and respected," soon were almost all closed.[23] St. John informed Lord Salisbury in March, 1887, that there were "no English importing houses of any standing either in Vera Cruz or the Capital."[24] Consul Biorklund said twelve years later that there were still no British commercial houses in Mexico City.[25]

The suggestion that the declining price of silver reacted adversely on Anglo-Mexican trade appeared frequently in British reports. When the world price of silver was comparatively high British merchants could exchange their silver earned in Mexico and get a fair return for their exports to Mexico.[26] When the value of silver fell in the 1890's to 22$d.$ the merchants felt they had to raise the price of their goods in silver to what ultimately became nearly a prohibitive level in order to make a profit. British consuls reasoned that under these circumstances the merchants lost "commercial confidence" in Mexico and often preferred not to risk the vagaries of the market.[27] The Mexican government agreed in 1893 that the falling price of silver was a potent force in determining the flow of European imports.[28]

The Mexican tariff was mentioned in diplomatic correspondence, letters from businessmen, and consular reports as a

[22] Kohzevar, pp. 152-53; Great Britain, Foreign Office, Commercial No. 18, *Report on British Trade with Mexico to 1885.*

[23] GBDCR, AS No. 2539, *Reports for the Years 1898, 1899, and part of 1900 on the Trade and Commerce of Vera Cruz* (London, 1900).

[24] St. John to Salisbury, No. 3 Commercial, March 27, 1877, FO 204, Vol. 194.

[25] GBDCR, MS No. 517.

[26] Tannenbaum, p. 203; Kohzevar, p. 148.

[27] Trench to Lord Kimberly (Lord President and Secretary for India), No. 12 Very Confidential, Jan. 19, 1894, FO 50, Vol. 492. Also see St. John to Rosebery, No. 35, Aug. 14, 1886, FO 50, Vol. 454; Consul Jerome to A. Bosomworth & Co., Hull, Dec. 14, 1902, FO 203, Vol. 140; GBDCR, MS No. 302, *Report on the Effect of the Depreciation of Silver on Mexico* (London, 1893).

[28] México, Secretaría de Hacienda y Crédito Público, *Memoria correspondiente al sexagésimo octavo año económico de 1° de julio de 1893 presentada por el secretario de hacienda al congreso de la unión* (México, 1893), p. 439.

possible reason for the loss of Britain's trading pre-eminence. The chief complaints were directed to the excessive duties and the intricate customs rules. During the early Díaz period the tariff was patterned after the Spanish regulations of the colonial era. Modifications in the incidence of the tariff were made in 1880, 1887, and 1890, but the Mexican government, pressured by industrial groups, remained wedded to the principle of high protection.[29] The British Board of Trade estimated in 1883 that duties amounting to as much as 150 per cent were levied on British manufactures.[30] Sir Spenser St. John reasoned that duties on specific goods were the same for all countries having most-favored-nation agreements, but Consul Baker at Veracruz insisted that although the favored-nation clause was accorded to Britain in principle, the Mexican tariff actually pressed more heavily on British goods than on those of any other nation.[31] The reason was that many of the British exports to Mexico such as cottons, linens, woolens, earthenware, and iron and steel were precisely those goods on which the highest duties were charged. In the mid-1880's the duty on all British goods averaged over 130 per cent, but duty on goods from the United States averaged 101 per cent, from France 98 per cent, and from Germany 78 per cent.[32]

Some British merchants believed that the bewildering array of Mexican laws regarding customs declarations, consular invoices, and ships's manifests were more important barriers to Anglo-Mexican trade than the high charges set forth in the tariff. Many British companies stopped trading with Mexico because they were unable to avoid being fined for violating the regulations.[33] Lionel Carden reported that the headings in the tariff regulations were so numerous that shippers had difficulty in deciding under which category certain goods should be placed. This made it impossible to estimate how much duty had to be paid until the shipments arrived in Mexico. There

[29] Tannenbaum, pp. 198-99; St. John to Salisbury, March 1, 1887, FO 204, Vol. 194.

[30] Griffin to Granville, June 13, 1883, FO 50, Vol. 443.

[31] St. John to Salisbury, No. 3 Commercial, March 22, 1887, FO 204, Vol. 194; St. John to Salisbury, Oct. 18, 1890, FO 50, Vol. 474; unsigned note on reverse of Baker to Salisbury, Oct. 18, 1890, FO 50, Vol. 474.

[32] Baker to Salisbury, No. 2 Commercial, Feb. 18, 1887, FO 50, Vol. 461; Baker to Salisbury, No. 1 Commercial, May 7, 1889, FO 50, Vol. 470.

[33] Carden to Rosebery, No. 2 Consular, April 29, 1883, FO 50, Vol. 490; GBDCR, AS No. 2527.

the rates often were subject to what Carden termed "the appraiser's caprice." Another problem was the difficulty of translating obsolete Spanish terms used in the tariff regulations.[34] When Consul Baker made a study of the customs house rules shortly after the renewal of diplomatic relations, he was annoyed to learn that fines up to 25 pesos might be imposed for miscellaneous mistakes in manifests, declarations, and invoices. He concluded that shippers did not understand the terminology used, were overwhelmed by the number of regulations, and were fined too much for minor offenses.[35]

When Díaz abolished a number of fines for mistakes in invoices in 1893, Baker and Carden hoped that the changes would lead to a rapid increase of British trade to the Republic. A Nottingham company indicated in 1896, however, that the main problems had not yet been solved. B. F. Stiebel, a partner in Stiebel, Kaufman and Company, wrote to the Foreign Office on June 18:

> I have just gone through the Mexican tariff and studied the regulations as to consular invoices, declarations, and classifications of goods, as we are beginning to do a little business in Mexico. I had heard about this tariff before, but I find that the regulations . . . are so complicated . . . that even a good Spanish scholar and a man experienced with declarations to Spanish countries like myself *finds the greatest difficulty* understanding many of them, and as the slightest error in any consular invoice which must be *written out* in triplicate or quadruplicate is visited with heavy customs fines, it seems to me that the object is to make trade with Mexico as difficult *as possible* for the *honest* trader.[36]

The Board of Trade added similar comments in December, 1896:

> The complications involved by 921 headings of the tariff are found to be serious obstacles to exporters in making out their Declarations in accord with the tariff headings. It must frequently be impossible to determine under which heading particular goods should be classed. . . . Attention must be drawn to the fact that Spain, which has more

[34] Jacob Behren (Chamber of Commerce) to Granville, June 12, 1883, FO 50, Vol. 443; Adams & Company to Foreign Secretary, Nov. 17, 1885, FO 50, Vol. 449.

[35] See "Schedule A Fines levied under Mexican General Order," in Baker to Iddesleigh, Sept. 29, 1886, FO 50, Vol. 457. Consul Biorklund disagreed with Baker, stating in 1899 that the tariff rules were not, and never had been, too difficult to comprehend. Biorklund believed that shippers were careless, did not study the tariff, and sometimes allowed junior clerks to make out important forms. See GBDCR, AS No. 2546.

[36] Stiebel to Sir Henry Burgne (Foreign Office), June 18, 1896, FO 50, Vol. 506.

than double the trade of Mexico, has a tariff embracing only about 370 headings. At present it is only possible for firms having skilled and technical knowledge of Spanish and of the distinctions between various classes of goods to make out a Declaration which they can be certain will be satisfactory to the Mexican authorities.[37]

The activities of the consular staff and the methods used by Britons who carried on commercial intercourse in the Republic were also examined by those seeking to explain Britain's inability to increase the value of her exports to Mexico as rapidly as her competitors. In 1886 the Foreign Office called the attention of its legations to complaints that diplomatic missions were often indifferent or unfriendly to British traders in certain "remote" countries.[38] Did the charge apply to the consuls in Mexico? Lionel Carden and others worked assiduously to improve the quality of the consular corps after 1884, but they were sometimes forced to appoint second or even third choices at some of the important posts.[39] Most British firms apparently did not feel that their interests were neglected.[40] Consuls answered inquiries concerning commercial conditions quickly and concisely, explaining the opportunities available to traders and directing the writers to persons and companies that could handle items such as chemical products, earthenware, machinery, electric lights, paint, soft drinks, dry goods, textiles, wire rope, beer, and coal.[41]

More attention must be given to contemporary statements indicating that British methods of carrying on trade in Mexico left much to be desired. When goods from England arrived in Mexico or Mexicans showed an interest in a given product, agents appointed by British companies were to push sales to retail and wholesale establishments in the Republic. Most

[37] Board of Trade to Salisbury, Dec. 3, 1896, FO 50, Vol. 506.

[38] Great Britain, Foreign Office, Commercial No. 16, *Correspondence Respecting the Question of Diplomatic and Consular Assistance to British Trade Abroad* (London, 1886).

[39] Baker to Salisbury, No. 17 Consular, June 29, 1890, FO 50, Vol. 475; Carden to Rosebery, Nov. 6, 1893, FO 50, Vol. 490; enclosures in Dering to Salisbury, Aug. 4, 1895, FO 50, Vol. 497.

[40] Only a few uncomplimentary letters regarding British consuls were received at the Foreign Office; see St. John to Rosebery, No. 12 Commercial Confidential, July 23, 1886, FO 50, Vol. 455; Denys to Salisbury, Dec. 8, 1887, FO 204, Vol. 194.

[41] See letters in 1886-87, FO 203, Vol. 107; 1888, FO 203, Vol. 113; 1890, FO 203, Vol. 115; 1895, FO 203, Vol. 123; 1899, FO 203, Vol. 138. Also see London Chamber of Commerce to Chapman, March 2, 1900, FO 50, Vol. 522; Chapman to Salisbury, March 19, 1900, FO 50, Vol. 522.

British firms did not employ their own countrymen for this job, but either by choice or necessity gave the jobs mainly to Germans, Americans, or Mexicans who also represented other European companies.[42] These commercial travelers took only a "very lukewarm interest in the success of the [British] companies or in the extension of British trade."[43] Sir Spenser St. John wrote in 1893: "The real cause of the smallness of the trade between Mexico and England is the supineness of the English merchants who are content to allow foreigners to carry on their trade."[44] Many of these men could not speak Spanish while others seemed unable to understand the habits of Mexican buyers. A British consul at Mazatlán said in 1900: "My experience is that the traveler who approaches the Mexican buyer in a leisurely way, leading gradually up to the business at hand, and studying the convenience of each customer, gets orders where the man who attempts to hurry matters loses customers, perhaps permanently."[45] Apparently the agents for British concerns usually were found in the latter category.

Other criticisms were levied against British companies that exported their wares to Mexico. While Americans flooded Mexico with advertisements, British goods were seldom pictured even in important newspapers.[46] Buyers could examine samples of American manufactures, but British firms seemed to feel that transportation costs were too high to make such procedure worthwhile unless a market practically was assured. Catalogues issued by British companies were written in English rather than Spanish. The description of many goods gave no indication of price or weight and often were too technical to be of much value in making the sale.[47] A British consul wrote this interesting but grammatically inept letter from Ensenada:

> It has been more than once brought to my notice the seeming difficulty in obtaining from British manufactures, information in regard to their prices, conditions of purchase, shipping facilities, etc., whereas American houses on application send a full list of the goods

[42] GBDCR, AS No. 2546; *ibid.*, AS No. 2527; St. John to Salisbury, No. 1 Consular, Jan. 20, 1890, FO 50, Vol. 474.
[43] St. John to Rosebery, No. 15, April 22, 1886, FO 50, Vol. 453.
[44] St. John to Rosebery, No. 1 Commercial, April 3, 1893, FO 50, Vol. 484.
[45] GBDCR, AS No. 2527.
[46] *Ibid.*, AS No. 3262; *ibid.*, AS No. 3285.
[47] *Ibid.*, AS No. 4215; *ibid.*, AS No. 3285.

which they have to sell, accompanied in a great number of cases with patterns, samples, etc., and give the intending purchaser all the necessary information, so as to enable him to see exactly what the good will cost delivered in his town, prices generally being quoted for large and small quantities.[48]

British diplomats and writers for London and Mexico City financial magazines stated that Britons made little or no attempt to adapt their goods to the needs of Mexican buyers. The Mexican *Journal of Commerce* advised British traders to supply customers with what they wanted rather than what the merchants considered good for them.[49] Mexican buyers, for example, preferred cheap machinery despite having to replace it in a few years. Miners wanted lightweight machines because freight rates to distant camps were high. They also demanded machinery with the greatest possible number of removable parts so that repairs would be inexpensive.[50] British machinery was expensive, heavy, and it was difficult to obtain parts in Mexican warehouses. By 1897 the distributing houses for machinery in Mexico were in American and German hands.[51] German manufacturers were especially zealous in studying the needs of the market, catering to the wishes of individual customers, and quickly supplying new products when a demand developed. Vice-Consul Nunn placed the issue squarely before British firms in the late Díaz period:

> The manufacturers of the United Kingdom who once had the major portion of Mexico's foreign trade, lost much of the business through inability to appreciate the Mexican's wants, and to understand the wisdom of falling in with his views. It may possibly be said that it would not suit manufacturers to vary their standards of production to meet the requirements of every small trader, but to do so is about the only way to hold onto the trade, as other manufacturers comply without question.[52]

The *Mining Magazine* added its comment in January, 1910:

> The English manufacturer is too conservative. He will not adapt the design of his goods to the requirements of the market. More

[48] *Ibid.*, AS No. 2527.
[49] Quoted in George Greville (British Minister to Mexico) to Lansdowne, No. 3 Commercial, March 5, 1902, FO 50, Vol. 528.
[50] *MM*, II (Jan., 1910), 29. Also see Mrs. Alec Tweedie, *Mexico as I Saw It* (London, 1901), pp. 456-57. Mrs. Tweedie was extremely biased but her views on some subjects coincided with those of contemporary British diplomats in Mexico.
[51] Carden to Jessop and Appleby Bros., Aug. 9, 1897, FO 203, Vol. 129.
[52] GBDCR, AS No. 3888.

money must be spent on the design and less on the manufacture; strength must be gained by scientific design, not by brute weight of cast iron; it must be remembered that at some mining camps freight costs more than the original cost of the machinery and hence it behooves the designer to avoid every unnecessary ounce of weight. Roughness of appearance and lack of finish count for nothing as against facilities for freight, erection, and freedom from breakdowns. It is also essential to build to standards in accord with the local system of measurement, and to study the customs laws and regulations so that shipments are properly classified and invoiced.[53]

* * * *

There was no agreement as to the reasons for Britain's loss of commercial pre-eminence in Mexico. Fluctuations in the price of silver, consular indifference, and Mexico's tariff regulations were blamed, but it is difficult to measure the impact of these factors. Whether or not the tariff actually pressed harder on British trade than on, say, American or German trade, is perhaps unimportant. If British merchants believed they did and accordingly ceased to push their manufactures in Mexico then that is the only important fact. Mexico's proximity to the United States was important, and companies in the United States took advantage of their position when the countries were linked by a railway system. However, Germany also moved ahead of Britain in the race for commercial supremacy despite her greater distance from the Republic. The Anglo-Mexican diplomatic imbroglio was also a significant factor since it was during the period 1867-84, while British representatives and merchants were absent, that the United States replaced Britain as the major exporter to Mexico. But it should be remembered that British diplomats were not absent, and British merchants need not have been absent, when Germany pushed Britain into third place in the market. In the final analysis it may have been the vigor of German and American agents and the adaptability and ingenuity of the manufacturers in their countries that overwhelmed the British. If so, it was a phenomenon that was not limited to Mexico.[54]

[53] *MM*, II (Jan., 1910), 29.

[54] The United States, Germany, and Great Britain may have had similar commercial clashes in other Latin American countries before World War I. For a study of their rivalry in Brazil, see Alan K. Manchester, *British Preëminence in Brazil* (Chapel Hill, 1933), chap. xii, especially pp. 329-33.

8. *The Balance Sheet*

Porfirio Díaz believed that the major barriers to Mexican greatness were economic in nature. Many of his policies were brilliantly successful. The number of railroads, mining companies, and banks operating in the country increased rapidly in a generation. More factories were built. Power plants were constructed and tram lines electrified. The valley of Mexico was drained; harbors from Tampico to Coatzacoalcos were improved; sewerage systems were installed in a few cities. Mexico moved into the ranks of the largest producers of petroleum in the world. Her credit rating improved in European countries. The value of her imports and exports jumped from 61,000,000 pesos in 1876 to almost 500,000,000 pesos in 1910.

The complete story of the American contribution to the economic transformation of Mexico before 1911 has not been told, but an examination of the role of other nationalities has long been needed. In 1910 Britain provided 14 per cent of Mexico's imports. From 1876 to 1911 Britons invested their capital in 304 limited companies registered to operate in Mexico and in at least 23 concerns formed by non-Britons for the same purpose. By 1910 a paid-up capital of over £77,000,000 was invested in Mexican railways, mines, real estate, ranching, and rubber companies, banks, factories, petroleum and public utility ventures, and in city, state, and federal government bonds.[1] These interests paled beside those of the United States. Three-

---

[1] A few Britons owned, or were employed by, insurances, pottery, glassware, and retail sales companies in Mexico City; see GBDCR, MS No. 517.

Table 8. British investments in Mexico, 1876-1910:
Amount of paid-up capital

Type of investment	1876 £	1884 £	1890 £	1900 £	1910 £
Government bonds	23,300,000	23,300,000	20,000,000	25,000,000	25,000,000
Railways					
in Br. cos.	5,816,730	7,820,780	8,500,000	11,000,000	14,357,045
non-Br. cos.				14,000,000	20,000,000
Mining					
in Br. cos.	1,435,348	1,642,902	2,760,835	3,790,319	4,522,775
Banks					
in Br. cos.	500,000	500,000	350,000	350,000	350,000
non-Br. cos.			590,000	590,000	590,000
Real estate					
in Br. cos.			3,367,158	3,259,873	3,658,053
Public utility					
in Br. cos.		100,000	100,000	1,108,000	630,607
non-Br. cos.					4,369,727 (shares) 4,887,663 (bonds)
Factories					
in Br. cos.				217,930	542,385
Petroleum				29,171	205,197 (shares) 16,800 (bonds)

				30,000,000 pesos (part share in Mexican Eagle Co.)
TOTAL	31,052,078	33,363,682	35,667,993	59,347,293	77,967,260 (plus Mexican Eagle)

Table 9. *Total registered British limited companies and non-British companies in which British capital was invested, 1876-1910[a]*

Type of investment	British (registered in London)	Non-Br.	Total	Br. Div. Company	Non. Br. Div. Co.	Total
Mines	224	?	224	16	—	16
Land cos.	32	—	32	2	—	2
Railroads	17	3	20	3	3	6
Factories	11	9 (?)	18	2	—	2
Public utils.	10	7	17	2	1	3
Petroleum	9	2	11	0	0	0
Banks	1	2	3	1	2	3
TOTAL	304	23	327	26	6	32

[a] Companies registered in Edinburgh, Scotland—23.

fourths of Mexico's trade was in American hands by 1910 and in that year citizens of the United States had over $1,000,000,000 invested in Mexican enterprises. Americans and Britons clashed in various fields, commerce, railways, and petroleum in particular, but the economic pre-eminence of the United States in Mexico was established before Díaz began his second term. Only in the utility and oil business was this supremacy seriously challenged before 1911.

The list of key organizers, directors, and investors in the important active British companies was small. Weetman Pearson was interested in mining syndicates, railroads, rubber, utility and petroleum companies, and construction jobs aimed at modernizing Mexican cities. Members of Baring Brothers, in association with the Rothschild family, helped to form and finance profitable mining and railway companies. The Antony Gibbs family, bankers in London, was involved in mining, railroad, and utility concerns. Delfín Sánchez, Manuel González, Romero Rubio, and President Díaz were prominent shareholders in the major railway ventures. Chandos Stanhope lent his support to the original Tehuantepec railroad in the 1880's and later held the controlling interest in five British companies. Dr. Samuel Machew, John MacDonald, and Robert Bird, Canadians from Montreal, were important figures in the organization and management of the Mexican Light and Power Company and Weetman Pearson's electrical and factory ventures. The name of Robert Symon was linked with most of the British railway concerns in western Mexico. Dr. Fred Stark Pearson was associated with railroads in Chihuahua and mining and power projects in the southern part of the Republic. Frederick Hawdon and Walter Maclachlan owned mines in three states and held directorships in four mining companies.[2]

The number of interlocking directorships further points to the dominance of a small group. In 1910 George Houghton sat on the board of six active Mexican ventures. Rawlinson Bayliss of the El Oro Mining concern was a director in three companies. Robert Price was chairman of four enterprises. John Body could attend the meetings of ten companies as a director while W. D. Pearson sat on the board of six concerns.

[2] See *Directory of Directors*, published yearly after 1881.

Sir Clarendon Hyde, another of Weetman Pearson's partners, was vice-president, chairman, and director in three enterprises. John MacDonald and Samuel Machew were vice-presidents and directors in all of Pearson's power companies operating in Puebla, Cédorba, and Veracruz. Fred Stark Pearson was president of three railroad, mining, and power concerns.

The task of carrying on business enterprise in Mexico also was in the hands of a comparatively small number of Britons. Ten thousand Americans, according to J. Fred Rippy, were engaged in ranching alone in Mexico in 1910. The diplomatic records and the inadequate census reports indicate that less than five thousand Britons worked or resided in the Republic at any time during the Díaz era. Most of this total, aside from the farmers, ranchers, and colonists, and the agents for British manufacturers, was made up of engineers, accountants, and foremen, and the executives such as Weetman Pearson who moved in the exclusive circle of Mexican officialdom, traveled in private railway cars, and wined and dined at the Jockey Club in Mexico City.

No company could operate in Mexico without working capital; and for most of the British concerns, although not all of them, this meant that the support of the investing public was needed. The renewal of diplomatic relations helped to foster the enthusiasm that many Britons had for things Mexican after 1884. There was considerable advantage in having diplomatic representation in Mexico. The consuls, twenty-two of them by 1910, answered a heavy correspondence from Britons asking about labor, wage, and living conditions. Reports on Mexican trade and commercial conditions, including the silver dilemma, were published regularly. Fortunately, no diplomatic difficulties after 1884 threatened to create a situation of the kind that led to the Anglo-Mexican break in 1867. During the discussions preceding the renewal of diplomatic accord the Mexican government indicated it would not in the future look with favor on official interference on behalf of those who lent their money or talents to Mexican enterprises. Concessions issued to Britons provided that disputes were to be settled in the Mexican courts. The Foreign Office adhered to these terms, although it was willing to have British diplomats use their influence unofficially to speed justice, smooth ruffled feelings, or give assistance to individuals or companies whenever it did not involve treading on the sensitive toes of the government.

There were other reasons for the increase of British activity after 1884. The settlement with the British bondholders and other claimants, although delayed, must have given many investors and traders confidence in the stability of the Mexican government. The modifications in Mexican laws that favored the foreigner was another factor. The opportunities for profitable enterprise were publicized by the Díaz government, promoters, directors of British companies, and the journals and newspapers of both countries. The fall in the price of silver may have influenced some Britons who saw in the cheap peso the chance to cut their expenses for labor and supplies purchased within Mexico.

The problems encountered by the British companies and merchants do not need to be repeated; the silver crisis proved especially harmful to many facets of British activity. The decline in the value of silver held back the rate of increase of British imports. The bad effects of the fluctuating peso were sometimes offset, and probably used to advantage, by British real estate, manufacturing, and mining companies, but the railway companies' earnings were entirely in silver. The railroads had to purchase foreign exchange in order to buy their rolling stock, other equipment, or fuel, and pay their debts and dividends abroad.

It is evident that the dividend records of the companies in which British capital was invested reflected, in part, the many problems faced in Mexico. Some British investors profited from their excursion into Mexican enterprises; most did not. Thirty-two of the 327 concerns noted in Table 9 paid dividends to their shareholders. Nearly one-half of these were mining ventures. Three were banks. Three of the public utility companies were dividend enterprises but Britons had to share credit for the success of these concerns with Canadians and Americans. A colonization company and a rubber venture managed to hand out returns for one year. Railway dividends were not high except those paid by the Mexican Railway in the early 1880's, but 33 per cent of the companies did make some returns. W. D.

Pearson's petroleum holdings gave promise of future profit but no dividends were paid before 1911. The two or three most prosperous limited companies, all mining ventures, were promoted, financed, and managed by men who brought previous experience in Latin America and unlimited capital to bear on their Mexican property.

The problem of determining exactly which Britons profited from the Mexican boom, and how much was earned, is almost unsurmountable. A few generalizations may be permitted. British contractors who built the railroads were in a position to earn a profit, as were the men who were paid salaries as managers, presidents, or directors by the companies. The promoter who resold property that he had purchased at low cost must have been more fortunate on occasion than investors. The bankers and brokers who sold Mexican shares in London did not have to assume the same risks as the ordinary investor. The Britons who sent machines, fuel, provisions, tools, and other gear to the British camps in Mexico did not regret the interests of their countrymen. The same was true of the shipping companies.

Most important from the Mexican standpoint is the question of the British impact on Mexico. Important contributions were made in the realm of public health. The joint hydroelectric project in Necaxa increased the industrial potential of a limited district, served as an example for other such ventures, and made the life of at least a segment of the Mexican population more comfortable. British technology was able to revive or open mining and oil areas. Mexico's railroad system was small in 1910 and perhaps, as some have argued, it was not well enough planned from the point of stimulating agricultural development. Yet it should be remembered that only in recent years have agricultural exports again come to comprise as large a percentage of Mexico's exports as in 1910, 1911, and 1912. The railroads joined with the fact of freedom for international trade and the flow of foreign capital to Mexico to stimulate commercial production for export by wealthy *hacendados*. The subsistence farmer, faced by high transportation costs and being for the most part outside the money economy, took little part in this development. However, the growth of foreign markets was followed by the widening of internal markets on a small scale, a fact proved by the increase in foreign freight carried by the Mexican Railway. The British railroads also hauled material for the construction of other lines, helped to relieve communities from isolation, brought agricultural raw materials, cotton, lumber, and vegetable oils, for example, to factories for processing, and gave employment to large numbers of Mexicans.

The historian must rely primarily on British sources for his information on the position of Mexican labor in the active mining, railroad, petroleum, utility, and factory enterprises. The Mexican press at times complained of the low wage paid to employees in the British companies and the policies of the Mexican Railway Company, which gave no right of seniority to native workers. This information must be compared with British reports which emphasized that their companies paid the same wages as other foreign companies, provided housing and sanitation facilities for Mexican labor and, in general, treated their employees so well that strikes were practically unknown. The British real estate and rubber companies seldom made any attempt to develop their holdings, and labor problems consequently did not develop. The Mexican or Indian who eked out an existence on British agricultural and rubber property in Lower California, Chiapas, Oaxaca, Sonora, or elsewhere technically lost what might be loosely defined as his right of ownership, but in fact he never knew in most instances of the existence of his landlord. If the British in the real estate field were guilty of anything it was neglect.

Porfirio Díaz reportedly spent his last days in Mexico at the Veracruz home of a close friend of Weetman Pearson, by then Lord Cowdray.[3] John B. Body, the owner, believed that Díaz' visit showed the warm feeling that the deposed leader had for the British and their contributions to Mexican progress. If Body was blessed with even a modicum of perspicacity he may have realized that the benefits accruing to Mexico from the foreigners who dominated the country had not often sifted down to the masses. If so, he had discovered at least one of the many pressures that brought the Díaz era to an end.

[3] Spender, p. 187.

Appendix

Table A. *British limited mining companies organized to work in Mexico prior to December 31, 1884, and on the Company Registrar's list on that date* —148

Table B. *British limited railway companies organized to work in Mexico, 1885-1910* —149

Table C. *British mining companies organized to work in Mexico, 1885-1910* —150-164

Table D. *British real estate, ranching, and rubber enterprise in Mexico, 1885-1910* —165-167

Table E. *British petroleum enterprise in Mexico, 1885-1910* —168-169

Table F. *British investments in Mexican public utilities, 1883-1910* —170-172

Table G. *British companies organized to build or operate factories in Mexico, 1885-1910* —173-174

Table A. *British limited mining companies organized to work in Mexico prior to December 31, 1884, and on the Company Registrar's list on that date*

Name of company	File	Location	Paid-up capital December 31, 1884 (£)
United Mexican Mining Company	2744	Guanajuato	1,230,398[a]
Almada and Tirito	4732	Alamos, Sonora	129,988[a]
Guerrerro[sic] Gold Mining Company	4478	Cozuca, Guerrero	19,911[a]
Esperanza Gold Mining Company	9241	No property	35
Trojes Mining & Smelting Co.	10768	Zitacuaro, Michoacán	109,320[a]
Providencia and New Rosario	11083	No property	—
Rio Grande and Dolores Silver	11895	Cutzeo, Michoacán	11,506[a]
La Gran Compaña Gold and Silver	15178	Las Nieves, Zac.	21,093
Zubiate Mining	17591	Hermosillo, Son.	—
Anglo-Mexican Mining Company	18783	80 Miles north of Culiacán, Sinaloa	b
Santa Rita	19108	Nieves, Zacatecas	—
Montezuma Silver Mines of Mexico	19209	Toluca, Federal District	11
North Mexican Silver Mining	19452	Cusihuiriachic, Chihuahua	b
Pinos Altos (Mex.) Mining Company	13015	Pinos Altos, Chihuahua	100,000[a]
Mexican Mining	19696	No property	2,540
La Trinidad	20507	Guaymas, Sonora	a

[a] Denotes active company on December 31, 1884.
[b] Denotes a company erecting machinery on its property, December 31, 1884.

Table B. *British limited railway companies organ-*
ized to work in Mexico, 1885-1910

Name of company	File	Paid-up capital 1890 £	Paid-up capital 1900 £	Paid-up capital 1910 £
Interoceanic Railraod (1888)[a]	26575	800,000	2,700,000	6,869,459
Mexican Mineral Railway Company (1888)[a]	27579	13,483	—	—
Mexican Pacific Railway (1888)	27725	29,364	899,930	—
Michoacan Mining and Railroad Company (1889)[a]	28137	92,030	97,886	97,886
Mexican Southern Railway (1889)[a]	28880	1,000,000	1,600,000	1,600,000
Mexican and Central American Railway (1890)	31661	—	—	—
Pachuca, Zacultipan, and Tampico Railway (1890)	31807	272,000	—	—
Western Railway Company of Mexico (1890)[b]	32279	—	23,100	—
Mexican Northern Pacific Railway (1891)	34391	—	—	—
Mexican North Western Railway (1891)	34430	—	—	—
Mexican Midland Railway (1894)	40426	—	—	—
Coahuila and Zacatecas Railroad (1896)	47580	—	—	—
Michoacan and Pacific Railway Company (1896)	50076	—	—	—
Vera Cruz (Mexico) Railways (1900)[b]	66525	—	60,007	500,000
Mexican Eastern Railway (1901)[b]		—	—	9,930
Mexican Union Railway (1910)[b]	107473	—	—	123,000

[a] Completed a railway line.
[b] Purchased railways built by non-British capitalists.

Table C. British mining companies organized to work in Mexico, 1885–1910

Name of company	File	Location of concession	Paid-up capital 1890 £	Paid-up capital 1900 £	Paid-up capital 1910 £
Almada and Tirito Company (1885)[a]	20992	Alamos, Sonora	dissolved 1890	—	—
Silver Queen United (1885)[a]	21101	Los Bronces, Sonora	—	—	dissolved 1906
Great Las Nieves (1885)	21087	Zacatecas	—	dissolved 1891	—
Trojes United Mining and Smelting (1885)[a]	21200	Angangueo, Michoacán	25,375	dissolved 1891	—
West Rosario Silver Mining Company	21333	Hidalgo	—	dissolved 1891	—
Mexican Mining, Exploration and Acquisition Co.	21415	—	dissolved 1888	—	—
Mesquital Del Oro Mining Company (1885)[a]	21604	Mesquital, Durango	49,998	49,998	dissolved 1904
Pinos Altos Bullion (1886)[a]	21996	Pinos Altos, Chihuahua	200,000	dissolved 1895	—
Le Velera (1886)[a]	22729	Sahuaripa, Sonora	28,836	28,836	dissolved 1904
Aztec Silver Mining Association (1886)	22962	Pachuca, Hidalgo	—	dissolved 1894	—

Company	No.	Location			
East Arevalo (Mexican) Mining Company (1886)[a]	22974	El Chico, Hidalgo	14,972	dissolved 1894	—
Palmarejo Mining Company (1886)[a]	22980	Near Chihuahua	253,899	253,899	dissolved 1903
San Pedro Gold and Silver Mines (1886)	23368	El Oro	—	dissolved 1892	—
San Ricardo Mining Company (1886)	23381	Batopilas, Chihuahua	—	dissolved 1892	—
Bravo Mining Syndicate (1887)	24074	Pinos Altos, Chihuahua	1,500	dissolved 1900	—
Smelting Company (1887)	24121	Chihuahua	66,271	dissolved 1895	—
Mexican Santa Barbara Mining Company (1887)	24330	Parral, Chihuahua	54,501	54,501	dissolved 1906
South Mexican Gold and Silver Mines (1887)	24456	Oaxaca	—	dissolved 1892	—
Batopilas Mining Company (1887)	24529	Batopilas, Chihuahua	—	dissolved 1892	—
Zacatecas Gold Company (1887)	24594	Pánuco, Zacatecas	dissolved 1889	—	—
Westminster Catorce Synd. (1887)	24618	Catorce, San Luis Potosí	2,410	dissolved 1892	—
Oaxaca Mining Company (1887)	24952	—	12,500	25,000	dissolved 1906
Mexican Mansfield Silver Mine (1887)	25029	Sonora	dissolved 1888	—	—
La Luz Mines of Mexico (1887)[a]	25285	Querétaro, Jalisco	—	dissolved 1897	—
Mexican Copper Company (1887)	25308	Michoacán	—	dissolved 1892	—

(Table C—*continued*)

Name of company	File	Location of concession	Paid-up capital 1890 £	Paid-up capital 1900 £	Paid-up capital 1910 £
El Gallo Mines (1887)[a]	25319	Guerrero	6,100	dissolved 1899	—
Santa Theresa Copper Co. (1887)	25603	Michoacán	150	dissolved 1891	—
New San Acasio Mine and Freehold Land Co. (1888)	25942	Zacatecas	—	dissolved 1894	—
Cerro Blanco Mines (1888)	26283	Sonora	dissolved 1890	—	—
Mexican Coal and Iron Company	26449	Monclova, Coahuila	—	dissolved 1894	—
Quintera Mining Company (1888)	26652	—	—	42,113	42,113
Arispe Gold Mines of Mexico (1888)	27184	Arispe, Sonora	3,017	dissolved 1896	—
Mina Grande (Querétaro) Mining Co. (1888)[a]	27199	Querétaro	—	94,715	dissolved 1908
Mexican Mines Development Co. (1888)	27251	Cusihuiriachic	—	dissolved 1896	—
North Mexican Milling and Mining Syndicate (1888)[a]	27389	Chihuahua	2,500	2,500	dissolved 1906
Sinaloa Mining Syndicate (1888)[a]	—				—
Pachuca Silver Mining Company (1888)	27675	Real del Monte, Hidalgo	app. 6,000	dissolved 1892	—

Mexican Inguaran Copper Company (1889)	29502	Michoacán	—	—	—
Chiapas Mining Co. (1889)[a]	28782	Saluschiapa Pichucalco, Chiapas	96,853	96,853	about the same
Chiapas Zone Exploration Company (1889)[a]	30027	Pichucalco, Chiapas	121,605 cash 7551	226,056 cash 7551	—
San Pablo (Mexico) Mining (1889)	30394	Real del Monte, Guanajuato	—	dissolved 1895	—
British-Mexican Exploration Synd. (1889)	30948	—	35	dissolved 1893	—
Torreón Silver Mining Co. (1889)	—	Torreón, Chihuahua	—	—	—
Mexican Rosario Company (1890)	23293	Nieves, Zacatecas	—	16,332	dissolved 1905
Princesa Gold Mining	—	Lower Calif.	—	—	—
Mexican Mineral and Exploration Co. (1890)	32401	—	—	dissolved 1895	—
Chiapas Syndicate (1890)	32791	—	—	dissolved 1893	—
Santa Beatriz Mining Synd. (1891)	33645	—	—	485	dissolved 1906
Santa Rosalia del Carmen (Mexico)	33930	Lower Calif.	—	—	dissolved 1905
El Refugio Mining Concessions (1891)[a]	34073	Guerrero, Chihuahua	—	dissolved 1896	—
New La Velera (1891)	34728	Sonora	—	—	dissolved 1904
Tominil Mines (1891)[a]	35379	—	—	14,338	dissolved 1907
El Progreso Native Copper Co. (1891)	35439	Michoacán	—	4,200	dissolved 1909

(Table C—*continued*)

Name of company	File	Location of concession	Paid-up capital 1890 £	Paid-up capital 1900 £	Paid-up capital 1910 £
Mexican Smelting Mining and Land Corp. (1891)	35517	—	—	dissolved 1898	—
New Pachuca Silver Mining Co. (1891)	35521	Pachuca, Hidalgo	—	45,424	dissolved 1901
New Imuris Mine (1892)[a]	36353	Sonora	—	dissolved 1899	—
Bacis Gold and Silver Mines (1892)[a]	36919	Bacis, Durango	—	127,864	dissolved 1904
Mexican Silver Mining Options (1892)	37505	Nieves, Zacatecas	—	dissolved 1897	—
Parral Consolidated Gold and Silver Mines (1892)[a]	37812	Parral, Chihuahua	—	dissolved 1900	—
New Pinos Altos Company (1893)[a]	38126	Pinos Altos, Chihuahua	—	dissolved 1900	—
La Yesca Gold and Silver Mines (1893)[a]	38888	Jalisco	—	66,513	dissolved 1905
Mexican Gold and Silver Recovery Co. (1893)[a]	39026	—	—	dissolved 1897	—
Almada and Tirito Company (1895)[a]	42980	Alamos, Sonora	—	dissolved 1897	—
United Mexican Mines (1895)[a]	43932	Guanajuato	—	17,801	dissolved 1908

New Guadalcazar Quicksilver Mines (1895)[a]	44875	San Luis, Potosí	—	119,000	dissolved 1904
La Bufa Mexican Gold Mines	44926	Batopilas, Chihuahua	—	105,000	dissolved 1908
Oaxaca Development Syndicate (1895)	45038	Oaxaca	—	567	dissolved 1902
Anglo-Mexican and Western Trust (1895)	45442		—	dissolved 1897	—
Mexican Gold and Silver Recovery Co. (1895)	45569		—	dissolved 1900	—
Tehuantepec Exploration and Development Co. (1895)[a]	45734		—	—	dissolved 1912
Mexican Trading Company of London (1895)	45767		—	dissolved 1897	—
Malacate Mining and Smelting Co. (1895)	46167	Toluca	—	400,000	dissolved 1908
Mexican Concessions Syndicate (1896)	47564		—	5,000	dissolved 1904
Mazapil Copper (1896)	47580	Mazapil, Zacatecas	—	—	—
New Mexican Rosario (1896)[a]	47688		—	29,000	29,000
Gold Fields of Mexico (1896)	48339	Huruapa, Chihuahua	—	—	dissolved 1906
Anglo-Mexican Colonization and Trading Co. (1896)	48493		—	—	dissolved 1906
San Juan Gold Mines (1896)	48767	Lower Calif.	—	dissolved 1898	—
Grand Central Mining (1896)[a]	49058	Sonora	—	100,000	dissolved 1909
Consolidated Gold Fields of Mexico (1896)[a]	49072	Arispe, Sonora	—	79,960	79,960 dissolved 1911

(Table C—*continued*)

Name of company	File	Location of concession	Paid-up capital 1890 £	Paid-up capital 1900 £	Paid-up capital 1910 £
Anglo-Mexican Properties (1896)	49745	—	—	2,500	dissolved 1906
British Gold Mines of Mexico (1896)	49866	Ures, Sonora	—	33,821	dissolved 1909
Mexico Ventura Syndicate (1896)	50465	—	—	40,000	dissolved 1913
Mesquital Del Oro Mining Co. (1896)[a]	50625	Mesquital, Durango	—	dissolved 1900	—
Canas Mines (1896)	50648	—	—	56,667	dissolved 1910
Campana Consolidated Gold Mines (1897)[a]	50129	Altar District, Sonora	—	20,000	dissolved 1903
Almada and Tirito (1897)	52209	Alamos, Sonora	—	dissolved 1899	—
Michoacan San Francisco Copper Trust Synd. (1897)	52980	—	—	15,000	dissolved 1902
El Mundo (Mexico) Gold Mining Company (1897)	53284	Altar District, Sonora	—	99,000	dissolved 1909
Mexican Minerals (1897)	54041	Hidalgo	—	—	dissolved 1910

Company (year)	Number	Location			
Avino Syndicate (1898)	56012	—	—	dissolved 1900	—
Palmarejo and Mexican Gold Fields (1898)[a]	57937	Near City of Chihuahua	—	16,805	91,327
Zaragoza Milling (1898)	58209	—	—	3,425	dissolved 1909
United Mexican Mines Association (1898)[a]	58553	Guanajuato	—	12,500	12,744 dissolved 1912
Mexican Copper Synd. (1898)	—	—	—	575	dissolved 1906
Buckland Synd. (1899)	60364	—	—	dissolved 1899	—
Avino Mines of Mexico (1899)[a]	60663	Durango	—	60,000	dissolved 1903
Sabinas Company (1899)	61012	—	—	—	dissolved 1904
Mexican Esperanza Gold Mine (1899)	61277	El Oro	—	dissolved 1899	—
Los Paras (Mexico) Gold Mines (1899)	61838	Oaxaca	—	—	dissolved 1902
Panuco Copper (1899)	62251	Monclova, Coahuila	—	264,910	dissolved 1910
Buena Vista Copper Mines (1899)	62252	Northern Dist. of Lower Calif., Dist. of Calmalli	—	—	dissolved 1907
Mesquital Mines (1899)[a]	63463	Mesquital del Oro, Zacatecas	—	—	dissolved 1906
Consolidated Copper Company (1899)	62510	San Luis Potosí	—	85,000	dissolved 1907

(Table C—*continued*)

Name of company	File	Location of concession	Paid-up capital 1890 £	Paid-up capital 1900 £	Paid-up capital 1910 £
Mexican Coal Fields (1899)	62546	—	—	—	dissolved 1902
El Oro Mining and Railway (1899)[a]	63105	El Oro	—	859,012	—
Sonoma Mines of Mexico (1899)[a]	64071	Avino, Durango	—	400	dissolved 1906
Zapoteca Mining (1899)	64363	Oaxaca	—	—	dissolved 1903
Mexican Gold and Silver Recovery (1899)	64443	Hermosillo, Arispe, Altar, Sonora	—	27,749	33,014
La Princess Gold Mines (1899)	64446	—	—	7,000	dissolved 1902
Mexican Oaxaca Syndicate (1900)	65664	Sierra Juárez, Oaxaca	—	—	9,006
San Ramon	—	Chihuahua, Ocampo	—	—	—
Gladys Proprietary Gold Mines (1900)[a]	66492	San Isidro de las Cuevas, Parral, Chihuahua	—	—	dissolved 1910
Compañía Minera de México (1900)	66651	—	—	—	dissolved 1907
Rosario Extension Syndicate (1900)	67492	—	—	—	2,269
Sierra Madre Exploration Synd. (1900)	67874	Artiaga District, Chihuahua	—	—	29,993
Mexican Rosario (1900)	69317	—	—	—	8,000
Mexican Mines Selection (1901)	69317	—	—	—	dissolved 1909

Company	Number	Location			
Parral Mines (1901)[a]	70043	Parral, Chihuahua	—	—	dissolved 1909
Dios T. Guie Mining (1901)	70110	Temósachic, Guerrero and Chihuahua	—	—	50,830
London Mexican Syndicate (1901)	71881	Parral, Chihuahua	—	—	dissolved 1909
Castellana Consolidated Mines (1901)	71954	Tepic, Aquascalientes	—	—	100,000
Cherokee (Mexican) Proprietary (1902)	72399	Parral, Chihuahua	—	—	dissolved 1906
Mechaco (Mexico) Mining and Milling Company (1902)	73372	Alamos, Sonora	—	—	79,993
Díaz Mines (1902)[a]	73385	Hidalgo, Chihuahua	—	—	dissolved 1904
Reform Mines Syndicate (1902)	73482	Michoacán	—	—	23,171
Abundancia (Mexico) Mining and Milling (1902)	73563	—	—	—	dissolved 1915
Waterson Mines (1902)	74124	—	—	—	dissolved 1908
British Mexican Syndicate (1902)	74470	—	—	—	dissolved 1909
Sinaloa Syndicate (1902)	74950	—	—	—	dissolved 1907
Anglo-Mexican Syndicate (1902)	75274	—	—	—	19,993
Encinillas Mines (1902)	75379	Santa Rosalia, Chihuahua	—	—	52,005
Avino Mines of Mexico (1903)[a]	76495	—	—	—	129,947
Oxnam Prospecting Company (no. 1) (1903)	76831	Huruapa, Chihuahua	—	—	39,977
Mexican San Felix Mines (1903)	76983	Durango	—	—	dissolved 1909

(Table C—continued)

Name of company	File	Location of concession	Paid-up capital 1890 £	Paid-up capital 1900 £	Paid-up capital 1910 £
San Francisco del Oro Mines (1903)[a]	77075	Near Parral, Chihuahua	—	—	330,000
Republican Mining and Metal Company (1903)[a]	77684	Zacatecas, San Luis Potosí and Querétaro	—	—	49,990
St. George's Syndicate (1903)	77983	Durango	—	—	dissolved 1907
Felton's Copala Mines (1903)[a]	78454	Copala, Sinaloa	—	—	dissolved 1907
Esperanza Limited (1903)[a]	78724	El Oro	—	—	455,999
Alice Santa Eulalia Mining Co. (1903)	78767	Santa Eulalia, Chihuahua	—	—	1,000
San Jorge Minillas Mining Co. (1903)	78773	Chihuahua City	—	—	3,000
Dolores (1904)[a]	79811	Chihuahua	—	—	dissolved 1909
Mexican Mines Development (1904)	80680	—	—	—	dissolved 1907
Bacis Gold and Silver Mining (1904)[a]	81168	—	—	—	14,536
Mesquital Gold Mines (1904)[a]	81172	—	—	—	dissolved 1910
North Dolores (1904)	81311	—	—	—	dissolved 1908
El Gallo Mining (1904)	81497	—	—	—	dissolved 1905

Company	No.	Location			
Mexico Mines of El Oro (1904)[a]	82292	Near El Oro	—	—	180,000
Ocampo Gold Mines (1904)	82293	—	—	—	dissolved 1909
Mexican Silver Lead Mines (1904)	82443	—	—	—	dissolved 1907
Mexican Premier Synd. (1904)	82605	Nepumoceno, Chihuahua	—	—	dissolved 1910
Premier Development Corp. (1905)	83636	Chihuahua	—	—	17,431
El Rosario (Taviches) Synd. (1905)	83662	Oaxaca	—	—	dissolved 1909
La Fortuna Mining Company of Santa Eulalia (1905)	83826	—	—	—	13,500
Oaxaca Gold and Silver Mine (1905)	83914	Oaxaca	—	—	dissolved 1910
Estado Mining Synd. (1905)	84122	—	—	—	—
Mexican and Colorado Synd. (1905)	85633	—	—	—	dissolved 1908
Waterson Gold Mining (1905)	85632	Ocampo, Chihuahua	—	—	100,000
Mexican Southern Mining Synd. (1905)	86345	—	—	—	dissolved 1908
Refugio Synd. (1905)	—	Cananea, Sonora	—	—	dissolved 1908
Somera Gold Mining (1905)[a]	86850	El Oro	—	—	dissolved 1909
Mexican Trust Co. (1905)	86771	—	—	—	1,335
Torres Mines (1906)	87551	—	—	—	—
Mazapil Copper Co. (1906)	—	—	—	—	dissolved 1907
Mexican and General Synd. (1906)	87768	—	—	—	dissolved 1909
New Anglo-Mexican (1906)	88019	Michoacán	—	—	

(Table C—*continued*)

Name of company	File	Location of concession	Paid-up capital 1890 £	Paid-up capital 1900 £	Paid-up capital 1910 £
L. H. Syndicate (1906)	88710	—	—	—	dissolved 1907
Guanacevi Co. (1906)	—	Durango	—	—	—
Consuelo Mines (1906)	88919	Hacienda de Yaxo, Oaxaca	—	—	14,937
Sierra Juárez Exploration Co. (1906)	89062	—	—	—	dissolved 1908
Congreso Copper Co. (1906)[a]	89237	Altar, Sonora	—	—	dissolved 1909
Reform Mine Syndicate (1906)	89846		—	—	17,325
Mexican Smelting Corp. (1906)	89999	Coahuila	—	—	107,950
Barranca (Mexico) Mines (1906)	90315	Hermosillo, Sonora	—	—	80,000
San Carlos Gold Mine (1906)[a]	90556	Durango	—	—	6,800
Marina Mines of Mexico (1906)	90765	—	—	—	4,975
Reina Victoria Mining (1906)	90868	Sombrerete, Zacatecas	—	—	—
Tominil (Mexican) Mining (1906)	91215	Tamajula, Durango	—	—	365,000
Dulces Nombres Silver Mining (1906)	91280	Dulces Nombres, Durango	—	—	—
Ventanas Mining and Exploration (1907)[a]	91867	Mazatlán, Sinaloa	—	—	125,000
British-Mexican Exploration Synd. (1907)	91888	Sonora	—	—	14,777

Company	No.	Location				
Tecolata Mines Synd. (1907)	91971	Durango	—	—	—	—
Mexican Mining and Industrial Corp. (1907)	93216	—	—	—	—	—
New Parral Mines Synd.	93217	Parral, Chihuahua	—	—	—	3,517
El Progresso Mexican Mines (1907)[a]	93833	Sinaloa	—	—	—	6,621
Encinillas Mines and Smelting Works (1907) of Santa Rosalia	94004	Encinillas, Chihuahua	—	—	—	45,647
British Mexican Copper (1907)	95882	—	—	—	—	—
Santa Maria (Mexico) Mines (1908)	100679	Minillas, Zacatecas	—	—	—	108,808
Mexico Mines of Chihuahua (1908)	100920	Santa Eulalia, Chihuahua	—	—	—	9,152
Avino Mines (1909)	101875	—	—	—	—	7,721
Exploration Company of England and Mexico (1909)	101888	—	—	—	—	43,750
Carmen Mines of El Oro (1909)[a]	102405	El Oro	—	—	—	120,007
Mexican Searchers (1909)	102820	Santa Eulalia, Chihuahua	—	—	—	1,575
Manta Mining (1909)[a]	103424	Chihuahua	—	—	—	23,500
Escondida (Mexican) Synd. (1909)	104038	—	—	—	—	1,305
Oaxaca Mines Development (1909)	104095	Oaxaca	—	—	—	1,175
Tominil Options (1909)	104292	—	—	—	—	—
Batopilas Mining Smelting and Refining (1909)	104397	Batopilas, Chihuahua	—	—	—	9,438
San Carlos Gold Mining Co. (1909)	105691	—	—	—	—	10,124
Santa Gertrudis (1909)[a]	106765	Santa Gertrudis, Pachuca	—	—	—	1,072,131
Hunson's Consolidated (1910)	107015	—	—	—	—	74,694
El Mayo Mines (1910)	—	—	—	—	—	—
West Mexican Mines (1910)	107108	Mina District, Chihuahua	—	—	—	—

(Table C—*continued*)

Name of company	File	Location of concession	Paid-up capital 1890 £	Paid-up capital 1900 £	Paid-up capital 1910 £
Esmeralda Consolidated Mines (1910)	—	Iguano, Nuevo León	—	—	—
Mexican Zacatecas Development Co. (1910)	108269	El Oro	—	—	—
Taxco Mines of Mexico (1910)[a]	108905	Taxco, Guerrero	—	—	—
Santa Gertrudis (South) (1910)	109315	—	—	—	—
Tominil (Mexican) Mining Corporation (1910)	111419	—	—	—	—

Total companies 210
Active companies 57
Total paid-up capital, end of 1890 £2,760,835
Total paid-up capital, end of 1900 £3,790,319
Total paid-up capital, end of 1910 £4,522,775
[a] Denotes active company.

Table D. *British real estate, ranching, and rubber enterprise in Mexico, 1885-1910*

Name of company	File	Paid-up capital 1890 £	Paid-up capitau 1900 £	Paid-up capital 1910 £
Mexican National Land Mortgage and Investment Co. (1886)[a]	23067	49,000	dissolved 1891	—
Mexican Land and Cattle Ranche Co. (1886)	21662	—	date of wind-up uncertain dissolved 1898	—
Mexican General Land Mortgage and Investment Co. (1887)[a]	24498	355,510		—
California (Mexico) Land Co. (1888)[b]	26608	53,966	55,084	suspended operations 1910
Mexican Land and Colonization Co. (1889)[b]	28841	2,555,390	2,712,540	2,712,540
Anglo-Mexican Land Corporation (1889)	29488	20,000	dissolved 1900	—
Mexican Explorations (1889)	30006	62,394	223,434	dissolved 1909
Mexican Tobacco Plantations (1889)[d]	30017	120,898	date of wind-up uncertain dissolved 1893	—
Mexican Subsidized Colonization and Land Co. (1890)	30620	—	dissolved 1893	—
Mexican (Anahuac) Government Concessions (1890)	31981	—	dissolved 1893	—
Mexican Estates and Trading Syndicate (1890)[c]	32230	—	4,380	dissolved 1907

(Table D—continued)

Name of company	File	Paid-up capital 1890 £	Paid-up capital 1900 £	Paid-up capital 1910 £
Lower California Development Co. (1890)[b]	32395	150,000	150,000	merged into Mexican Land and Colonization Co., 1907
Chiapas Land Co. (1891)	34150	—	date of wind-up uncertain	—
Agricultural and Fruit Growing Colonies of Mexico (1892)	35636	—	date of wind-up uncertain	—
Anglo-Mexican Planting and Trading Corp. (1892)[c]	37841	—	dissolved 1896	—
Mexican Isthmus Co. (1896)	49911	—	—	dissolved 1902
Durango Estates (1897)[a]	52122	—	20,000	dissolved 1907
Mexican Rubber Co. (1897)	53361	—	10	dissolved 1909
Zaragoza Milling Co. (1898)	58209	—	3,425	dissolved 1909
Mexican Syndicate (1899)	60641	—	2,000	dissolved 1902
Mexican Coffee Syndicate (1899)	61461	—	70	dissolved 1904
Yaqui River Land and Development Co. (1900)[b]	66438	—	40,000	40,000
New Sabinas Co. (1901)	72156	—	48,310	48,310
Chilean Exploration and Development Syndicate (1903)[c]	72239	—	—	80,000
Cotton Estates of Tlahualilo (1903)[d]	77927	—	—	250,000
Land Company of Chiapas (1905)[c]	86790	—	—	220,000

San Cristobal (Mexico) Rubber, Tobacco, and Estates Co. (1909)c	104031	—	—	50,000
Guerrero (Mexican) Land Syndicate (1909)a	104413	—	—	7,733
Tepehuacan (Mexican) Syndicate (1910)	108907	—	—	—
Guayule Rubber Co. (1910)c	108932	—	—	250,000
North Mexican Land and Timber Co. (1910)	109004	—	—	70
Anglo-Mexican Land Co. (1910)	109096	—	—	—
TOTAL (32 cos.)		3,367,158	3,259,873	3,658,053

a Companies interested mainly in ranching enterprise.
b Companies interested mainly in colonization.
c Companies interested mainly in producing rubber.
d Companies interested mainly in agriculture (cotton, etc.).

Table E. *British petroleum enterprise in Mexico, 1885-1910*

Name of company	File	Location of concession	Paid-up capital 1900 £	Paid-up capital 1910 £
Mexican, Asphalt Pitch, and Oil Wells (1893)	38845	Formed to acquire areas in San Luis Potosí, Veracruz, Tamaulipas.	dissolved 1897	—
Oil Fields of Mexico (1898)	55665	Tampico and Tuxpan	—	dissolved 1904
Mexican Properties (1898)	58600	Formed to receive an oil concession, location not specified.	—	—
Mexican Petroleum and Liquid Fuel Company (1899)	62420	Buy property "in Mexico" from a New York owner, Albert Johnston.	29,171	dissolved 1901
Mexican Oil Corporation (1904) Anglo-Mexican Oil-fields (1907)	81999 93276	Tuxpan Pichucalo, Chiapas	— —	dissolved 1910 205,197 (Eng. shares) 16,800 (Eng. bonds)
Mexican Eagle Oil Company (1908)	3615- 130054	Tuxpan and Tampico	—	$30,000,000 (Mexican)
Tampico Oil (1910)	110314	Pánuco, Veracruz	—	—

Oil Fields of Mexico (1910) Standard Oil Company (1910)[a] of Mexico	110611 Not a limited company	Pánuco, Veracruz Tampico	no reports published	— —
Elektra Oil Syndicate (1910?)[b]	Not a limited company	75 miles south of Tampico	no reports published	—
TOTAL (11 cos.)			29,171	205,197 (Eng. shares) $30,000,000 (Mexican shares held in part by shareholders in Mexican Eagle Co.) 16,800 (Br. bonds)

[a] There is no report of such a company in the Bush House files and no reference to the concern in the diplomatic correspondence, consular reports, or other official documents. The sole reference discovered is in *Oil* (May 13, 1911), p. 237.

[b] *Ibid.*, (April 22, 1911), p. 191.

Table F. British investments in Mexican public utilities, 1883-1910[a]

Name of company	File	Location of concession	Paid-up capital 1900	Paid-up capital 1910
Mexican Gas and Electric Light Co. (1883)	18223	Mexico City and a plant in suburb of San Lazaro	£ 100,000	£ 100,000
San Luis Potosí Water Co. (1891)	33830	San Luis Potosí (water supply)	dissolved 1900	—
Mexican Electric Works (1897) Mexican Public Works and Finance Corporation (1897)	52281 52988	Mexico City	£ 400,000	dissolved 1905
The City of Mexico Electric Power Syndicate (1897)	55438	Transmitting electric power from waterfall near Mexico City. Gave up concession.	—	dissolved 1904
Mexico Electric Tramways (1898)	56932	Acquired shares in a Mexican-controlled tram company in the Federal District.	—	—
MET (1898) taken over by a Canadian Company, the Mexican Consolidated Electric Co. (1906 under Canadian Law) MCEC changed its name to Mexico Tramways Company in 1908.	—	See MET, above	—	£1,770,197 (shares)

Mexican Light and Power Co. (1902). Registered under Canadian Law. Became part of the Mexico Tramways Company in 1910.	—	Plant at Nonoalco, suburb of Mexico City, and Necaxa, 92 miles from M. C. Supplying power to Capital, El Oro mining district.	£1,862,094 (bonds) $22,000,000 (Mexican) £1,389,387 (Br. shares) £1,229,710 (bonds)
Mexican Power Development Syndicate (1905)	83992	—	dissolved 1909
Mexican Electric Light Co. (1905). Registered under Canadian Laws. Organized by the Mexican Light and Power Company, it took over the Mexican Electric Works, Ltd. (See above)	—	Supplying electric lights to Mexico	$12,000,000 (Mexican)
Anglo-Mexican Electric Co. (1906)	87403	To supply some electric power in Puebla. Took over concession of an Illinois Company. Was a subsidiary of Puebla Tramway, Light and Power Co., registered in Canada.	Company placed £180,607 in PTL and P Co.
Puebla Tramway, Light and Power Co. (1906)	—	See above statement on AME Co.	$8,750,000 (Mexican) £ 333,881 (Br. shares) £ 445,859 (bonds)

(Table F—*continued*)

Name of company	File	Location of concession	Paid-up capital 1900	Paid-up capital 1910
Vera Cruz Electric Light, Power and Traction Co. (1906)	89686	To provide electric lights for VC. Also was to instal tramways and various public works.	—	£ 350,000 (Br. shares) £ 350,000 (bonds)
Monterrey Railway Light and Power Co. (1908). Registered in Canada.	—	Took over existent electricity and tram system. Built waterworks and sewer system.	—	£ 236,000 (Br. shares) £1,000,000 (bonds)
Vera Cruz Telephone Construction Syndicate (1910).	Private concern	To supply 450 wall phones in Veracruz.	—	£ 9,655
TOTAL (16 cos.)			£1,108,000	£4,369,727 (Br. shares) £4,887,663 (Br. mortgage debentures) $42,750,000 (shares, in Mexican dollars, held in Mexico, Canada, U. S.)

[a] Only one company, the Mexican Gas and Electric Light, Limited, was formed before 1890; its paid-up capital in that year was £100,000.

Table G. British companies organized to build or operate factories in Mexico, 1885-1910[a]

Name of company	File	Location of concession	Paid-up capital 1900 £	Paid-up capital 1910 £
North Mexican Foundry (1886)[b]	22464	Chihuahua	dissolved 1894	—
Mexican Portland Cement Company (1890)[c]	31471	—	dissolved 1897	—
Anglo-Mexican Saw Mills (1890)[d]	32749	Orizaba	dissolved 1899	—
Santa Gertrudis Jute Mill Company (1893)	38820		130,930	152,730
San Quintin Milling Company (1893)	39830	Lower California (flour)	19,980	Merged with Mexican Land and Coloniza- tion Company.
L. and H. Pinto (1897)	54109	Factories in Tuxtla (VC), Teziutlán (VC), Jalapa (VC), Veracruz (city), and Oaxaca (cigars- boxes)	67,020	67,023
The Mexican Government Explosives Concessions (1899)	60745	—	—	dissolved 1904
Michoacan Lumber Company (1901)	70244	Erongaricuaro, Michoacán, 10 miles from the Mexican National Railway	—	—

(Table G—continued)

Name of company	File	Location of concession	Paid-up capital 1900 £	Paid-up capital 1910 £
ML Co. was merged into The Lumber and Development Company of Michoacan (1905)	86194	See above, ML Company	—	39,000, but just before Díaz was overthrown the property was sold at auction
Salinas of Mexico (1906)	88222	North of city of San Luis Potosí (salt)	—	280,632
Mexican Industrial Syndicate (1910)	113082	—		
TOTAL (11 cos.)			217,930	542,385

[a] There was some British capital in factories in Mexico that were not controlled by British limited companies. Information on such factories is lacking but some British pounds were probably invested in the Mexican National Packing Company, which had slaughtering houses and processing plants in Vera Cruz, Michoacán, and Mexico City. British pounds were in the Linen Company of Mexico and the San Rafael y Anexas Paper Company. Britons also had interests in the Monterrey Wire Nail Company (Monterrey), Encarnación Iron Works, San Miguel Iron Works, and the Apulco Foundry, all located in the state of Hidalgo, and the Comanja Iron Works in Guanajunto. Weetman D. Pearson owned and operated his own oil refinery after 1904 in Minatitlán. This was part of his oil development program in southern Mexico. Brief mention of these concerns may be found in Carleton Beals, *Porfirio Díaz; Dictator of Mexico* (Philadelphia, 1932), pp. 336–37; GBDCR, AS No. 4215; C. Reginald Enock, *Mexico* (London, 1909), p. 338; *Oil* (Feb. 3, 1911), p. 58.

[b] The North Mexican Foundry was one of three factory companies organized. Its paid-up capital in 1890 was £379. The company carried on no business before its dissolvement in 1894.

[c] The Mexican Portland Cement Company was one of three factory companies organized between 1885 and 1890. Its paid-up capital in 1890 was £1,680. The company was never active.

[d] The Anglo-Mexican Saw Mills, another non-active concern, was the third factory company to be formed between 1885 and 1890. Its paid-up capital in the latter year was £65.

Selected Bibliography

Books

Aubertin, J. J. *A Flight to Mexico*. London: Kegan Paul, French & Company, 1882.

Bancroft, Hubert H. *History of the North Mexican States*. 2 vols. San Francisco: The History Company, Publishers, 1884-89.

Beals, Carleton. *Mexico: An Interpretation*. New York: B. W Huebach, Inc., 1923.

———. *Porfirio Díaz, Dictator of Mexico*. Philadelphia: Lippincott, 1932.

Bowles, Charles. *The Petroleum Industry*. Kansas City: Schoolery Stationery & Printing Co., 1921.

Bulnes, Francisco. *La deuda inglesa—colección de artículos publicados en el Siglo XIX*. Mexico, 1885.

Casasús, Joaquín. *Historia de la deuda contraida en Londres*. México, 1885.

Cline, Howard F. *The United States and Mexico*. Cambridge, Mass.: Harvard University Press, 1953.

Cubas, Antonio. *Mexico in 1876*. Mexico, 1877.

Cumberland, Charles Curtis. *Mexican Revolution: Genesis Under Madero*. Austin: University of Texas Press, 1952.

Directory of Directors. London, 1876-1911.

Dublán, Manuel and Lozano, José María, eds. *Colección legislativa completa de las disposiciones legislativas expedidas desde la independencia de la República*. 44 vols. México, 1876-1912.

Enock, C. Reginald. *Mexico*. London: T. Fisher Unwin, 1909.

Ensor, R. C. K. *England, 1870-1914*. Oxford: Oxford University Press, 1936.

Fabela, Isidro. *Belice: Defensa de los derechos de México*. México: Editorial Mundo Libre, 1944.

International Bureau of the American Republics, ed. *Mexico.* Washington: Government Printing Office, 1904.

Jones, Chester L. *Mexico and Its Reconstruction.* New York: D. Appleton and Company, 1922.

Kohzevar, Edward. *Report on the Republic of Mexico to the Council of Foreign Bondholders.* London, 1886.

Long, W. Rodney. *Railways of Mexico.* Washington: United States Bureau of Foreign and Domestic Commerce, 1925.

Manchester, Alan. *British Preëminence in Brazil.* Chapel Hill: University of North Carolina Press, 1933.

Mathieson, F. C., and Sons, eds. *Stock Exchange Ten Year Record of Prices and Dividends.* 2 vols. London, 1907, 1915.

McCaleb, Walter Flavius. *Present and Past Banking in Mexico.* New York: Harper & Brothers, 1920.

Mexican Year Book. London, 1908-12.

México. *Informe que sus compatriatos el ciudadano General Díaz acerca de los actos de su administración, 1884-1888.* México, 1889.

Mining Laws of the United States of Mexico. México, 1901.

Mining Manual, 1886-1911. London, 1887-1912.

New Mining Laws of the United States of Mexico. Nogales, 1910.

Nordhoff, Charles. *Peninsular California.* New York. Harper & Brothers, 1888.

Ober, Frederick. *Travels in Mexico.* Boston: Estes and Lauriat, 1883.

Parkes, Henry Bamford. *A History of Mexico.* Cambridge, Mass.: Houghton Mifflin Company, 1938.

Powell, Fred W. *The Railroads of Mexico.* Boston: The Stratford Publishing Company, 1921.

Rippy, J. Fred. *Latin America and the Industrial Age.* New York: G. P. Putnam's Sons, 1947.

———. *The United States and Mexico.* New York: F. S. Crofts & Company, 1931.

Rodríquez, Ricardo. *Historia auténtica de la administración de Sr. Gral Porfirio Díaz.* 2 vols. México, 1904.

Romero, Matías. *Geographical and Statistical Notes on Mexico.* New York: G. P. Putnam's Sons, 1898.

———. *Railways in Mexico.* Washington: H. W. Moore, 1882.

Simpson, Eyler. *The Ejido, Mexico's Way Out.* Chapel Hill: The University of North Carolina Press, 1937.

Spender, J. H. *Weetman Pearson, First Viscount Cowdray, 1865-1927.* London: Cassell and Company, Ltd., 1930.

Stock Exchange Year-Book, 1876-1911. London, 1877-1912.

Tannenbaum, Frank. *Mexico: The Struggle for Bread and Peace.* New York: Alfred Knopf, 1950.

Turlington, Edgar. *Mexico and Her Foreign Creditors.* New York: Columbia University Press, 1930.

Tweedie, Mrs. Alec. *Mexico as I Saw It.* London: Hurst and Blackett, Ltd., 1901.

Valadés, José C. *El porfirismo, historia de un régimen: El nacimiento, 1876-1884.* México: Jose Porrua e Hijos, 1941.

Villegas, Daniel Cosío, ed. *Historia moderna de México: La república restaurada. La vida economica por Francisco Calderón.* México, 1955.

Williams, Sir John. *International Law and International Financial Obligations Arising from Contract.* 2 vols. Leyden, 1923.

Wolf, Howard and Ralph. *Rubber: A Story of Glory and Greed.* New York, 1936.

Public Documents

Great Britain. Diplomatic and Consular Reports. *Memorandum on Imports from the United Kingdom and Germany.* Miscellaneous Series No. 662. London: His Majesty's Printing Office, 1907.

Great Britain. Diplomatic and Consular Reports. *Report for the Year 1888 on the Trade of Vera Cruz.* Annual Series No. 604. London: Her Majesty's Printing Office, 1888.

Great Britain. Diplomatic and Consular Reports. *Report for the Year 1893 on the Trade of the Consular District of Vera Cruz.* Annual Series No. 1342. London: Her Majesty's Printing Office, 1894.

Great Britain. Diplomatic and Consular Reports. *Report for the Year 1896 on the Trade of Vera Cruz.* Annual Series No. 1870. London: Her Majesty's Printing Office, 1897.

Great Britain. Diplomatic and Consular Reports. *Report for the Years 1898, 1899 and part of 1900 on the Trade ana Commerce of Vera Cruz.* Annual Series No. 2539. London: Her Majesty's Printing Office, 1900.

Great Britain. Diplomatic and Consular Reports. *Report for the Year 1899 on the Trade and Commerce of Mexico.* Annual Series No. 2546. London: Her Majesty's Printing Office, 1900.

Great Britain. Diplomatic and Consular Reports. *Report for the Year 1900 on the Trade of Mexico.* Annual Series No. 2693. London: Her Majesty's Printing Office, 1901.

Great Britain. Diplomatic and Consular Reports. *Report for the Year 1902 on the Trade and Commerce of Mexico.* Annual Series No. 2951. London: His Majesty's Printing Office, 1903.

Great Britain. Diplomatic and Consular Reports. *Report for the Year 1902 on the Trade and Commerce of Vera Cruz.* Annual Series No. 3039. London: His Majesty's Printing Office, 1903.

Great Britain. Diplomatic and Consular Reports. *Report for the Year 1902 on the Trade of Mexico.* Annual Series No. 3112. London: His Majesty's Printing Office, 1904.

Great Britain. Diplomatic and Consular Reports. *Report for the Year 1903 on the Trade and Commerce of the Consular District of Vera Cruz.* Annual Series No. 3262. London: His Majesty's Printing Office, 1904.

Great Britain. Diplomatic and Consular Reports. *Report for 1903 on the Consular District of Mexico.* Annual Series No. 3285. London: His Majesty's Printing Office, 1904.

Great Britain. Diplomatic and Consular Reports. *Report for the Year 1903 on the Trade of Mexico.* Annual Series No. 3332. London: His Majesty's Printing Office, 1905.

Great Britain. Diplomatic and Consular Reports. *Report for the Year 1904 on the Trade and Commerce of the Consular District of Mexico.* Annual Series No. 3429. London: His Majesty's Printing Office, 1905.

Great Britain. Diplomatic and Consular Reports. *Report for the Year 1906 on the Trade and Commerce of Mexico.* Annual Series No. 3888. London: His Majesty's Printing Office, 1907.

Great Britain. Diplomatic and Consular Reports. *Report for the Year 1907 on the Trade and Commerce of the Consular District of Tampico.* Annual Series No. 4051. London: His Majesty's Printing Office, 1908.

Great Britain. Diplomatic and Consular Reports. *Report for the Year 1907 on the Trade and Commerce of the Consular District of Vera Cruz.* Annual Series No. 4021. London: His Majesty's Printing Office, 1908.

Great Britain. Diplomatic and Consular Reports. *Report for the Year 1908 on the Trade and Commerce of the Consular District of Tampico.* Annual Series No. 4215. London: His Majesty's Printing Office, 1909.

Great Britain. Diplomatic and Consular Reports. *Report for the Year 1910 on the Trade of Mexico.* Annual Series No. 4742. London: His Majesty's Printing Office, 1911.

Great Britain. Diplomatic and Consular Reports. *Report for the Year 1911 on the Trade of Mexico.* Annual Series No. 4976. London: His Majesty's Printing Office, 1912.

Great Britain. Diplomatic and Consular Reports. *Report on Investments for British Capital in Mexico.* Commercial No. 18. London: Her Majesty's Printing Office, 1886.

Great Britain. Diplomatic and Consular Reports. *Report on Railway Concessions in Mexico.* Miscellaneous Series No. 170. London: Her Majesty's Printing Office, 1890.

Great Britain. Diplomatic and Consular Reports. *Report on the British Trade to Mexico, 1897.* Miscellaneous Series No. 486. London: Her Majesty's Printing Office, 1898.

Great Britain. Diplomatic and Consular Reports. *Report on the Commerce of Vera Cruz and the Future of that Port.* Miscellaneous Series No. 65. London: Her Majesty's Printing Office, 1887.

Great Britain. Diplomatic and Consular Reports. *Report on the Cultivation of Coffee in Mexico.* Miscellaneous Series No. 393. London: Her Majesty's Printing Office, 1896.

Great Britain. Diplomatic and Consular Reports. *Report on the Customs Tariff and Railway Rates as Affecting the Import Trade of the State of Vera Cruz, Mexico.* Miscellaneous Series No. 13. London: Her Majesty's Printing Office, 1886.

Great Britain. Diplomatic and Consular Reports. *Report on the Effect of the Depreciation of Silver on Mexico.* London: Her Majesty's Printing Office, 1893.

Great Britain. Diplomatic and Consular Reports. *Report on the Federal District of Mexico.* Miscellaneous Series No. 517. London: Her Majesty's Printing Office, 1899.

Great Britain. Diplomatic and Consular Reports. *Report on the Mexican Budget for the Fiscal Year 1908-09.* Annual Series No. 3958. London: His Majesty's Printing Office, 1908.

Great Britain. Diplomatic and Consular Reports. *Report on the Mexican Isthmus (Tehuantepec) Railway.* Miscellaneous Series No. 658. London: His Majesty's Printing Office, 1908.

Great Britain. Diplomatic and Consular Reports. *Report on the Mexican Tariff, 1890.* Annual Series No. 786. London: Her Majesty's Printing Office, 1890.

Great Britain. Diplomatic and Consular Reports. *Report on the Mines and Minerals of the State of Vera Cruz, 1887.* Miscellaneous Series No. 66. London: Her Majesty's Printing Office, 1887.

Great Britain. Diplomatic and Consular Reports. *Report on the Railroad and Customs Duties at Vera Cruz, 1886.* Miscellaneous Series No. 13. London: Her Majesty's Printing Office, 1887.

Great Britain. Diplomatic and Consular Reports. *Report on the Railways of Mexico.* Miscellaneous Series No. 116. London: Her Majesty's Printing Office, 1899.

Great Britain. Diplomatic and Consular Reports. *Report on the Trade and Agriculture of Sonora.* Annual Series No. 2464. London: Her Majesty's Printing Office, 1900.

Great Britain. Diplomatic and Consular Reports. *Report on the Trade of Vera Cruz, 1903.* Annual Series No. 3262. London: His Majesty's Printing Office, 1904.

Great Britain. Foreign Office. *Correspondence Respecting the Question of Diplomatic and Consular Assistance to British Trade Abroad.* Commercial No. 16. London: Her Majesty's Printing Office, 1886.

Great Britain. Foreign Office. *Report on British Trade with Mexico to 1885.* London: Her Majesty's Printing Office, 1886.

Great Britain. *Hansard's Parliamentary Debates* (3rd series), Vols. CXCV-CCXCIII.

Great Britain. *House of Commons Sessional Papers.* Vol. LXXIII (Accounts and Papers, Vol. II). Cmd. 3989. 1867-68.

Great Britain. Public Record Office. Customs and Excise Documents. *Annual Statement of the Trade of the United Kingdom with Foreign Countries and British Possessions for the Year 1890.* London, 1890.

Great Britain. *State Papers.* Vols. LXXIX, LXXV. London, 1885, 1889.

México. Ministerio de Comunicaciones y Obras Públicas. *Contrato celebrado entre Francisco Z. Mena en representación del ejecutivo de la unión y el Señor John B. Body, represente de S. Pearson and Son, Limited.* México: Imprenta, Lit. Y Encuadernación De I. Paz, 1902.

México. Ministerio de Fomento, Colonización, Industria, y Comercio. *Decretos de concesión.* México, 1877.

México. Ministerio de Fomento, Colonización, Industria, y Comercio. *Modificaciones hechas en 11 de noviembre de 1868 al decreto de 27 de 1867.* México, 1868.

México. Secretaría de Comunicaciones y Obras Públicas. *Ferrocarril nacional de Tehuantepec.* México, 1908.

México. Secretaría de Comunicaciones y Obras Públicas. *Memoria por el secretario de estado y del despacho de comunicaciones y obras públicas Leandro Fernández corresponde al período transcurrido del 1° de julio de 1902 a 30 de junio 1903.* México, 1904.

México. Secretaría de Fomento. *Exposición que hace el secretario de fomento sobre la colonización de la Baja California.* México, 1887.

México. Secretaría de Hacienda. *Exposición de la secretaría de hacienda de los estados unidos mexicanos, de 15 de enero de 1879 sobre la condición actual de México.* México, 1879.

México. Secretaría de Hacienda. *Memoria correspondiente al ejército fiscal de 1885 a 1886 presentada al congreso de la unión por el ministro Lic. Manual Dublán.* México, 1887.

México. Secretaría de Hacienda. *Memoria correspondiente al sexagésimo octavo año económico de 1° de julio de 1893 presentada por el secretario de hacienda al congreso de la unión.* México, 1894.

México. Secretaría de Relaciones Exteriores. *Correspondencia diplomática cambiada entre el gobierno de la república y el de su majestad britanica con relación del territoria llamado de Belice, 1872-1878.* México, n. d.

México. Secretaría de Relaciones Exteriores. *Correspondencia diplomática cambiada entre el gobierno de los estados unidos mexicanos y los de varias potencias extranjeras desde el 30 de junio de 1881 a 30 de junio de 1886.* Vols. IV-VI. México, 1887.

México. Secretaría de Relaciones Exteriores. *Memoria que en cumplimiento del precepto constitucional presenta al duodécimo congreso de la unión El C. Ignacio Mariscal.* México, 1885.
United States. *Consular Reports.* Vol. XXXI. Washington, 1889.

Articles and Periodicals

Anglo-American and Mexican Mining Guide. Vols. VIII-XIII. Mexico City, 1905-11.
Anglo-Colorado and Mexican Milling Guide. Vols. VIII, XIII. Denver, 1905, 1910.
"Cyanide Practice at Esperanza," *Mining Magazine,* III (July-December, 1910), 298.
Economist. Vols. XXXVIII-LXIX. London, 1880-1909.
Financier. London, 1907.
Halse, Edward. "Deep Mining in Mexico," *Mining Journal,* LXV (July 6, 1895), 694.
————. "Gold Mining in Mexico," *Mining Journal,* LXVIII (December 10, 1898), 1394.
Hardy, Osgood. "Ulysses S. Grant, President of the Mexican Southern Railway," *Pacific Historical Review,* XXIV (May, 1955), 111-21.
Herapath's Railway and Commercial Journal. Vols. XXX-XLVII. London, 1876-1885.
Hindry, W. E. "Esperanza Mine, El Oro Mexico," *Mining Magazine,* I (September-October, 1909), 131.
India Rubber World. Vols. XXVIII-XLII. New York, 1908-10.
Investor's Monthly Manual. Vol. XIII. London, 1883.
Mexican Financial Review (Mexico City). Mexico, 1890.
Mexican Financier. Vols. VI-XXIX. Mexico City, 1885-97.
Mexican Mining Journal. Vol. VI. Mexico, 1908.
Mining Investor. Vols. I-II. Colorado Springs, 1909-10.
Mining Journal. Vols. XLVI-LXXXIX. London, 1880-1910.
Mining Magazine. Vols. I-III. London, 1909-10.
Mining Record. Vol. I. New York, 1889-90.
Mining World and Engineering Record. Vols. XXVI-LXXX. London, 1884-1911.
Modern Mexico. Vols. XV-XX. Mexico City. 1902-6.
Oil. Philadelphia, 1911.
Pletcher, David. "The Building of the Mexican Railway," *Hispanic American Historical Review,* XXX (February, 1950), 26-62.
————. "The Development of Railroads in Sonora," *Inter-American Economic Affairs,* I (March, 1948), 3-44.
————. "The Fall of Silver in Mexico, 1870-1910, and Its Effects on

American Investments," *The Journal of Economic History,* XVIII (March, 1958), 33-55.
Prichard, W. A. "Looking for Mines in Mexico," *Mining Magazine,* I (November, 1909), 205.
Railroad Gazette. Chicago, 1885.
Railway Times. Vol. XLVIII. London, 1885.
Rippy, J. Fred. "English Investments in Mexico: A Study of Bonanzas and Heartbreaks," *Journal of Business,* XXVI (October, 1952), 228-42.
———. "Latin America and the British Investment 'Boom' of the 1820's," *Journal of Modern History,* XIX (March, 1947), 122-29.
Skertchly, Sydney A. R. "Oil in Mexico," *Mining Magazine,* III (July-December, 1910), 283.
South American Journal. Vols. XX-LXXII. London, 1883-1911.
Tischendorf, Alfred. "British Investments in Colorado Mines," *The Colorado Magazine,* XXX (October, 1953), 241-46.
———. "British Investments in Latin-American and African Mines: A Study in Contrasts," *Inter-American Economic Affairs,* VI (Spring, 1953), 29-38.
———. "North Carolina and the British Investor, 1880-1910," *North Carolina Historical Review,* XXXII (October, 1955), 512-18.
———. "The Anglo-Mexican Claims Commission, 1884-1895," *Hispanic American Historical Review,* XXXVII (November, 1957), 471-79.

Reports

Corporation of Foreign Bondholders. *Annual Reports.* London, 1877-1911.
Mexican Bondholders' Committee. *Report of March 3, 1876.* London, 1876.
Mexican North-Western Railway Company. *First Annual Report for the Year Ending December 31, 1910.* No place of publication.
Mexican Railway Company. *Half-Year Reports of the Directors.* London, 1880-1911.
Mexican Railway Company. *A Review of the Mexican Railway, 1879-1884.* London, 1885.

Unpublished Material

Company Record Office. Bush House, London. File of British Limited Companies.

Great Britain. Public Record Office, London. Foreign Archives Series 50. Despatches from British Ministers in Mexico. Vols. 434-528, 1869-1902.

Great Britain. Public Record Office, London. Foreign Archives Series 203. Mexico, Consular Despatches. Vols. 105-138, 1886-99.

Great Britain. Public Record Office, London. Foreign Archives Series 204. Mexico, Consular Despatches. Vols. 138, 207, 217, 1889, 1892.

Great Britain. Public Record Office, London. Foreign Archives Series 205. Vol. 42, 1897.

United States. National Archives, Washington. Consular Despatches, Mexico. Mazatlán, Vol. 5, 1883-98.

United States. National Archives, Washington. Consular Despatches, Mexico. Matamoras, Vol. 23, 1889.

United States. National Archives, Washington. Diplomatic Despatches, Mexico. Vols. 158-59, 1902.

Newspapers

El Época. 1877.
Las Novedades. 1886.
La Patria. 1881.
La República. 1885.
Mexican Herald. 1885-1902.
Pall Mall Gazette. 1883.
The Times (London). 1876-1911.
Two Republics. 1876-1910.

Other Sources

The Stock Exchange Library. London. Prospectuses for British Limited Companies. 1876-1910.

Index

Acapulco to Veracruz railroad, 46
Admiralty. *See* Navy, British
Adit system at Palmarejo Mining Company, 83. *See also* Mining, Mexican
Advertisements. *See* Trade, Mexican
Agua Caliente, 105
Almada and Tirito Silver Mining Company: organization of, 24; location of, map 1, 26; control of shares in, 1876, 28; distance of from railroads, 29; dividend paid by in 1876, 31; closeness of to backruptcy in 1884, 31
Allsopp, A. P., 101-2
Altata, 64
Altata-Culiacán Railway: location of, map 3, 37; on the brink of bankruptcy, 64. *See also* Symon, R. R.
American-Hawaiian Steamship Company, 67. *See also* Tehuantepec Railroad
American Mining Company, 86-87
Anglo-American and Mexican Mining Guide, 75
Anglo-Mexican Electric Company purchases plants in Puebla and Córdoba, 119
Anglo-Mexican Mining Company: brings labor and equipment to camp, 65; dividends of, table 7, 72; history of, 78-81 *passim*; location of, map 4, 79. *See also* Chinese labor; Hopkins, George
Anglo-Mexican Planting and Trading Corporation, 107
Anthony, Charles, 102
Applegarth, Edgar, and the promotion of the Palmarejo Mining Company, 82-83
Aqueducts, plans for in Mexico, 18

Archbold, Ralph, 84-85
Arteaga, Francisco, and railroad from Irolo to Puebla, 46
Association of Chambers of Commerce. *See* Chambers of Commerce
Australia, 87

Baker, Consul Alfred, on Mexican tariff, 133, 134
Banco Nacional de México. *See* National Bank of Mexico
Bandits and the Pinos Altos Mining Company, 81-82
Bank of England, 31
Banks: survey of British interests in Mexican, 23 n.; increase of in Mexico, 1876-1910, 139; British and non-British operating in Mexico, 140; amount of British investment in, 140-41
Bankers' Investment Trust Corporation, 101
Baring Brothers, 31, 87; summary of activities of in British enterprises, 142
Baring, Francis, 88
Barriga, Manuel, and the Mexican Information Bureau, 76-77
Barrón, William: and the Mexican Railway Company, 34; and the concession to supply Mexico City with gas and electric lights, 112
Bayliss, Rawlinson: and management of El Oro Mining and Railway Company, 89; and a philosophy of mining, 89; cited as successful manager, 92; as director of three British companies, 142
Berlin, 109, 115

B. F. Stiebel and Company, 134
Bird, Robert, 118, 119; position of in
British companies summarized, 142
Birmingham, England, 75
Board of Trade, 133, 134
Body, John B., 118, 124; holds director-
ships in ten companies, 142; has Díaz as
guest in home, 146
Bonds, Mexican, total invested by Britons
in, 140. *See also* Bondholders; English
Convention of 1851; London bond-
holders
Bondholders: settlement with prerequisite
to British investment, 10, 12; relation
of settlement with to British invest-
ment after 1884, 144. *See also* Bonds;
English Convention of 1851; London
bondholders
Boston, 114
Braniff, Thomas, 112
Brazil, 27, 47
Brill, J. C., 116
British Golf Club, 71
British Honduras: and the renewal of
Anglo-Mexican diplomatic relations,
15; instructions to Mexican envoy con-
cerning, 16
Browne, James T., and the promotion of
Guaymas, Sonora mines, 25
Bumerango and Anexas Mining Com-
pany, 90

C. T. Bowring Company, 123
California (Mexico) Land Company: loca-
tion of, map 6, 98; dividends paid by,
100 n.
Campbell, Albert J.: acquires concession
to build Mexican Southern, 49; and
hopes for future of line, 50
Campeche, 123
Canada, 90; engineer from, and the Mexico City tram lines, 116; company formed
under laws of in Monterrey, 119, 127;
Mexican Light and Power Company
organized under laws of, 149
Canals, 18
Capital invested by British companies in
Mexico, 1876-1910, 140-41, 148-74
Carden, Lionel: prepares report on Mexican commerce, 15; delivers note to
Mexican foreign minister, 15; appointed
consul in Mexico City, 74; uses influence, 74; discusses Díaz land policies,
99; gives advice to Britons going to
Mexico, 102; on consular candidates,
102; and rubber enterprise, 108; warns
of increasing United States trade with
Mexico, 129-30; on trade with Mexico,

133-34; and quality of British diplo-
mats, 135
Casasús, Joaquín, 116
Cassell, Sir Edward, 65
Castilloas tree. *See* Rubber
Catalogues issued by British companies
in Mexico, 136
Cattle. *See* Ranching
Caustic soda. *See* Trade, Mexican
Central Europeans, 100
Chambers of Commerce: memorial from
Association of to Foreign Office, 9; and
Mexican trade, 14, 128; on lack of
diplomatic relations, 17
Chamier, Adrian, 121, 122
Chancery Court, 93
Chemical products. *See* Trade, Mexican
Chiapas, 97, 100, 101, 105, 106, 107, 123,
146
Chiapas Mining Company: dividend rec-
ord of, table 7, 72; location of, map 4, 79
Chicago, 81, 119
Chihuahua, 88, 97, 102; promotion of
state of in *Mining Journal*, 27
Chile, 108
Chinaware. *See* Trade, Mexican
Chinese labor: at Anglo-Mexican Mining
Company, 65; contract for with Hong
Kong firm, 80; arrival of in Mexico, 80-
81. *See also* Anglo-Mexican Mining
Company; Hopkins, George
Chinipas River, 63, 83
Cholula, 41
Christian Murietta and Company, 47
Científicos, 61, 97
Cigars produced by British companies, 111
Córdoba, 119, 143
Ciudad Juárez, 35, 65
Claims of British citizens against Mexico:
nature of in 1876, 16; and the renewal
of diplomatic relations, 16; foreign of-
fice and the abrogation of, 18; new
arrangements to be made regarding, 18;
new arrangements for settling, 18-19.
See also Complaints of mistreatment by
Britons against Mexico
Clarendon, Lord, 8
Coahuila, 97, 102
Coahuila and Zacatecas Railroad, 63;
location of, map 3, 37
Coatzacoalcos, 66, 67, 139
Coffee, 108; British interests in, 96 n.
See also Farming
Colchester, England, 112
Colonization: of Britons in Mexico, 97;
location of British ventures in Mexico,
map 6, 98; British interest in acquiring
land for, 99; attempts by British sum-

marized, 110. *See also* Emigration; Farming; Immigrants; Ranching
Colorado, 27
Compañía de Ferrocarriles del Distrito Federal de México, 115
Company Registration Office, London, 21, 120
Complaints of mistreatment by Britons in Mexico, 1876-1880, 10-11. *See also* Claims of British citizens against Mexico; Diplomatic intervention
Consolidated National Debt, 101
Consuls, quality of British in Mexico, 135
Convention bondholders. *See* English Convention of 1851
Cotton industry in Mexico, 96, 108, 120, 127 n.
Cottons. *See* Trade, Mexican
Cowdray, Lord, 146. *See also* Pearson, Weetman Dickinson
Crawley, George, 34
Cuban Line, contract with Tehuantepec Railroad, 67. *See also* Tehuantepec Railroad
Culiacán, 65, 80, 81
Cusihuiriachic, Chihuahua, 81
Cyanide process: at Palmarejo mine, 83; at Esperanza, 91. *See also* Mining, Mexican

Daily Express, 75
Dam: at junction of Necaxa and Tenango rivers, 114; repairs on after rain, 115
Derby, Earl of, 19; and British investors on subject of diplomatic break, 11; sends message to Mexico City, 12
Dering, Sir Henry, 113
Díaz, Mrs. Porfirio, 20
Díaz, Porfirio, 21, 53, 70, 71, 81, 87, 88, 89, 108, 117, 120, 121, 127, 130, 134; enters Mexico City, 3; becomes President, 8; victory of and hope for renewal of diplomatic relations, 9; and British investment as counterpoise to northern imperialism, 15; asked to construct breakwater at Veracruz, 43; sees danger to Veracruz trade position, 44; promises attack on yellow fever, 44; and Interoceanic Railroad, 46; as shareholder in Interoceanic Railroad, 46; at Mexican Southern inauguration ceremonies, 50, 52; disapproves of rate fixing by railroads, 53-54; and improvement of Veracruz, 58-60; at inauguration of Veracruz port works, 60; and National Railways of Mexico, 61; and rebuilding of Tehuantepec Railroad and isthmus cities, 66; and opening of Tehuantepec

Railroad, 67; establishes Mexican Information Bureau, 76; sends troops to Pinos Altos, 82; land policies of, 97, 99; letter to from Governor of Lower California, 103; and Lower California annexation plot, 104; and rubber enterprise, 105; as shareholder in Mexican Eagle Oil Company, 124; success of policies of, 139; position of in major British railroad companies, 142; and last days in Mexico, 146
Díaz Revolution, 8, 108, 109, 118
Díaz' son, 116
Dilke, Sir Charles, 13
Diplomatic intervention: on behalf of Britons in Mexico by foreign office, 8-9; increase in requests for, 10-11; request for by Mexican Railway refused by foreign office, 47; and cases involving requests from British mining interests in Mexico after 1884, 73-74; by British diplomats making private visits to Mexican leaders, 74; on behalf of public utility, factory and petroleum companies, 125; summary of by British foreign office and diplomats, 143-44. *See also* Foreign Office; Protection of British subjects
Diplomatic relations, Anglo-Mexican: first attempt to renew, 9; requests for renewal of, 11; signing of Preliminary Agreement to renew, 19; renewal of and relation to Mexico City gas and electric light system, 112; lack of and the decline of British trading pre-eminence in Mexico, 132; effect of renewal of on drawing capital into Mexican enterprise, 143-44
Directors, summary of in active British companies in Mexico, 142-43
Directorships, interlocking: in public utility, factory, and petroleum enterprises, 117-20 *passim,* 126-27; summary of in British companies, 142-43
Dividend record: of United Mexican Mining Company, 30; of Almada and Tirito Silver Mining Company, 31; of Mexican Railway Company, 35, 48; of Interoceanic Railroad, 59; lack of by Tehuantepec Railroad, 68; of Mexican Southern, 70; of fifteen mining companies, 72; of two real estate and rubber companies, 97; of California (Mexico) Land Company, 100 n.; of Guayule Rubber Company, 109; of utility, factory, and petroleum companies, summarized, 125; of all British companies in Mexico, summarized, 144-45
Doheny, Edward, 125

Dolores (mining company): dividend record of, table 7, 72; location of, map 4, 79

Dos Bocas: oil found at, 124; fire at, 124

Drought, J. A., implicated in plot to annex Lower California to U. S., 103-4

Dublán, Manuel, 46

Dunlop-Aldham Convention, 5, 6. *See also* English Convention of 1859; London bondholders

Durango, 97

Durango Estates, location of, map 6, 98

Earthenware. *See* Tariff, Mexican

Ebano, 125

Economic crisis of 1890, 102

Economic crisis of 1893, 102

Electric lights: at Palmarejo Company, 84; in Mexico City, 112-14; W. D. Pearson contracts to install in Veracruz, 118. *See also* Electricity

Electricity: installation of at El Oro, 89; for kitchen stoves, 111; lines from Necaxa to Mexico City and El Oro, 115; rates set by British companies, 115; to Orizaba factory, 119; amount of available in Mexico about 1941, 127

El Época: on renewal of Anglo-Mexican relations, 8

El Ferrocarrilero: on passenger travel on Mexican Southern, 51; criticizes tramway facilities in Mexico City, 116-17

El Oro Mining and Railway Company, 95; Golf Club at, 71; dividend record of, table 7, 72; location of, map 4, 79; history of, 86-90; detailed map of, 87; electrical power to, 115

El Paso, 35, 52

El Portzuelo Light and Power Company, 119

Emigration, foreign office discourages British to Mexico, 102. *See also* Colonization; Immigrants

England, 50, 88, 124

English Convention of 1851: history of, 4-6 *passim*; necessity to recognize validity of, 11-12; foreign office views on, 14; and decision of Law Officers of the Crown, 17; and new arrangements with Mexican government, 19; settlement of, 20 n. *See also* Bondholders; London Bondholders

Ensenada, 104; plans for hotel at, 100; mail service from San Quintin to, 102; mining at, 106; hotel at, 106; letter from consul at, 136-37

Erlanger, Baron Emile, 77

Errazu, Luis, 122

Escandón, Antonio: transfers railroad concession to Englishmen, 31; holds heavy interests in Mexican Railway Company, 34. *See also* Mexican Railway Company

Escandón, Guillermo, 120, 124

Esperanza, Limited, 95; dividend record of, table 7, 72; location of, map 4, 79; history of, 90-91

Europe, 38, 123

Exploration Company, 87. *See also* El Oro Mining and Railway Company

Factories, 110; salt producing, 111, 122; burlap sack, 119; history of British activity in development of in Mexico, 120-22; summary of British activity in Mexican, 125-27 *passim*; and Díaz policies, 139; total investment by British in Mexican, 140-41, 173-74

Fall in the price of silver: problem of the, 29-31; 1876-1903, 30; and the Mexican Railway, 35, 36, 38, 39, 41; and relation to Mexican Railway receipts, 1884-92, 45; Mexican Southern takes advantage of, 50; and effect on dividends of Mexican Southern, 51; and the meeting of the major Mexican railroad companies, 53; and relation to investment in Mexican land, 99; and British factory, petroleum, and public utility enterprise, 126; and Anglo-Mexican trade, 132, 138; effects of summarized, 144. *See also* Silver; Treatment of silver ore in Mexico

Far East, 108

Farming: British interest in acquiring land for in Mexico, 99; summary of British activities in, 110; list of British companies engaged in Mexican, 165-67. *See also* Coffee; Colonization; Cotton industry in Mexico; Immigrants; Ranching; Rice; Sugar cane; Tobacco

Federal district, 102, 117. *See also* Mexico City

Fernández, José: gives views on renewal of diplomatic relations, 17; signs Preliminary Agreement renewing diplomatic relations, 19

Filibuster raid against Lower California, 103

Financier, 76

Fish, Hamilton, 7. *See also* Seward, William H.

Fitzmaurice, Lord Edmund: and question of taking initiative in renewing relations, 15; on British claims and the renewal of relations, 17; on renewal and

trade, 17; and Pauncefote present renewal plan to Law Officers, 18; and position of U. S. in Mexican trade, 129
Foreign Office: and London bondholders, 6; and Mexican Bondholders' Committee, 7; expresses willingness to renew relations, 8; and complaints of Britons in Mexico, 9, 10; believes Mexico wishes to offset United States influence, 12; and possibility of more direct contact with Mexican government, 12-13; opinion of men in on diplomatic stalemate, 13-14; and claims of London and Convention bondholders, 14; letter to from Chambers of Commerce, 14; position of on claims of British citizens against Mexico, 16-17; expects settlement of claims after renewal of relations, 20; and George Hume's claims, 64; and W. D. Pearson and the Tehuantepec Railroad, 66-67; gives information on Mexican mining, 74; El Oro Company requests aid from, 89; and protection of British mining interests, 94; receives letters from investors, 99; discourages British emigration to Mexico, 102; discourages investment in Sonoran companies, 106; and prospective rubber investments, 107; and assistance requested from utility, factory, and petroleum enterprises, 126; receives letters on trade opportunities in Mexico, 128; receives letter from Stiebel, Kaufman, and Company, 134; and complaints about British consuls, 135; summary of position taken by in disputes involving Britons in Mexico, 143-44. *See also* Diplomatic intervention
France, 88; renews diplomatic relations with Mexico, 12; Mexican tariff on goods from, 133

Galvanized iron sheets. *See* Trade, Mexican
Geddes, Robert: manager of London Bank of Mexico and South America, 12; takes letter from Lord Derby to Mexico City, 12
Germany: ambassador from to Mexico and renewal of Anglo-Mexican diplomatic relations, 12; ambassador from in Paris arranges Anglo-Mexican talks, 13; capitalists from control United Mexican Mining Company, 77; scientists from and the guayule rubber shrub, 109; lighting concession in Mexico City and a firm from, 113; investments in tramways by citizens of, 115; technicians in Monterrey from, 119, 127; per cent of all goods by value sent to Mexico from, 1876, 128; and value of her trade with Mexico, 1900 and 1910, 130; nature of goods to Mexico from, 130; Mexican tariff on goods from, 133; and control of distributing houses in Mexico, 137
Gibbs, Alban, 113
Gibbs, Antony, 34, 112, 142
Gibbs, George, 34, 80
Gibbs, H. H., 112
Glennie, Frederick, 3
Gold: mined at El Oro, 88; value of extracted at Esperanza, 91; mined by most prosperous British companies, 92, 94; lures foreigners to Lower California, 100; gives out in Lower California, 100; possibility of finding on rubber estates, 108
Gold Standard: adopted by Mexico, 1905, 61. *See also* Limantour, José Y.
González, President Manuel, 39; shareholder in Interoceanic Railroad, 47; prominent shareholder in major British railroad companies, 142
Gould, Jay, 49
Governor of Veracruz, 120
Grand Central Mining Company: dividends paid by, table 7, 72; location of, 78, map 4, 79
Grant, Alexander, 10
Grant, Ulysses S., and the Mexican Southern, 49
Granville, Lord, and the Anglo-Mexican diplomatic break, 15-16
Great Britain: and Mexican recognition of old conventions, 6; and United States trade rivalry, 129, 130; Mexican tariff on goods from, 133; and German trade rivalry, 130, 131; inability of to maintain her share of Mexican trade, analyzed, 131-38. *See also* Trade, Mexican
Guadalajara, 26, 84
Guadalcazar Quicksilver Mines. *See* New Guadalcazar Quicksilver Mines
Guaymas, 24, 25, 105
Guayule Rubber Company, 109. *See also* Rubber
Guerrero (Mexican) Land Syndicate: location of, map 6, 98
Guggenheim family, 90, 91

Hacendados, 145
Halse, Edward, 74
Hammond, John Hays, 90
Harbors, 18
Hardware trade. *See* Trade, Mexican

Harvey, Captain Charles, 85
Hawdon, Frederick: controls various British mining ventures, 85-86; summary of activities of, 142. *See also* Maclachlan, Walter
Hayne, J. C., 112
Hemp and jute sacks. *See* Trade, Mexican
Hertslet, Edward, 14
Hidalgo, 85
Highland Land and Livestock Company, map 6, 98. *See also* Scottish companies
Hockin, George, 24
Honduras. *See* British Honduras
Hong Kong, 80. *See also* Chinese labor; Hopkins, George
Hopkins, George: chairman of Anglo-Mexican Mining Company, 80; signs contract for Chinese labor, 80; mentioned as successful manager, 92. *See also* Anglo-Mexican Mining Company
Hotels. *See* Ensenada
Houghton, George, 121; on board of six Mexican enterprises, 142
Hudson River tunnel, 58
Hüller, Louis, 100, 101
Hume, George, 64, 70
Huntington, Collis P., 107
Huntley, Lord, 11
Hyde, Sir Clarendon, 143
Hydroelectric power. *See* Mexican Light and Power Company; Necaxa

Immigrants: few remain in Lower California after 1889, 100-01; exempt from federal taxes in Mexico, 101; in Chiapas, Sonora, and Lower California, 98, 102. *See also* Colonization; Emigration
Impact of British capital on Mexico, summary of, 145-46
Imperial Mexican Railway. *See* Mexican Railway Company
Imports, Britain's inability to maintain her proportionate share of Mexico's, summary of reasons for, 131-38. *See also* Fall in the price of silver
India Rubber World, 107, 110
Industrial development, 97, 111. *See also* Factories
Influenza at British camps, 85. *See also* smallpox
International Company of Mexico, 100
Interoceanic Railroad, Limited, 45; Díaz announces construction of, 44; early history of, 46-49; location of, map 3, 37; attempt to stop construction of, 47; arranges to carry Mexican Southern freight, 49; leasing of Mexican Southern to, 51; opens from Veracruz to

Mexico City, 52; dividend record of, table 6, 59; chairman of on the fall in price of silver, 57; history of from 1903-10, 58-63 *passim*; merger with National Railways of Mexico, 61-62; absorbs Mexican Eastern, 64
Investment, total British in Mexico, 139, 140-41; compared to United States, 139, 142
Investors, British: urge renewal of diplomatic relations, 11; organize thirteen companies, 1876-1880, 11; meet with Earl of Derby, 11; types of in pre-1885 companies, 27
Irolo, 38, 46
Iron. *See* Trade, Mexican
Issacson, Frederick, 47
Isthmus of Tehuantepec, 64; railroad across, 66; labor problems on, 66-67. *See also* yellow fever
Italy, minister in Mexico and Anglo-Mexican diplomatic relations, 8

Jalapa, 34, 43, 46, 121
Jampa River, 118
Japan, 29
Jefferis, James, 75
Jeffrey, George, 122, 123, 124
Jenkinson, Sir Edward: plans to acquire twenty million acres in Lower California, 99; and formation of Mexican Land and Colonization Company, 99-100; transfer of property to, 101; implicated in plot to annex Lower California, 103. *See also* Mexican Land and Colonization Company
Jenner, George, 99
Jockey Club, Mexico City, 143
Jojutla: location of, map 3, 37; railroad from Mexico City to, 49
Juárez, Benito: and attitude toward powers who recognized Archduke Maximilian, 3; announces Anglo-Mexican diplomatic break, 3; cancels prior agreements with Great Britain, 6; willing to consider new arrangements with British creditors, 7; and view of old treaties and conventions, 8
Juchipila, 84

Kalgoorlie, Australia, 93
Kansas City, 65
Kinnell, Thomas, 120
Kohzevar, Edward, 131

L. and H. Pinto Company, 121
Labor: wages paid at British mines to Mexican, 76; lack of Mexican at Anglo-Mexican mine, 80; use of soldiers at

Pinos Altos as, 82; at Palmarejo mine, 83; at Mesquital mine, 85; shortage of at El Oro, 88; strikes absent at El Oro, 88-89; at Esperanza mine, 91; and problems of absenteeism, 91; aid of Díaz in relations of management and, 92; companies ruined by lack of, 93; at Mano Marques estate, 108; establishment of town and facilities by Mexican Light and Power Company for, 114-15; on Mexican Railway, 50; use of Chinese, 65; on W. D. Pearson construction jobs on isthmus, 67; and its position in British enterprises in Mexico, 146; and the electrification of Mexico City tramways, 116; at salt factory near San Luis Potosí, 122; unskilled at Pánuco, 123

La Compañía del Ferrocarril Interoceánico de Acapulco a Veracruz, 46. *See* Interoceanic Railroad, Limited

Lake Temiahua, 124

Land: policies of Díaz, 97; price of in Mexico, 99; offered to Americans and Europeans in 1886, 100. *See also* Colonization; Farming

Land Company of Chiapas, 106

Laredo, 36, 52, 123

La República, 42, 43

La Paz, 11

La Trinidad, Limited: organizers buy from London promoters, 25; problems of before 1885, 28

Law Officers of Crown, 18

Laws, Mexican: as barrier to Anglo-Mexican trade, 9, 133-34; change of in regard to mining, 74. *See also* Litigation

Leland-Harrison Line, 67. *See also* Tehuantepec Railroad

Lerdo de Tejada, Sebastián, 34

Limantour, José Y., 120; concerned with bimetalism, 60-61; and Gold Standard, 61; and formation of National Railways of Mexico, 61-62

Linen goods. *See* Trade, Mexican

Lipton, Sir Thomas, 107

Litigation by Mexican Land and Colonization Company to obtain title to land, 101. *See also* Laws, Mexican

Liverpool, 131

London, 82, 91, 94, 106, 109, 115, 119, 120, 137

London Bank of Mexico and South America, 12, 21, 118

London Bondholders: early history of, 4-8 *passim*; and foreign office on question of diplomatic relations, 8; continue to press for assistance from foreign office, 1876-1880, 10; and direct negotiations with Mexican government, 10; and possiblity of agreement with Mexican government, 12; negotiate with Mexican government but reach impasse, 14-15, 16 n.; not included in arrangements for renewal of diplomatic relations, 18; arrange settlement with Mexico, 20 n. 62. *See also* Bondholders; English Convention of 1851

London City and Midland Bank, 124

London Evening Standard, 75

Los Bronces, Sonora, 78

Lower California, 97, 99, 100, 102, 146

Lower California Development Company: location of, map 6, 98; organization of, 102; near collapse of, 102; and plot to annex Lower California to United States, 103-04; reselling property to Mexican Land and Development Company, 104

Lyons, Lord: discussions with Mexican minister to Paris on renewal of diplomatic relations, 13-14

MacDonald, John, 118, 119, 121; position of in British enterprises in Mexico summarized, 142, 143

Machew, Dr. Samuel, 118, 119; position of in British enterprises in Mexico summarized, 142, 143

Machinery. *See* Trade, Mexican

Mackenzie, Mann, and Company, 119

Maclachlan, Walter, controls various British mining ventures, 85-86, 142. *See also* Hawdon, Frederick

Madero, Francisco, 84

Manchester, England, 75

Mano Marques Estate, 108

Marcos, 46

Marshall, William, 24

Mariscal, Ignacio, 17, 120; meets with Lionel Carden on Anglo-Mexican diplomatic break, 15; is selected as special envoy to London, 16; receives instructions from Mexican government, 16; appointed Minister to Great Britain, 20; at opening of Mexico Electric Tramways service in Mexico City, 116

Maximilian, Archduke Ferdinand, 3, 6, 13

Mazapil Copper Company: dividend record of, table 7, 72; profits of, 78; location of, map 4, 79

Mazatlán, 80, 136

Mesquital Del Oro Mining Company. *See* Mesquital Mines

Mesquital Mines: dividend record of, table 7, 72; location of, map 4, 79; history of, 84-86

Mexican Bondholders' Committee, 7. *See also* Perry, E. J.

Mexican-British trade relations. *See* Trade, Mexican

Mexican Central Railroad, 38, 42, 43; and the dividend record of the Mexican Railway Company, 34; location of, map 3, 37; cuts rates in 1885, 44; opens branch to Tampico, 52; and the pooling arrangements, 1892-1902, 52-58 *passim*; merges with National Railways of Mexico, 61, 65; survey of activities and problems of, 69

Mexican Eagle Oil Company: registered in Mexico, 124; board of directors of, 124; established as leading oil producer, 125

Mexican Eastern Railroad: location of, map 3, 37; taken over by Interoceanic Railroad, 64

Mexican Electric Works: organized, 113; pays first dividend, 114

Mexican Financier, 42, 77

Mexican Fuel Oil Company, 125

Mexican Gas and Electric Light Company, 112, 113

Mexican General Land Mortgage and Investment Company, location of, map 6, 98

Mexican-German trade relations. *See* Trade, Mexican

Mexican Gold and Silver Recovery, Limited, 90

Mexican Herald, 107, 111

Mexican Information Bureau, 76

Mexican Land and Colonization Company: location of, map 6, 98; organization of, 99-100; appoints Jenkinson as General Manager, 101; history of, 100-106 *passim*; accused of being agent of British government, 102-3; condition of in 1910, 110. *See also* Jenkinson, Sir Edward

Mexican Light and Power Company, 127; sends electrical energy to El Oro and other areas, 89; role of British capital in, 111; history of, 111-20 *passim*; list of important men in, 142. *See also* Pearson, Fred Stark

Mexican Mines Selection Syndicate, 86

Mexican National Land Mortgage and Investment Company; location of, map 6, 98

Mexican National Railroad, 38, 43, 65, 109; and the dividend record of the Mexican Railway Company, 34; location of, map 3, 37; opens from Laredo to Mexico City, 52; and pooling and rate fixing, 1892-1902, 52-58 *passim*; merges

with National Railways of Mexico, 61; summary of position of, 69

Mexican North-Western Railway Company: location of, map 3, 37; registered as Canadian concern, 65

Mexican Pacific Railway, 64

Mexican Railway Company, 21, 22, 52, 80, 112, 121, 144; letter from delegate of to foreign office, 17; route of, map 2, 33, map 3, 37; history of before 1885, 31-41; and dividend record of, 1876-1884, 35; and effect on Mexico before 1885, 40; condition of in 1885, 42; and passenger travel, 43; and argument concerning rates, 43; cuts rates, 44; gross returns of and freight carried on, 44-45; effect of the fall in price of silver on from 1884 to 1892, 45; dividend record of, 1885-1910, 48; dividends of and relation to building of Mexican Southern and Interoceanic lines, 45, 49; and competition, 46; attempts to halt construction of Interoceanic, 47; and pooling and rate fixing, 52-58 *passim*; and the fall in the price of silver, 1902, 57; history of, 1903-10, 58-63 *passim*; summary of activities and problems of, 69-70. *See also* Escandón, Antonio

Mexican Santa Barbara Company, 93

Mexican Southern Railroad, 45, 121; route of, map 3, 37; early history of, 49-52; fiesta to open, 50; dividend record of, 51; effect of the fall in the price of silver on, 51-52; and pooling and rate fixing, 52-58 *passim*; leased to Interoceanic in 1909, 61, 63; summary of activities of, 69-70

Mexican Tramways Company: dividend record of, 117

Mexican-United States trade relations *See* Trade, Mexican

Mexico: aware of need to attract foreign capital, 10; allegedly favoring American dollars, 13; anxious for British investment, 15; defaults on subsidies to railroads, 38, 39, 47; adopts Gold Standard, 52; agricultural products sent from, 145

Mexico City, 47, 48, 52, 54, 71, 78, 82, 84, 110, 111, 118, 137: Díaz enters, 3; British consul appears before judge in, 3; press responds to diplomatic break in 1867, 4; arrival of E. J. Perry in, 1876, 7; arrival of British envoy to restore diplomatic relations, 16; mention of plans for harbors, railroads, canals, aqueducts in, 18; shipment of salt to, 122; railroads from northern border to, 131-32; Jockey Club in, 143

Mexico Electric Tramways operates in Mexico City, 115-17, 121-22

Mexico Mines of El Oro: dividend record of, table 7, 72; location of, map 4, 79

Michoacan Mining and Railroad Company, 63; location of, map 3, 37

Minantitlán, 123, 124

Mining, Mexican: British activity in before 1885, 23-31; technological aspects of, 24, 28 n., 80, 83, 91, 123; British companies in, 71; history of British dividend companies in, 77-91; dividend record of British companies in, table 7, 72; summary of British activity in, 92-95, 140-41; and Díaz' policies, 137; list of British companies in, 1876-1910, 148, 150-64

Mining Journal, 93; containing advertisement for La Trinidad Limited, 25; on Mexican Railway's dividend record, 36; on political stability in Mexico, 73; on the caution exercised by British investors, 92

Mining Magazine: on caution of British investors, 92; tells readers of mining opportunities, 95; on British merchants and Mexican trade, 137-38

Mining World: on Mexican stability in 1885, 73; on Palmarejo Company, 83; on selection of mines by Americans, 92

Modern Mexico, 107

Monterrey, Canadian company in, 119, 127

Monterrey Electric Tramways and Power Company, 119

Moody's Magazine quoted, 89-90

Morgan, J. Pierpont, 101

National Bank of Mexico, 49, 61

National Railways of Mexico: organization of, 61-62

Nationalists, Mexican, 100

Navy, British: anchors off Veracruz in 1889, 5; deserter from, 11; and alleged annexation plot in Lower California, 103; in Parliament disavows interest in San Quintin, 103

Necaxa, 91, 115, 117, 145; location of hydroelectric plant at, 89; serves Esperanza Limited, 90

Necaxa River, 114

New Guadalcazar Quicksilver Mines: dividend record of, table 7, 72; location of, map 4, 79

Newspapers: of Mexico City respond to diplomatic break in 1867, 4; in Mexico fear electric rate increase, 115. *See also* names of individual newspapers

New York City, 25, 54, 67, 90, 105

Niagara Falls, 114

Nonoalco, 112, 113, 114

Norwegians, 100

Nottingham, 134

Number of Britons in Mexico: in 1867-1876, 8-9; in 1890, 102; in Díaz era, 143

Nunn, Vice-consul, 137

Oaxaca, 46, 49, 50, 51, 97, 121, 146

Oil. *See* Petroleum

Oil Fields of Mexico, 123, 124

Organizers of British companies in Mexico, number and nature of analyzed, 142-43

Otway Convention, 1859, approved by British government, 5

Orizaba, 119, 120

Otway, L. C., 5

Oxnam, E. H.: manager of Palmarejo Mining Company, 84; mentioned as successful manager, 92

Ozomacin, Oaxaca, 121

Pachuca, 91, 102, 127

Pachuca, Zacultipan, and Tampico Railway, 64

Pall Mall Gazette on stability in Mexico, 73

Palmarejo, 83

Palmarejo and Mexican Goldfields. *See* Palmarejo Mining Company

Palmarejo Mining Company: lays railroad tracks to Chinipas River, 63; dividend record of, table 7, 72; location of (under Palmarejo and Mexican Goldfields), map 4, 79; history of, 82-84

Paris, 109, 115, 122

Pánuco, 123

Parral, Chihuahua, 63, 85

Passengers: on Mexican Railway, 1877-78, 34; on Tehuantepec Railroad, 66; on Mexico Electric Tramways in Mexico City, 1901-5, 116-17

Pauncefote, Sir Julian, receives appraisal of diplomatic situation, 15

Pavy, Francis, 105, 106, 110

Pearson, town of in Chihuahua, 65

Pearson, town of in Salina Cruz, 65

Pearson, Annie, 120

Pearson, Fred Stark: early career of, 65, 114; as President of Mexican North-Western Railway Company, 65; heads Mexican Light and Power Company, 89; announces electricity rates, 115; heads Mexican Tramways Company, 117; on board of Puebla Tramway Light and Power Company, 119; and activities in Mexico summarized, 142-43. *See also* Mexican Light and Power Company

Pearson, Weetman Dickinson (Lord Cowdray), 106, 110, 127, 146; early career of, 58; and the draining of the valley of Mexico, 58, 60; and work on Veracruz harbor, 60; and opening of Veracruz port works, 60; and the Tehuantepec Railroad, 66-68; and the foreign office and admiralty, 70; and the organization of Esperanza Limited, 90; in rubber enterprises, 105-06; sees collapse of rubber ventures, 108; and electric power development in Mexico, 117-20 *passim*; and his burlap sack factory in Orizaba, 120-21; and petroleum enterprise in Mexico, 123-25; and the effect of the fall in the price of silver on his factory in Orizaba, 126, 127; summary of interests of in British enterprise in Mexico, 142, 146

Perote, 46, 48

Perry, E. J., 7, 10

Peru, 123

Petroleum, 110, 111, 139; survey of British activity in, 122-25; first British consular report on, 122; Peruvian, 122; use of rotary drill to search for, 123; and relations of W. D. Pearson and United States capitalists, 125; summary of British activities in, 125-27 *passim*; and price of silver, 126; total British investments in, 140-41; companies organized by Britons, 168-69

Pierce, Henry Clay, 125

Pinos Altos Company, 78; dividends of, table 7, 72; located on map 4, 79; history of, 81-82

Pinos Altos Bullion Company. *See* Pinos Altos Company

Pinto, Lionel and Herbert, 121; and their tobacco enterprise and the fall in the price of silver, 126

Pletcher, David M., comments on the declining price of silver, 29-30

Pochutla, Oaxaca, 107

Political stability in Mexico, evidence of in British press, 73

Pools and rate fixing and the British railroads in Mexico, 1892-1902, 52-58 *passim*. *See also* names of British railway companies

Potrero gusher, 125

Potts, John, 24, 25

Preliminary Agreement renewing Anglo-Mexican diplomatic relations, 22, 99; signed, 19. *See also* Diplomatic Relations

Price, Robert J., 90, 142

Prietas, Sonora, 64

Problems of British companies, 22; in mining field, 28-31; in railroad ventures, 34, 35, 40, 41, 42-70 *passim*; 78-95 *passim*; in real estate business, 100-101; in rubber, 103-4, 106-9; summarized, 144. *See also* Fall in the price of silver; names of particular British companies

Promotion: techniques used by British companies, 1867-1884, 22, 24-25; in *Mining Journal*, 25; in prospectuses, 27; lack of by British railroad companies, 69; and the sale of Mexican mines, 74-76; in quotation by Cecil Rhodes, 75; by E. W. Toye, 76; by Mexican Information Bureau, 76-77; of mining company by Edgar Applegarth, 82-83; and relation to mining investments in Mexico, 94; of Mexican land in consular reports, 99; of rubber ventures, 107; lack of in petroleum, factory, and utility concerns, 126; and relation to increased British activity after 1884, 144. *See also* Prospectuses

Prospectuses: format of before 1884, 27; issued by North Mexican Silver Mining Company, 27; issued to promote Mexican mine sales, 75; of Mesquital Mines, 85; of Yaqui River Land Company, 105

Protection of British subjects, 103. *See also* Diplomatic intervention

Public Utilities: history of British activity in enterprises in Mexico, 112-20; and Díaz policies, 139; total British investment in, 140-41; companies listed, 170-72

Puebla, 41, 43, 46, 48, 49, 51, 119, 143

Puebla Tramway Light and Power Company, 119

Pure water and sewerage. *See* Public Utilities

Quintera Mining Company: dividend record of, table 7, 72; capital and dividends of, 77; located, map 4, 79

Railway Journal gives stock quotation for Mexican Railway, 37

Railways: opportunities for extension of in Mexico, 18; through agricultural areas, 32; located on map 3, 37; open rate war, 52; and their pooling and rate fixing, 52-58 *passim*; and the adoption of the gold standard by Mexico, 61; miles of in Mexico, 1876-1911, 68; activities of summarized, 68-70; in northwestern Mexico, 100; and W. D. Pearson's petroleum, 125; total British investment in, 140; affect Mexican life, 146; list of British companies organizing, constructing, or buying, 149

See also names of particular British companies; National Railways of Mexico

Ranching by Britons in Mexico, 96, 97, 98, 110, 165-67. *See also* Colonization; Emigration; Farming; Immigrants

Rand, 93

Read, H. Rudston, 49, 50

Real Estate: ventures of Britons in Mexico, 110, 139-41, 165-67. *See also* Colonization; Farming; Ranching

Rendon, Francisco, 121

Revolution. *See* Díaz Revolution

Rhodes, Cecil, quoted, 75

Rice. *See* Farming

Rippy, J. Fred, 143

River Plate Trust Company, 101

Romero, Matías: on effect of Mexican Railway on Mexico, 40; and appraisal of rubber enterprise, 107

Rothschild family, 87, 142

Rothschild, Lord Nathan, 88

Rubber, 111; history of British companies organized to produce, 105-09; and investors in the United States, 106; production by the *castilloas* tree, 106-7; Romero's opinion on opportunities in, 107; experiments on guayule shrub by Germans, 109; list of British companies involved in, 165-67. *See also* Guayule Rubber Company

Rubio, Romero, 19; holds shares in Interoceanic Railway, 47; in Oaxaca for opening of Mexican Southern, 50; position of in major railroad companies, 142

Russell, Lord, 6

Sahlberg, August, 90

St. Andres, 121

St. John, Sir Spenser: appointed special envoy, 16; arrives in Mexico to discuss diplomatic relations, 16; confers with Fernández, 16-17; and Preliminary Agreement renewing Anglo-Mexican relations, 18-19; hopes of for Anglo-Mexican accord, 19; appointed Minister to Mexico, 19; announces party for Mrs. Díaz, 20; plans to increase economic ties, 21; refuses to halt construction of Interoceanic Railroad, 47; and problems of British companies, 73, 74; and murder of Captain Harvey, 85; and plot to annex Lower California, 104; and United States-British rivalry, 129; on inability of Britain to maintain proportionate share of Mexico's trade, 131; quoted, 136

Salina Cruz, 65, 67

Salinas of Mexico: salt produced by, 121-22

Salisbury, Lord, 104

Salt. *See* Salinas of Mexico

Saltillo, Coahuila, 78, 109

San Angel, 116

San Carlos, 121

Sánchez, Delfín, 142; completes line from Mexico City to Irolo, 46; and financing of Interoceanic line, 46; holds shares in Interoceanic Railroad, 47; hires laborers and contractors, 47

San Cristóbal, Veracruz, 123

San Diego, 102

San Francisco, 80

San Juan Bautista, Chiapas, 107

San Lazaro, 112, 113

San Luis Potosí, 78, 86, 97, 109, 122

San Quintin, 101, 102, 103

Santa Barbara, 85

Santa Gertrudis Jute Mill Company, 120-21; and fall in the price of silver, 126

São Paulo, Brazil, 114

Scott, Captain Buchanan, 105

Scottish companies in Mexico, 141. *See also* Highland Land and Livestock Company

Scott, Read, Campbell & Company, 48-49

Seward, William H., 7. *See also* Fish, Hamilton

Siemens and Halske, 113

Silk manufactures. *See* Trade, Mexican

Sillem, Augustus, 34; and concession to supply Mexico City with gas and electric lights, 112

Silver: production of, 1851-61, 1881-90, 29. *See also* Fall in the price of silver; Treatment of silver ore in Mexico

Silver Queen United: dividend record of, table 7, 72; location of, map 4, 79

Sinaloa, 65, 80, 88

Sisson, George, 100; abandons Mexican land project, 101

Smallpox, 85. *See also* Influenza

Sonora, 28, 29, 80, 88, 97, 100, 102, 105, 106, 146

Sonora Railroad, 64; completed to Almada mine, 29; location of, map 3, 37; and the Yaqui River Land and Development Company, 105

South Africa, 88

South America, 87

South American and Mexican Company, 82

South American Journal: quoted on the renewal of diplomatic relations, 19; on the price of silver and the Mexican Southern, 51-52; on the price of silver and the Mexican Railway, 57

Spain, 134
Stamping equipment at Esperanza, 91.
    See also Mining, Mexican
Standard Oil Company, 125
Stanford, Vice-consul, 119
Stanhope, Chandos, 121; and the Te-
    huantepec Railroad, 66; and opening of
    tramway services in Mexico City, 116
Stanley, Lord, 4; announces diplomatic
    break with Mexico, 3; declares Britain
    not responsible, 7
State Department, United States, 107
Steamboats, 67
Stevens, Simon, 11
Stilwell, Arthur E., 65
Stock Exchange, 36
Straits of Magellan, 67
Streetcars. *See* Public Utilities
Strikes. *See* Labor
Subsidy: promised by Mexican govern-
    ment to Mexican Railway, 31-32; failure
    of Mexican government to pay to
    Mexican Railway, 34, 38; failure of
    Mexican government to pay to Mexican
    Southern, 51
Sugar Cane. *See* Farming
Sullivan and Hampson Contractors Com-
    pany, 49
Sunday Sun presents appraisal of Mexico,
    75
Switzerland, 41
Symon, Robert R.: and railways in west-
    ern Mexico, 64-65; mentioned as leading
    railroad promoter, 142. *See also* Altata-
    Culiacán Railway

Tabasco, 123
Tampico, 5, 52, 54, 55, 123, 139
Tapachula, Chiapas, 108
Tariff, Mexican: and failure of Britain to
    maintain proportionate share of Mexi-
    co's import trade, 132-33; high on
    cottons, linens, woolens, earthenware,
    iron, and steel, 133; on British, United
    States, French, and German imports,
    133
Tehuantepec Railroad, 123; letter from
    investor in to foreign office, 11; com-
    pleted in 1894 from Salina Cruz to
    Coatzacoalcos, 66; history of to 1910,
    66-68. *See also* American-Hawaiian
    Steamship Company; Cuban Line;
    Pearson, Weetman Dickinson
Tejería, 32
Tejar, 118
Telegraph, 80
Telephone, 80
Temósachic, 65
Tenterden, Lord, 13-14

Terrazas, 65
Texas, 25, 124
Textiles. *See* Trade, Mexican
Teziutlán, 64, 121
The Times: on the Mexican Railway, 41
Tlanepantlo, effect of Mexican Railway
    on city of, 39
Tobacco. *See* Farming
Tokyo, 67
Tonala, 64
Topolobampo, 65
Toronto, 114, 117, 119
Torres, Governor Luis, sends letter to
    Díaz revealing plot to annex Lower
    California, 103
Torres, Sonora, 64
Toye, E. W., 75-76
Trade, Mexican: regulations for carrying
    on, 9; Carden prepares report on, 15;
    expansion of, 54-55; value of (imports
    and exports), 61, 137; 128-38 *passim*;
    British report in 1884 on, 129; British
    methods of carrying on, 135-36; com-
    parison of advertising methods of Brit-
    ish and others involved in, 136-37; and
    the failure of Britain to adapt to needs
    of Mexican buyers, 137; and the rivalry
    of Great Britain and United States,
    129, 130, 142; and the rivalry of Great
    Britain and Germany, 130-31; and the
    value of British imports compared to
    those of United States and Germany,
    128; and the nature of British imports,
    128, 133, 135. *See also* Fall in the
    price of silver; Germany; Great Britain;
    United States
Tramways. *See* Mexico Electric Tram-
    ways; Public Utilities
Treaties and Conventions: Juárez an-
    nounces abrogation of, 3-4; Clarendon
    says Mexico must recognize, 8; recogni-
    tion of prerequisite to renewal of
    relations, 12; new arrangements for old,
    20 n. *See also* English Convention of
    1859; Otway Convention, 1859; Treaty
    of peace, commerce, and navigation,
    Anglo-Mexican
Treatment of silver ore in Mexico, 28 n˙
Treaty of peace, commerce, and naviga-
    tion, Anglo-Mexican: lack of during
    diplomatic break, 17; St. John prepares
    in April, 1884, 18; signed in 1887, 20 n.
Trojes Mining and Smelting Company, 11
Tufts, 89
Tuxpan, 124
Tuxpan-Furbrero pipeline, 124
Tuxtla, 64
Two Republics, 107

United Mexican Mining Company: listed as active concern in 1876, 21, 24; location of, map 1, 26, map 4, 79; control of shares in 1876, 28; railway in area of, 28; and fall in the price of silver, 29, 30-31; dividend record of, table 7, 72; control of by Germans, 77-78

United States, 87, 88, 90; and interest due to Mexico's creditors, 6; and Mexican desire to offset influence of, 12; Mexico favors dollars from, 13; produces silver coin to replace peso, 29; trade from to Mexico, 38; railroad rates to Mexico from, 55; selection of mines by investors in, 92; and alleged plot to annex Lower California, 100, 103; and the rubber boom in Mexico, 106; plan to send petroleum to, 123, 124; position of in Mexican trade, 1876, 128; commercial influence in Mexico, 1883, 129; trade with Mexico in 1900, 1910, 130; control of distributing houses by, 137; interests of in Mexico, 139, 142. *See also* El Oro Mining and Railway Company; Esperanza, Limited; Mexican Central Railroad; Mexican National Railroad; Trade, Mexican

University, plans for in Lower California, 100

Valley of Mexico, draining of by W. D. Pearson Company, 58, 60, 139

Vancouver, 67

Velasco, Emilio: appointed Mexican minister to France, 12; meets with Lord Lyons, 13; attitude of toward British bondholders, 14

Venture Corporation, 90

Veracruz, 5, 36, 38, 42, 47, 49, 54, 55, 97, 108, 133, 143; contract for constructing dock at, 32; yellow fever at, 38; merchants in and the Mexican Railway rates, 43; chamber of commerce demands lowering of railroad rates, 43; dwindling of complaints from against Mexican Railway, 44; modernization of by British capital, 58, 60; traffic from Tehuantepec to, 67-68; public utilities in, 118-21; and concessions to W. D. Pearson, 123

Vera Cruz Electric Light, Power, and Traction Company, 118

Vera Cruz (Mexico) Railway, Limited, 68

Waters, H. C., 118

Water tunnel: at Palmarejo mines, 84

Wehrner Beit and Company, 115

Welles, Edgar, 105

West Virginia, 86

Woolen goods. *See* Trade, Mexican

Worswick, W. E., 116, 118

Yaqui Indians, 105

Yaqui River, 105

Yaqui River Land and Development Company, 106; location of, map 6, 98; organization of, 105

Yellow fever: in Veracruz, 38; on isthmus of Tehuantepec, 66

Yorke, Vincent, 118

Zacatecas, 91

Zuloaga, General Felix, 5

DATE DUE